The Six-Day Financial Makeover

THE
Six-Day
Financial
Makeover

TRANSFORM YOUR FINANCIAL LIFE IN LESS THAN A WEEK!

ROBERT PAGLIARINI

ST. MARTIN'S GRIFFIN ✹ NEW YORK

www.stmartins.com

Library of Congress Cataloging-in-Publication Data

Pagliarini, Robert.
    The six-day financial makeover : transform your financial life in less than a week! / Robert Pagliarini.
        p. cm.
    ISBN-13: 978-0-312-37774-8
    ISBN-10: 0-312-37774-6
    1. Finance, personal. I. Title.

HG179.P16 2006
332.024—dc22

                                                        2006024819

First St. Martin's Griffin Edition: January 2008

10 9 8 7 6 5 4 3 2 1

A Note to the Reader

The goal of this book is to provide accurate and useful information to the reader about personal financial planning. It is designed to help the reader focus on goals and actions that are important to address in the financial planning process. The book is intended to provide general guidelines that are for informational purposes only and is sold with the understanding that the publisher and author are not engaged in rendering professional services or in providing specific investment advice.

The application of general guidelines involving regulatory, accounting, and legal practices, which may differ from locality to locality and which are constantly changing, is highly dependent on an evaluation of individual facts and specific circumstances. With regard to any decisions that can potentially have significant financial, legal, tax, or other consequences, no book can take the place of individualized professional advice. Readers should not regard this book as a substitute for consulting with a competent lawyer, accountant, or other financial professional, as appropriate to the nature of their particular situation.

Throughout the book are presented various investment strategies and products that may or may not be appropriate for any individual reader's specific situation. It is also important to keep in mind that different types of investments involve varying degrees of risk, and there can be no assurance that the future performance of any specific investment, investment strategy, or product discussed in this book will be profitable or suitable for any one reader's portfolio. Also, in order to help the reader consider investment options, certain assumptions as to future investment returns are provided. These projections are based on a number of factors including past performance of various asset classes. While the past sometimes repeats itself, there is no assurance that past investment performance will be indicative of future results. Consequently, future investment performance for asset classes and portfolios cannot be guaranteed. If readers have any questions regarding the applicability of any investment strategy or product discussed in this book to their particular financial situation, they should consult with a professional advisor.

References in the book to products, service providers, and potential sources of additional information do not mean that the publisher or the author can vouch for such products or services or the information or recommendations in such sources. Neither the publisher nor the author is responsible for any third-party product or service or content over which they do not have control. Also, references in this book to the SixDay FinanacialMakeover.com website do not mean that St. Martin's Press sponsors or endorses that site, which is exclusively owned and operated by Robert Pagliarini. St. Martin's Press has no association with, has no control over, and is not responsible for the content or policies of that website, including any advice or advisory services that may be rendered in connection with the site.

To Gavin ... my beautiful baby boy
May 29, 2004–December 29, 2004

Contents

Acknowledgments

I will be forever grateful to these three guys . . . Tim Sanders, Michael Broussard, and Ethan Friedman. First, let me say how incredibly great Tim Sanders is. He wrote the *New York Times* bestselling book *Love Is the Killer App* and most recently, *The Likeability Factor*. Tim's credo is that even in a dog-eat-dog business world, it's best to spread love and help others as much as possible. And guess what? He doesn't just write about this stuff, he actually lives it. From out of the blue, he connected me with super agent Michael Broussard.

Michael is one in a million. He has unsurpassed energy and enthusiasm. The first time I talked to him, I knew I'd made a friend for life. Against all odds, he promised me we'd get a book deal. During the highs and during the lows, I knew I could count on Michael to come through. And come through he did, for he introduced me to editor extraordinaire Ethan Friedman.

Ethan saw the *Six-Day* vision from the beginning. It didn't take any convincing or selling. He got it and he loved it. He's an "author's editor"—supportive, inspiring, and open-minded.

While these three guys were instrumental in making this book possible, there were countless others who contributed to whom I will also be forever grateful:

Allyson Laughlin, president of Youngnsavvy Media, a dear friend who never once had a doubt this book would be written, published, and become a success. She's everything you could ask for in a friend, and she's also a public relations master and brilliant strategist.

John Murphy at St. Martin's Press. I loved this guy from the first meeting. He truly cares about his authors and is passionate about his work. He's a public relations genius, and I am fortunate to have him on my side.

Thanks to Jan Miller and Nena Madonia at Dupree Miller & Associates.

Jan "über-agent" Miller took a shot on me and I can't thank her enough. Nena is a joy to work with—full of energy and insight. I couldn't ask for a better team.

Thank you to the Financial Planning Association, the National Association of Personal Financial Advisors, and The American College for their continued support.

Special thanks to those who diligently reviewed the book, including (in alphabetical order) Lance Alston, Phil Cook, Dennis DeYoung, Kevin Dorwin, Curtis Estes, Seth Gilman, Jeff Lewis, George Padula, J. D. Roth, and Tony Steuer.

Thanks to Andrew Erie of Hybrid Logic Media for his great ideas about the book cover.

I am blessed for knowing David and Helen Price and honored to call them friends. Their kindness, generosity, and willingness to help others achieve their dreams are remarkable.

Thank you to my mother and stepdad for their unwavering emotional support at a time when I didn't know what I wanted, but knew exactly what I didn't want. They gave me the encouragement to pursue a vision beyond what was immediately in front of me.

A very special thank-you to my family. My deepest thanks to my wonderful wife, Liz, for letting me become the person I am. As cliché as it sounds, she makes me want to be a better man. Regardless of my crazy ideas, I can count on her to support me. She's a "why not?" kind of gal, and I love her for that. Thank you to my son, Gavin. You were (and still are) an inspiration for me. Daddy misses you very much and will see you soon. Thank you to my beautiful daughter, Alexandra ("Bean"), for providing me with joy and happiness every single day.

And thank you to Jesus Christ, my Lord and Savior. Help us not forget that while a financial transformation can last a lifetime, a transformation of our soul lasts for eternity.

Introduction

Thank you for buying this book. I am thrilled to be your guide through your financial transformation. Regardless of who you are and however confused or frustrated you may be with your finances, don't worry. Help is on the way!

Through this journey, I promise you these five things:

1. **You will learn new and powerful financial strategies.** The world doesn't need another personal finance book rehashing the same old tips and rules of thumb. This book contains brand-new strategies that will revolutionize the way you think about money and how you invest.

2. **You will implement the advice you read.** This is a personal finance book, not a novel! If you read it but don't implement any of the strategies, I have failed. To experience a true financial makeover, you must take what you read and apply it in your life. I'm going to do everything I can to make implementing the advice easy for you. The book's patent-pending website, www.SixDayFinancialMake over.com, is unlike any other. It was designed to do one thing—help you implement the advice you read in this book. It will track your progress and remind you of exactly what you need to do. If you use the website, you will absolutely implement the advice you read.

3. **You will understand what you're reading.** These chapters are filled with action-based financial advice that cuts through "financial fog"— the complex jargon and wishy-washy advice that can make it hard for the average person to understand and improve his or her finances.

4. **You won't feel overwhelmed.** Transforming your financial life in less than a week is a tall order, but it won't feel like a lot of work. Everything is presented in bite-sized pieces. One step, one chapter, and one day at a time.

5. **You won't feel guilty about your past financial decisions.** Nobody's perfect. I'm the financial "expert," but I've made questionable financial decisions, too. Your current financial situation or what you've done in the past doesn't matter. The focus of your financial makeover is on transforming your financial life . . . beginning today!

Here's all I ask from you . . . read the book, follow the Action Steps, and use the free website. That's it. If you do, you will experience a financial makeover, and you will transform your financial life!

Robert Pagliarini

P.S. One more thing. I want to hear your success stories. Go to www.SixDay FinancialMakeover.com and share what you've been able to accomplish and how your financial life has been transformed.

The Six-Day Financial Makeover

CHAPTER 1

Do You Need a Financial Makeover?

Do you want more from life? Are you working harder and putting in longer hours but don't feel financially secure or satisfied with your progress? Many of us are making more money but we still don't feel that we've *made it*. What do you think about when you're alone? When the phones aren't ringing and the television is off, what occupies your thoughts? What questions or concerns do you have just before falling asleep at night? In those quiet moments when you are able to reflect, are you satisfied with your financial situation or do you yearn for more?

Regardless of your present situation, you can achieve the life you've always dreamed of. It doesn't matter who you are or where you live. It doesn't matter if you had a privileged childhood of abundance or one of hardship and scarcity. With this book, you can improve your life and chart your own destiny in six short days.

This chapter is your wake-up call. Do you feel that you are maximizing your potential? Do you feel that you are living the life that you've always wanted? If you are financially frustrated, insecure, or just plain scared, you *can* feel financially secure and realize all of your dreams with a financial makeover.

Should I read this chapter?

	TRUE	FALSE
1. I thought I would have a more fulfilled life than I do right now.	☐	☐

	TRUE	FALSE
2. I think making money is the most important goal to have.	☐	☐
3. I don't know what it would take to have a balanced life.	☐	☐
4. I don't know why financial independence is a worthwhile goal.	☐	☐
5. I'd like to learn about the incredible opportunity I have to improve my finances and my life through a financial makeover.	☐	☐

If you answered any of these questions TRUE, you should read this chapter.

Chapter Toolbar

Cost to Implement Advice	Likelihood of Needing Strategies in Chapter	Need Professional Advice?	Website Tools
$0	1 2 3 4 5 6 7 8 9 10 Not Likely Very Likely	↑ ↑ ↑ ↑ ↑ No Definitely	Yes

---

What Is a Financial Makeover?

Maybe you're not sure what to expect from a financial makeover. That's fair. It's good to be a little skeptical. If you're familiar with fashion makeover, you know the successful ones don't stop with a facial or a new wardrobe. Successful makeovers require a total transformation—from head to toe and inside and out. Likewise, your financial makeover won't stop with just a budget or an investment plan. Your financial transformation will include all of the critical areas of your financial life—creating a spending and savings plan, protecting assets, investing wisely, risk management, insurance, estate planning, and much, much more.

Over the next six days, your financial makeover will strip away everything that is not working—maybe you're spending too much, sabotaging your own success, taking too much risk, not investing wisely, or leaving yourself and your loved ones financially exposed—and replace it with a solid foundation from which you can immediately start to see success and feel a sense of confidence. Your financial makeover will also maximize what you're already doing well. If you have powerful and inspiring goals, are saving diligently, and investing well, your Six-Day Financial Makeover will help you maximize and optimize your strengths.

I will walk with you, step by step, throughout the six-day transformation. Together we will turn the complexities of budgeting, investing, insurance, and estate planning into something understandable and practical. We're going to take the "pie-in-the-sky" theories and turn them into bite-sized pieces that you can implement in your life immediately.

Do You Need a Financial Makeover?

Maybe you're not convinced you need a financial makeover. Are you nervous, frustrated, unsure, concerned, or just plain scared of your financial situation? Are you tired of feeling sick every time you think about investing, retirement planning, life insurance, estate planning, and paying the bills? What if I said you don't have to feel that way anymore? No, you won't get rich or magically accomplish all of your goals in six days, but *The Six-Day Financial Makeover* will help you feel better and more confident about your financial situation and provide practical steps that are easy to understand and will make a dramatic and immediate impact on your life. If you're still not convinced you need a financial makeover, take the short quiz below or online at www.SixDayFinancialMakeover.com to quickly determine how well you're really doing.

Financial Satisfaction Quiz

Name _____   Date _____

Circle the number that corresponds to how you feel today.

| I feel negative and pessimistic about my future. | 1 2 3 4 5 | I feel extremely positive and optimistic about my future. |

I am not sure what I want to achieve or obtain in life.	1 2 3 4 5	I know exactly what I want out of life.
I have no idea what it would take to become financially independent.	1 2 3 4 5	I have made plans and have developed strategies to become financially independent.
I feel that no matter what I do I won't be able to get ahead.	1 2 3 4 5	I feel completely in charge of my success and my destiny.
I do not have a system in place to consistently save and invest money each month.	1 2 3 4 5	I have a system in place to consistently save and invest money each month.
I have never invested before, or if I have, I make decisions without having an overall investment strategy.	1 2 3 4 5	I know the subtleties of investing and have an overall strategy for all of my investments.
I am not sure if I would lose all of my assets if I was sued.	1 2 3 4 5	I feel confident that if I was involved in a lawsuit my assets would be protected as much as possible.
I am not satisfied with the amount of money that I save and invest on a regular basis.	1 2 3 4 5	I am satisfied with the amount of money that I save and invest on a regular basis.
I have heard of identity theft but am not sure how to protect myself.	1 2 3 4 5	I have taken all of the necessary steps to protect myself from identity theft.
I am not sure where my assets will go when I pass away.	1 2 3 4 5	I know exactly where my assets will go when I pass away.
I think I may be taking too much risk with my investments and do not think that my investment portfolio is properly diversified.	1 2 3 4 5	I am taking an appropriate amount of risk and am extremely comfortable that my investment portfolio is properly diversified.

I have not taken any steps to ensure my family's well-being in the event of a tragedy.	1 2 3 4 5	In the event of a tragedy, I know that I have taken the proper steps to ensure my family's well-being.

TOTAL: _____

Scoring the Financial Satisfaction Quiz

Add your scores to see how you've done:

Score 12–34 = Overall, you're not satisfied with your current financial situation. By completing the Six-Day Financial Makeover, you will see the greatest improvement. At the end of the six days, you will feel more confident and secure—you will experience a financial transformation!

Score 35–47 = You're doing some things right, but there is a lot more you can do. Maybe you've got a great handle on investing but are neglecting other areas of your financial life. Whatever the case, there is significant room for improvement. You can and will feel energized and on top of your financial situation at the end of your financial makeover!

Score 48–60 = You're doing a lot of things right. You've got a good handle on many aspects of your financial situation. Now it's a matter of optimizing what you're already doing well and making sure you've covered all of the bases.

Take the quiz online at www.SixDayFinancialMakeover.com if you haven't done so already.

The Importance of Financial Independence

Financial independence is a phrase that gets tossed around too often and usually without any understanding of what it really means—often by salespeople on late-night infomercials hocking "get rich quick" real estate schemes, home-based businesses, or investment trading programs. My goal is to take the mystery out of financial independence and to show you exactly what it is and what it provides and to explain what financial independence is not. Financial independence should be your primary financial goal, and here's why.

At the root of financial independence is the freedom to choose. The ability to choose between several options puts you in control of your finances and your life. It allows you to shape your life rather than being at the mercy of someone else's vision of your future. It takes you out of life's passenger seat and puts you behind the wheel. Suddenly you can choose the kind of work that stimulates and inspires you without worrying about how much money you will earn. It also allows you to pursue your hobbies without regard to their cost or time commitment. For many, financial independence allows them to volunteer their time and money to worthy causes.

Financial independence also provides security. How would you feel if you could live the lifestyle of your dreams without worrying about being downsized, having to work two jobs, or sacrificing time with your family? When you become financially independent, your sense of security comes from having control over your life and your future. Without financial independence, your life is dictated by someone else—usually your employer. Your security is in the hands and at the whim of an organization or an individual with their own best interests at heart—not yours.

What Is Financial Independence?

Financial independence means different things to different people. To some, it means being able to pay the bills. For others, it means being able to eat out every night. Yet for some, it means being able to have three vacation homes and a yacht. I define financial independence as being able to support the lifestyle you desire without having to work.

There are two important pieces to this definition. First, you need to differentiate the lifestyle you desire from your current lifestyle. This is a signficant distinction. Too often, we reduce our lifestyle to fit within our means.[1] Financial independence is not about limiting or reducing your lifestyle, but about living the life you want and having the means to support it.

---

1. Worse yet, we create a lifestyle that is above our means by using credit cards and taking home equity loans. Chapter 4 will expose this kind of financial suicide and will show you concrete steps to take back control of your spending.

Don't Let This Happen to You

Josh grew up with his three sisters and one brother in a home that barely had enough resources to support two children, let alone five. There was never quite enough to go around. The family never took vacations or had enough for the "extras" other families could afford. Josh used his childhood experience to fuel his growing ambition. He vowed that he would never go without again and that his family would have everything they wanted. He didn't want his kids to suffer the ridicule he experienced growing up.

Josh's ambition and drive helped him climb the corporate ladder. When the new line of BMWs came out, he upgraded. His twenty-five-foot boat was replaced with a larger, faster version when his golfing buddy purchased a better one. From the outside, it appeared that Josh and his family had it all—a large house, two luxury cars, an expensive boat, plus they frequently took cruises and family vacations.

On the inside, it was a much darker picture. Josh was borrowing against his future to support the extravagant lifestyle he chose to live today. He racked up credit card debt and borrowed against his home. His monthly expenses greatly exceeded his income. Even with a big promotion and year-end bonus, he couldn't continue at this pace. When creditors began calling him at his office, he knew his choices were limited.

The bankruptcy was hard on his family and placed stress on his seven-year marriage. His wife was not upset that they lost nearly everything, but she was horrified that Josh—who managed all of their finances—could have let it get so out of control.

Second, financial independence means you don't need to work to support your lifestyle. This just means that the income generated by your assets can fully support your expenses.

Income from labor is *earned income*. It requires your participation, effort, and energy. If you decide to take a year off, your earned income ceases. Earned income is how most of us receive money. Our alarm clock wakes us in the morning, we have our cup of coffee, we take a shower and get dressed, and we drive to work. We put in our day and drive home. Every couple of weeks, we get a paycheck. This is the earned income cycle.

Earned income is an exchange of time for money. Through education and experience, we can increase the value of our time and be compensated accordingly. Even high-powered attorneys or surgeons who make hundreds or thousands of dollars an hour still exchange their time for a paycheck. The minute they stop this exchange, they stop earning income.

Financial independence breaks this cycle. It replaces earned income with *passive income*. Passive income includes the following sources of income[2]:

- Investment income (e.g., dividends, interest, capital gains)

- Rental real estate income

- Royalties

- Licenses

- Partnership and business income (if you don't have to work or manage anything to receive it)

- Social Security and pension income

Passive income is the Holy Grail of personal finance. Why? You don't have to trade your time for it. Passive income gives you the freedom to do what you want. Earned income is a chain that restricts what you can do and when you can do it. Passive income liberates us from nine-to-five jobs and two-week vacation limitations.

Contrary to its name, accumulating passive income is not a passive endeavor! Accumulating the assets to generate passive income requires skill, education, and diligence. You can't expect to sit back and have massive amounts of passive income deposited into your bank account every month. Generating passive income from dividends and interest requires you to select and to monitor the appropriate investments. Rental income requires purchasing and maintaining commercial or residential real estate. Royalties and licenses require the development and sale of a product. Partnership and business passive income, like investments, requires the careful selection of investments and monitoring them diligently.

There are two important advantages to passive income. First, passive income doesn't take as much effort to maintain. To earn a salary, you typically have to put in forty or more hours of work a week. Maintaining the same amount of passive income takes a fraction of the time.

---

2. For accounting and taxation purposes, there are three types of income: earned income, passive income, and investment income. In this book, unless stated otherwise, I combine investment income with passive income because both share the same characteristic—they do not require active involvement.

Second, you can outsource what little time it takes to maintain passive income to somebody else. You can hire a financial advisor to select and monitor your investments, an accountant to monitor your royalty and license fees, and a property management company to collect rent and fill vacancies. This is an advantage that just doesn't exist with earned income. Can you imagine hiring a temp to take your place at work?

Financial independence does not mean that you *can't* work; it simply gives you the *option* of working. Most of us want to continue working—our contribution to the world provides a sense of accomplishment and esteem.

Are You Financially Independent?

Now that you know what financial independence is and why it is important, it is just as important to understand what it is not. Financial independence is not about being "rich." To be rich, you only need to have a lot of money. This definition ignores a critical part of the equation—expenses.

Financial Independence Versus Retirement

Financial independence is about having enough investments so you don't have to work another day in your life. Basically, it gives you the option of retiring early. Retirement, on the other hand, usually is what happens after working for more than forty years. In a recent survey by the Vanguard Center for Retirement Research, two-thirds of respondents admitted that they were not saving enough for retirement.[3] Retirement doesn't guarantee financial security, but financial independence can!

Financial independence involves earning enough passive income to support the kind of lifestyle you desire. As a result, there is no "magic" amount of passive income that is required—it is entirely dependent on your expenses. If

---

3. James Choi, David Laibson, Brigitte Madrian, and Andrew Metrick, "Defined Contribution Pensions: Plan Rules, Participant Decisions, and the Path of Least Resistance," NBER Working Paper 8655, 2001, p. 6. Quoted in Olivia Mitchell and Stephen Utkus, "Lessons from Behavioral Finance for Retirement Plan Design," Pension Research Council Working Paper, 2003. http://fic.wharton.upenn.edu/fic/papers/03/0334.pdf.

you earn $100,000 in annual passive income and have expenses of $85,000 per year, you are financially independent. If you have $500,000 in annual passive income but have $750,000 in expenses per year, you are not financially independent. Expenses are an equally important part of the equation.

Take the quiz below to find out if you are financially independent!

Determine Your Independence Factor™ Financial Independence Quiz

(You can also take this quiz online at www.SixDayFinancialMakeover.com.)

Step 1—Approximate how much you spend per month. Include everything—entertainment, mortgage, rent, taxes, insurance, food, etc.   **Monthly Expenses**   (A) $_____

TOTAL MONTHLY EXPENSES	(A) $_____

Step 2—Add all of your sources of passive income per month, not including investment income

Rental Income	(B) $_____
Royalties/Licenses	(C) $_____
Social Security/Pension/Partnership Income	(D) $_____
MONTHLY NON-INVESTMENT PASSIVE INCOME	(E) $_____

Step 3—Total all of your investment accounts (e.g., 401(k), IRA, savings) and multiply by 0.33%* (i.e., 0.0033):

$_____ × 0.33% = Enter total →   **Monthly Investment Income**   (F) $_____

MONTHLY INVESTMENT PASSIVE INCOME	(F) $_____
TOTAL MONTHLY PASSIVE INCOME (E+F)	(G) $_____

Step 4—Divide your Total Monthly Passive Income by your Total Monthly Expenses (G ÷ A)   **Passive Income Ratio**   (H) _____

Step 5—Multiply your Passive Income Ratio by 31 (H × 31)   **Independence Factor**   (I) _____

---

* Why 0.33 percent? This calculation assumes you can withdraw 4 percent of your portfolio each year, a fairly conservative amount you should be able to take out, year after year, without depleting your assets.

Scoring the Financial Independence Quiz

Your Independence Factor represents the number of days per month you could survive with your current lifestyle without working. In other words, if you stopped working tomorrow, your Independence Factor tells you how many days you could live off of your passive income. If your goal is to have the freedom and flexibility of financial independence, you need to make sure you have enough passive income to last you through the whole month.

Independence Factor 0–7=A score in this range means that if you stopped working tomorrow, the income you generate from your passive investments wouldn't cover you for more than a week every month. Life would be good for those first few days. You could sit back, spend time with the family, maybe enjoy a round of golf. But before you know it, your passive income would run out. What would you eat the rest of the month? Where would you live? Don't worry if you fall into this category. It just means you need to increase your passive income, reduce your expenses, or both. You have some work to do, but the good news is that you will quickly see results from your financial makeover.

Independence Factor 8–23=Keep up the good work—you're not quite there but the finish line is in your sights. By controlling your expenses, setting up automatic savings plans, and investing with a purpose, you will be able to last two weeks a month, then three, then the entire month.

Independence Factor 24–30=You're well on your way to becoming financially independent. By saving a little more and investing wisely, you will soon experience the joy of financial independence.

Independence Factor 31+=Congratulations! You are financially independent. If you stopped earning a paycheck you'd be just fine. You'd be able to pay your mortgage, your gas bill, and still have money left over for food and entertainment. You could pay for all of this from the passive income you generate—month after month, year after year.

Check your Independence Factor every six months or so, especially if your expenses increase and/or your income or assets decrease.

How Do I Increase My Independence Factor?

If your Independence Factor isn't quite as high as you'd like, don't worry, you've come to the right place. The chapters that follow will provide you with step-by-step instructions and guidance to help you increase your Independence Factor!

What Financial Independence Doesn't Guarantee

We've all heard the saying, "Money doesn't buy happiness." Well, it's true—money doesn't buy happiness, and financial independence doesn't guarantee happiness, either. Personal income in the United States has almost tripled since 1956, but the number of Americans who claim to be "very happy" hasn't increased—it has remained at about 30 percent year after year.

Income is up, yet the level of happiness is flat. Why? While there are thousands of factors that contribute to happiness or unhappiness, it appears that simply earning more money isn't enough to ensure happiness.

Academic research suggests that our current actions are based on predictions of future emotional consequences. Our decision to order a double bacon cheeseburger, compete in a marathon, work late nights and weekends, or purchase a larger house, is based on how we think we will feel once we've accomplished these things.

If we were good predictors of our emotional reactions to these events, this wouldn't be a problem. According to Harvard psychology professor Daniel Gilbert, we do a poor job of determining how we will feel as a result of something—we tend to overestimate the future positive effect of an action and how long we are going to feel good. We think the brand-new car will make us feel much happier and for a longer period than it actually will. In other words, we overestimate those things that we think will make us happy. Gilbert's research tells us that whatever we think will make us happy won't make us as happy as much as we estimate or for as long as we estimate.[4]

---

4. For someone who studies happiness, Gilbert's work seems pretty depressing. The good news is that we also overestimate how badly we are going to feel and how long we are going to feel bad. We think we are going to feel horrible forever if we lose our job, but in reality the fall is not as deep or as prolonged.

Does this make financial independence an unworthy goal? Absolutely not. It means that financial independence is a means to an end, a tool. Financial independence alone will not make you happy. It's what you do once you become financially independent that determines your level of happiness.

Most people know what they *should* want to make them happy. Our brain is powerful beyond comprehension, but it is constantly trying to make things easier for us. As a result, we simplify and streamline what we think will make us happier. We are susceptible to ads that promise excitement and satisfaction without thinking critically about whether the product really will or not. If we did, I would venture to say jeans ads with scantily dressed models (*not* even wearing the jeans being advertised!)—just oozing sex appeal—would not be as effective.

As a result of this overly simple approach to happiness, it is no wonder that we are poor predictors of our happiness. If we stop and honestly evaluate what will make our lives richer and more fulfilling, we might experience happiness. The next chapter will help you determine what will make you happy—in effect, it will make you think, maybe for the first time, about what drives you.

Because of the billions of dollars spent on advertisements and marketing campaigns, we incorrectly assume that our happiness is linked directly to material possessions. Too often, we set goals about what we want to own. While these things can add to our level of satisfaction, happiness will ultimately come from accomplishing goals and growing as people. Advertisements trick us into thinking that a product will satisfy our needs. A Hummer will make us a rebel. A Rolex will make us sophisticated. Chapter 2—Design the Life of Your Dreams—will strip away the ads and products and will help you determine what you truly want to accomplish and who you want to be.

Armed with the knowledge of what it will take to enrich our lives and add excitement, we can use financial independence as a tool to help us achieve our other goals. What's the worst-case scenario? We become financially independent, get the things we want, accomplish what we want, and become who we want to be—and are no happier than when we started. Whoever said, "If I had a choice, I'd rather be rich and unhappy than poor and unhappy," was on the right track! In our pursuit of financial success, though, it is important not to neglect the other areas of our lives.

The Importance of a Balanced Life

In working with individuals and families from diverse backgrounds, I've discovered a universal truth. If you take time to step back from the details of your daily life and focus on the bigger picture, you will find that there is probably at least an area or two in your life that is going well—maybe your job, your marriage, or your relationship with your kids. Most people can usually find some satisfaction in their lives.

On the other hand, there may be an area or two that causes dissatisfaction, maybe even frustration or anger. You may be able to pinpoint those areas that make you unhappy, or if you are like many people, you may not be able to easily identify these troubled areas.

In an effort to advance in one area of our lives, we often neglect another. Marital problems can destroy a good career, just as career problems can derail a good marriage. By neglecting certain parts of our lives, we allow these areas to infect the areas where we are satisfied. These problems have the potential to undermine our success and overall happiness in life.

A balanced life is comprised of different Life Zones™, the major areas of your life that are most meaningful and important to you. What I value may not be what you value—it is common for different people to have different Life Zones. The following graph represents the most common Life Zones for most people.

Common Life Zones

This book focuses on improving one of the Life Zones—your financial health. The importance of good financial health cannot be overemphasized. Like poor physical health, financial health can have an immediate and dramatic impact on the other areas of your life. Financial difficulties can split marriages, tear families apart, and can be a catalyst for health problems.

Financial problems may well be the number one cause of divorce and relationship breakups. Immediately following the terrorist attacks on September 11, 2001, nearly twice as many adult Americans who had difficulty sleeping were worried more about their finances than about national security.[5] Our nation had been attacked. Thousands of innocent men, women, and children had been murdered. Our sense of security had been jeopardized, but we continued to worry about our finances. Few other things in life have the power of money.

Money is the fuel that propels you to your goals. It is your ticket to the best schools, it provides the best health care—in short, money provides the *opportunity* for you to have the things you want, to accomplish your goals, and to grow as an individual.

Make no mistake, money does not provide a *guarantee* that you will get what you want, accomplish what you desire, or become a better person. In fact, it is not necessary for you to have a lot of money to achieve success in life. Mother Teresa had very little financial wealth, but had immense happiness and satisfaction with her life.

Remember—money is not evil, the *love* of money is. Dr. Martin Seligman writes in his insightful book *Authentic Happiness,* "People who value money more than other goals are less satisfied with their income and with their lives as a whole."[6] While the pursuit of money is not unhealthy, the unrelenting pursuit of money at the expense of the other Life Zones is terribly unhealthy.

Sound financial health opens doors easily and quickly. My wife and I tried for two years to get pregnant with no results. We sought the counsel of a fertility specialist and eventually adopted. Anyone who's gone through fertility treatments and/or adopted knows it isn't cheap! Without a clear understanding of our financial situation and the assets to pay for treatment (insurance usually doesn't cover infertility or adoption), we may not have the beautiful girl we have today.

Another benefit of working on your financial health is that you have total control over it. When you make improvements in other areas of your life the

---

5. McNeil Consumer Healthcare, "Americans Awake and Worried—Personal Finance More Disconcerting Than National Security Issues." *PRNewswire,* December 13, 2001. www.prnewswire.com/cgi-bin/stories.pl?ACCT=104&STORY=/www/story/12-13-2001/0001633188&EDATE= (accessed July 25, 2006).

6. Martin Seligman, *Authentic Happiness* (New York: Free Press, 2002), 55.

results are often slow to see. When you improve your finances, results can be visible immediately. Once you make a commitment to improve, your past decisions and behaviors are irrelevant.

You've already made that commitment by completing this chapter! If you want to experience a financial transformation, there's more work to be done, though. There are so many books on the market that provide the quick sensation that things are fine and that you can accomplish anything. Momentarily, you feel invincible—things aren't as bad as you imagined and you can accomplish anything you want. Within days of finishing the book, however, the rush subsides and reality sets in and you realize that nothing has changed. By reading and following the Action Steps in this book, you will not only *feel* better, your financial health will actually be better: You *can* and *will* experience a financial transformation in six days!

Once our mind is open we can focus with precision on what we want to own, what we want to accomplish, and who we want to be. Hang on tight because we're just getting started. The next chapter will show you exactly how to design the life of your dreams!

Action Steps

Right here, right now is where you can transform your financial life. Nothing was ever achieved without action. Reading about financial independence won't get you closer to achieving it unless you take the quizzes, complete the worksheets, and implement the advice in this chapter. Some of the most successful people in the world didn't complete college or even high school—but what they lacked in formal education they more than made up in action!

Go through the Action Steps below and put a check mark in one of the following boxes for each one:

- **Completed**—Check this box if you've already completed the Action Step. (Nice work!)

- **Need to Complete**—Check this box if you still need to complete this Action Step. (To make sure you complete these Action Steps, update your account at www.SixDayFinancialMakeover.com.)

- **Does Not Apply**—Check this box if the Action Step does not apply to your situation. (That's okay! Not every Action Step will apply to everyone.)

Create Your Online Financial Makeover Account

1. ☐ Completed   ☐ Need to Complete   ☐ Does Not Apply

Before you do anything else, create a free online account at www .SixDayFinancialMakeover.com. You'll be able to take all of the quizzes and get access to free templates and forms that you can use to help you throughout your financial makeover.

More important, you will have "someone" that will track your progress and help you take what you've learned and help you implement it in your life. If all you do is read this book, you won't transform your financial life. The only thing that will improve your finances and peace of mind is taking what you've learned and implementing it in your life. The free and patent-pending online assistant will guide you through the implementation process. It doesn't forget and doesn't take no for an answer, so go ahead and register right now at www.SixDay FinancialMakeover.com.

Log in regularly to your account and update it with your progress.

Financial Satisfaction Quiz

2. ☐ Completed   ☐ Need to Complete   ☐ Does Not Apply

Take the Financial Satisfaction Quiz on page 3 or online at www .SixDayFinancialMakeover.com to determine how satisfied you are with your current financial situation.

Determine Your Independence Factor

3. ☐ Completed   ☐ Need to Complete   ☐ Does Not Apply

Take the Financial Independence Quiz on page 10 or online at www .SixDayFinancialMakeover.com to determine your Independence Factor.

CHAPTER 2

Design the Life of Your Dreams

This chapter will help you determine exactly what motivates you and will act as your road map in creating a purposeful and fulfilling life. This chapter doesn't contain the typical goal-setting exercises that have left so many people frustrated and unfulfilled. Instead, this chapter has unique exercises that will help you identify and clarify what you want to own, what you want to accomplish, and who you want to be. This chapter provides the purpose and the fuel to propel your financial makeover.

Should I read this chapter?

	TRUE	FALSE
1. I don't have a clear vision for my future.	☐	☐
2. I am "successful" by society's standards, but I feel like I'm missing something.	☐	☐
3. I don't have clearly written goals.	☐	☐
4. I want my life to be different, but I'm not sure where to start.	☐	☐
5. I want to design my life by determining what I want to own, accomplish, and be.	☐	☐

If you answered any of these questions TRUE, you should read this chapter.

Chapter Toolbar			
Cost to Implement Advice	Likelihood of Needing Strategies in Chapter	Need Professional Advice?	Website Tools
$0	1 2 3 4 5 6 7 8 9 10 Not Likely Very Likely	🕴 🕴 🕴 🕴 🕴 No Definitely	Yes

We can choose to survive or to thrive. We can choose a life of emptiness or a life of fulfillment. Where you are today doesn't have to be where you are tomorrow. Your financial makeover must begin by igniting your drive to achieve your dreams.

Unfortunately, we've forgotten how to have fun thinking about what we want. We've forgotten how to think big—to see the larger picture. When we're children, everything is a possibility and nothing limits us. We want to be movie stars and astronauts, race-car drivers and ballerinas.

Then life happens, and suddenly we realize that we must work hard to achieve our goals. We quickly learn that taking risk involves failure and disappointment. By the time we are teenagers we've heard "no" a hundred times more than "yes." We temper our desires and conform to what we think we *should* want (or worse, what others want). At the end of Day 1, you will know exactly what motivates you and precisely the kind of future you desire—we will uncover what it is you really want and will show you how to get it.

So what's the first step? Should we create a list of stuff we want? Our gut reaction is to say we want a big house, nice cars, and to travel the world. While these are worthwhile goals for a financial makeover, they don't provide a direction. If you immediately jump into setting goals, you may find that you work hard to accomplish your goals but are left unfulfilled once you achieve them. A popular and true saying is, "When climbing the ladder of success, make sure it is leaning against the right building." In other words, don't focus all of your time and energy accomplishing goals that don't fulfill you.

So if setting goals is not the first step, where do we start? The five Power Exercises to designing and achieving a fulfilling and rewarding life are:

1. Create a perfect *Vision* for your future.

2. Define your *Want List.*

3. Create and prioritize *IMPACT-Goals*™.

4. Calculate how *Money* can help.

5. Use *Pictures* for motivation.

I know how easy it is to read a chapter or a strategy and think, "That won't work for me," or, "I'll implement it later." I personally struggled with this issue. For many years, my objective in reading a book was to finish it. My focus was on completing the book, and not on learning and expanding my knowledge. I approached these opportunities as tasks—literally to-do items on a list. When it came time to complete the exercises or quizzes, I rationalized that I would get around to them later. "The exercises are all the same," I used to think, "I'll just read ahead and figure out the gist of the chapter."

After years of reading, I was no better off. I'd read hundreds of theories and had been exposed to some of the best minds in the world, but I was still the same person I had always been. I learned a lot, but I never converted the theories, knowledge, or advice into anything useful. I spent thousands of dollars and dedicated hundreds of hours but I didn't take the extra ten minutes to work through an exercise or to implement any of the knowledge. (I changed my ways when someone asked me what I thought of a book I'd just finished and I had no idea.) Don't make the same mistake. Your financial makeover requires action! Finish these exercises. The energy you invest in this chapter will propel you in the direction of your dreams.

When You Met Sally

To help you better understand how to design the life of your dreams, you can look over the shoulder of Sally Smith as she completes the exercises in this chapter.

Power Exercise #1—
Create the Perfect *Vision* for Your Future

Where there is no vision, the people perish.

—Proverbs 29:18

Everything starts with your vision. Your vision is the foundation that supports everything that you do. Without a firm understanding of your vision, you will have an unsteady structure that will eventually crumble. This exercise will help you create the perfect vision for your future by looking into the future and examining how you want to be remembered. You will create the vision of your perfect future and identify what you value most in your Life Zones—again, the major areas of your life that are most meaningful and important to you.

My Life Zones

Remember, your Life Zones might not match the Life Zones I value most. Such a list can vary widely from person to person. Some areas may not even apply to your life. If, for example, you are retired, you might not have a Business and Career category. Feel free to add or remove other categories to better create a list that matches accurately with your life. Without further ado, let's get started!

Everyone is wearing black. There are so many people present, you are surprised it is so quiet. Everyone has their backs to you. No one looks up as you make your way to the front of the room. Suddenly you see an old college friend whom you haven't seen in years. "This is great!" you think—it will give you some time to catch up. Then you notice your neighbor, your mother-in-law, and your boss. "What's he doing here?" you wonder. In fact, "What is everyone doing here?" Just as you're about to say something to your old college friend, you notice your family seated near the front of the room. Something is wrong. Your wife is seated and you can see her trembling; she's crying. Then it hits you. Someone has died—this is a funeral. You immediately notice the casket. Cautiously, you make your way to the open casket. You don't want to look in, but you have to. Your body lies in the casket!

It's a scene straight out of a movie. You have died. Everyone is here for your funeral. There's nothing you can do. You're witnessing your own funeral! Barely able to move, you sit down as the eulogies begin.

- Your spouse/partner, children, and/or close relatives slowly walk to the podium. What do you want your spouse to say about you? Were you there when he needed you? Were you exciting and romantic? Did you adore him? Were you a good friend? Did you praise her accomplishments and hold her when she failed? Were you respectful and compassionate? What do you want your children to say about you? Were you the best parent you could be? Were you always there for them? Did you give your all? Did you help them grow and learn? Did you teach them important values? Were you a good role model? Were you available to them? What do you want your brothers, sisters, and close relatives to say about you? Were you supportive and encouraging? Were you there for them when they needed you?

  *Write **"Family"** at the top of a blank sheet of paper and think about the answers to those questions. Are you happy or disappointed with what you hear? Regardless of what you think your spouse, children, and family might say today, write what you'd like them to say at your funeral—either in a bullet point list or in full sentences.*

- Your friends stand at the podium. How do you want them to remember you? What do they say about you? Could they count on you? Were you true to your word? Did you support them and encourage them to become better people? Were you honest and direct with them?

  *Write **"Relationships"** at the top of a blank sheet of paper and think about the answers to those questions. Are you happy or disappointed* *with what you hear? Regardless of what you think your friends might say today, write what you'd like them to say at your funeral— either in a bullet point list or in full sentences.*

- Your boss, colleague, or business partner stands at the podium. What do you want him to say about you? Did you always give 100 percent? Were you honest and ethical? Did you treat your coworkers or employees with the same respect you would give your family? Were you in a position that regularly challenged you? Were you doing something you loved and felt passionate about? Did you seek to improve the company?

  *Write "**Business and Career**" at the top of a blank sheet of paper and think about the answers to those questions. Are you happy or disappointed with what you hear? Regardless of what you think your boss, colleagues, or business partner might say today, write what you'd like them to say at your funeral—either in a bullet point list or in full sentences.*

Just when you think the ceremony is over, a good friend wheels a large television to the front of the room. He takes a DVD from his jacket and announces he edited the highlights from your home videos. He pushes "play" and everyone watches the screen. . . .

- Do you look healthy and in good shape? Did you take care of your body? Is there footage of you crossing a finish line or playing sports? What does your body look like? Are you embarrassed when they show you playing with the kids by the pool in your bathing suit or are you proud of your body? Do you look powerful and full of energy? Do you look like you could conquer the world?

  *Write "**Physical Health**" at the top of a blank sheet of paper and think about the answers to those questions. Are you happy or disappointed with what you see? Regardless of what the video might show today, write what you'd like the video to highlight of your physical body, your health, and your energy level.*

- Is there footage of you receiving awards? Are you speaking another language? What are your hobbies? Are there graduation ceremonies? Are you traveling in other countries? Are you on safari? Are you participating in a play? Is there footage of you preparing for a dance recital or a concert? Are you reading, learning, and growing?

Write "Personal Growth" at the top of a blank sheet of paper and think about the answers to those questions. Are you happy or disappointed with what you see? Regardless of what the video might show today, write what you'd like the video to highlight of your personal achievements, hobbies, and passions.

- Is there footage of you volunteering at a homeless shelter? Did someone secretly tape you smiling as you wrote a big check to a charity? Does the video show you involved at your place of worship? Are you praying before meals? Does it show footage of you reading the Bible to your children?

  Write "Spirituality" at the top of a blank sheet of paper and think about the answers to those questions. Are you happy or disappointed with what you see? Regardless of what the video might show today, write what you'd like the video to highlight of your generosity, unselfishness, and spirituality.

- How much footage is there of you at work? Do you have the time and money to take long vacations with your family? Are you able to attend all of your kids' plays and games? Are you an escort for your children's field trips? Are you driving a car that makes you proud? Are you living in the home of your dreams? Do you have the home "extras" you always wanted such as a pool, Jacuzzi, and gym? Are you filled with pleasure knowing you've saved and invested appropriately when you have to write the check to pay for your child's college tuition or your parents' health care? Do you have the look of confidence that comes from knowing you'd be fine financially if you didn't work another day in your life?

  Write "Financial Health" at the top of a blank sheet of paper and think about the answers to those questions. Are you happy or disappointed with what you see? Regardless of what the video might show today, write what you'd like the video to highlight of your passion for the work you do, free time away from work, flexibility, independence, and the lifestyle you live.

Your perfect vision is a look into the future to see the kind of life you would like to achieve. The power of having a clear vision cannot be overemphasized. If you don't define your vision for your future, I guarantee someone will impose their vision on you. By actively defining your vision, you are able to build a life that is right for you.

There's a famous story that illustrates the power of a clear vision. Walt Disney died before Disney World in Florida was completed. On opening day, a newspaper reporter asked Walt's brother, Roy, who oversaw completion of the park, "Isn't it a tragedy that Walt never got to see Disney World?" Roy replied, "Walt did see it. He saw it in his imagination. That's why you're seeing it now."

Complete Power Exercise #1 Now!

Sally's Financial Vision

Sally used the standard Life Zones featured earlier in the chapter because they each represented important areas of her life. Sally's vision for her financial health is about as far from reality as can be, but that's okay—that's why they call it a *vision*. Sally is working a full-time job and has recently started a part-time job at night and on weekends to pay off the $13,827 in credit card debt she has racked up over the years. That's her reality, but her vision for financial health is to work only one job, to travel a lot, to be debt free, to live in a big house, to put her kids through college, to have a 35 Independence Factor, and to have a great retirement.

Now that you have created a vision for your perfect future and identified the Life Zones most important to you (remember, you can go back and change this list at any time), it's time to dream BIG!

Power Exercise #2—Define Your *Want List*

> *If one advances confidently in the direction of his dreams,*
> *and endeavors to live the life which he has imagined, he will*
> *meet with a success unexpected in common hours.*
> —Henry David Thoreau

Now that you have identified a vision for each Life Zone, it's time to open the floodgates and unleash your creativity. Answer these three questions for each Life Zone:

- What do you want to own?
- What do you want to accomplish?
- Who do you want to be?

Start with the first category, Family. Take a couple of minutes to list as many items as you can for each of the three questions. For example:

- **What do you want to own?** Complete the sentence, "To support the vision I have for *Family*, I want to own _____." For example, your list might include a pool, a top-of-the-line sports car, a lakeside cabin, a fishing boat, an RV, a tennis court, a big-screen TV, a six-bedroom house, a $500,000-investment account dedicated exclusively to education, a two-carat diamond ring, and so on.

- **What do you want to accomplish?** Complete the sentence, "To support the vision I have for *Family*, I want to accomplish _____." For example, your list might include one international educational trip per year, three two-week vacations a year, having time to help your children with homework every night, being able to attend your children's sporting events and recitals, taking your spouse on a date every week, taking the family on a monthly shopping spree, being able to deliver Thanksgiving baskets to needy families, and so on.

- **Who do you want to be?** Complete the sentence, "To support the vision I have for *Family*, I want to be someone who _____." For example, your list might include being generous, setting a good example, having flexibility and free time, being a good listener, being supportive, being able to teach values, and so on.

Write the answers to these questions on paper as quickly as they come to you. Don't worry about spelling, punctuation, or listing them in any particular order. The goal is for you to have more than twenty things on your list for each question at the end of the two minutes. Force yourself to keep thinking and writing for the entire two minutes.

For this exercise, anything is possible and no want is too small, big, impractical, ridiculous, silly, or unachievable. There will be plenty of time to place limitations on yourself and your Want List but, for just a moment, make the commitment to dream big.

Don't feel bad if you've never thought about what you want to own, accomplish, and be. It is easy to get caught up in the day-to-day stuff. The here and now occupies so much of our mental focus and energy that we never get around to planning our future. Turn off the TV, unplug the phone, and shut your door. This is your chance to define what *you* want!

Complete Power Exercise #2 Now!

Sally's Financial Want List

Sally had fun escaping her current financial reality and coming up with items on her Financial Want List. Here are three of them: (1) To support the vision I have for *Financial Health,* I want to *own* an investment account worth enough so I never have to work another day in my life again; (2) To support the vision I have for *Financial Health,* I want to *accomplish* an Independence Factor of 35; and (3) to support the vision I have for *Financial Health,* I want to *be* debt free.

You have now created a vision for each area in your life that matters most and have followed this by creating a list of what you want to own, accomplish, and be for each of these areas of your life. Congratulations, you are further along than most people but you aren't done quite yet. The list you created in Power Exercise #2 is a raw and unfinished product at this point. With a little more work, you will turn these desires into powerful goals. Not just any goals, but IMPACT-Goals.

Power Exercise #3— Create and Prioritize *IMPACT-Goals*

> *If you aim at nothing, you'll hit it every time.*
> —Author unknown

This exercise will help you transform your Want List into concrete, action-oriented goals. The difference between an average goal and an IMPACT-Goal is like the difference between a car on empty and a car with gas. A car without fuel might be nice to look at and sit in, but it isn't going to take you anywhere. Having a list of goals might look good on your bathroom mirror, but if they are not designed to move you closer to your destination, they are meaningless.

The difference between a "good" and an "average" goal lies in how the goal is designed, not in the value of the goal itself. Don't set just any kind of goal, set IMPACT-Goals. IMPACT-Goals are designed to maximize the likelihood of their being accomplished, and as a result, make an *impact* on your life.

Regardless of your current situation or your aspirations, your life is headed in a certain direction. Whether you are the CEO of a large corporation working eighty hours a week or a stay-at-home mom, your energy and focus are pointed in a certain direction. Even if you feel you are confused and your life is going nowhere, you are still headed in a direction.

This concept can be hard to grasp. Many people say, "My life is headed *nowhere*! Why are you telling me that it is going in a certain direction?!" Don't confuse direction or effort with destination. We can drive nonstop for days in the wrong direction and never make it to our destination. Goal setting gives us the destination *and* the direction.

Consider the captain of a cruise ship. Once he leaves port, he must have the exact coordinates of his destination. He may need to change course to avoid storms or to navigate around islands, but he never loses sight of the ship's destination.

Before we start Power Exercise #3, I want to clear up any confusion and misunderstanding surrounding goal setting. Many of you have listed your goals in the past and have been disappointed with the results. There are many reasons why you may not have had success with goal setting in the past. Maybe you expected results from simply identifying your goals. Most often, though, I find that unachieved goals have not been properly designed for success.

Have you ever been taught how to design a good goal? If you are like most people, you probably haven't. Goal setting is not taught in schools, even though it is one of the tools that can make the most impact on success. We learn the Periodic Table of Elements and how to dissect a frog, but we don't learn the easy process of setting good goals. Once you complete this section, you will have a Ph.D. in goal setting. You will learn how to set IMPACT-Goals—goals that are designed to be accomplished. But before you can create IMPACT-Goals, you need to know what they are.

The Top Five Excuses We Use for Not Setting Goals!

1. I shouldn't have to set goals. An aspiring young musician attended a concert with his father. After a brilliant performance by a world-renowned pianist,

the young boy exclaimed to the performer, "I'd give my life to play like you."
The old pianist smiled and remarked, "I have."

*Too many people fall into the trap of thinking that they should get what
they want because they deserve it. Nothing gets me fuming faster than
people who feel they shouldn't have to work for their dreams. The sooner
you learn that life isn't fair, the more control you will have over your happiness. If you sit back and wait for your dreams to come true, you will likely
be sitting a long time. Be the person that not only deserves it, but earns it
and gets it.*

2. **If I reach my goals, I will get bored.** In 1969, Buzz Aldrin—one of the
world's most famous astronauts—landed on the moon. It was one of the
single greatest goals ever set and accomplished in history. It was a monumental achievement for our nation and for an individual. If you were an as-
tronaut in the 1960s, flying to the moon was not a goal, it was *the* goal. In
the weeks and months after Aldrin returned from this successful space
flight, he sank into a deep depression. In a 2001 interview with *Psychology
Today* magazine, Buzz reflected on this time period and said the following:

"What am I doing? What is my role in life now? I realized that I was experiencing a melancholy of things done. I really had no future plans after re-
turning from the moon. So, I had to reexamine my life."

Buzz set a huge goal and accomplished it, but instead of feeling satisfaction, he felt empty.

*When you direct so much of your mental energy to accomplishing one
goal, a void can replace the daily struggle and challenge when you succeed. The problem Buzz faced was that his entire identity was wrapped up
in going to the moon. Once he accomplished it, he lost his identity and his
sense of purpose. This is one of the reasons why it is so important to have
a balanced life (see Chapter 1).*

*It is also important to set new and challenging goals as you begin to
reach existing goals. If you reach one destination, but already have a map
and route planned for the next adventure, you are less likely to experience
emptiness and lack of purpose.*

3. **If I set goals, I could fail.** Nobody likes to fail, and goal setting has all of
the trappings for failure. When you take time to set goals, write them down,
and pursue them, it is easy to determine if you've failed in reaching those
specific goals. Why would anyone want to set themselves up for such an
obvious indication of failure? Most choose not to take the risk and either
don't set goals or, if they do, they set such easily attainable goals that failure
is impossible.

What they don't understand is that failure is the one thing that separates winners from losers. Winners fail and losers don't. Yes, you read that correctly. The key characteristic of a winner is that he fails miserably, and some fail quite often. Thomas Edison failed more than a thousand times trying to invent the lightbulb, but—because of his commitment to this goal— finally succeeded.

Losers never fail because they never do anything challenging or risky enough to cause them to fail. Losers either don't set goals or, if they do, they lower the bar on those goals so that success is virtually guaranteed. You cannot achieve worthwhile, challenging, and deeply personal goals without experiencing failure.

4. **If I set goals, I'm admitting I'm not happy.** Not true. Goal setting involves taking an honest look at your current situation and thinking about what you would like to improve. By setting a goal to spend more time with your family, it implies that the amount of time you are currently spending with your family is not as much as you would like.

   If this belief prevents you from setting goals, your view of happiness is flawed. Admitting you'd like areas of your life to improve does not automatically mean you are admitting unhappiness. Happiness is not like a lightbulb with only two choices—on or off. Happiness is a continuum. You may feel marginally happy, fairly happy, or even very happy. Saying that you'd rather spend more time with your family does not mean you are not happy with the amount of time you spend with your family, it just means that you would feel even happier by spending more time with them.

   You may discover through the goal-setting process that there are areas in your life where you truly are unhappy. If this is the case, wouldn't you rather identify these areas and improve instead of burying your head in the sand and pretending nothing is wrong? Psychologists tell us that we can only suppress unhappiness or dissatisfaction for so long until it inevitably surfaces. It may come out in an explosive burst, or it may slowly creep out over time. Dissatisfaction is like a virus. It often spreads and infects the healthy and happy areas of our life. Don't be afraid to expose the unhappy areas of your life. Use this mental uncovering as your wake-up call.

5. **I don't like to plan.** Would you rather take a vacation or plan one? Most of us would rather *do* than *plan*. We want to see immediate results. Planning, by definition, is about future results. The time we "waste" planning something that may or may not occur in the future could be spent doing something right now with an instant payoff. Why plan for tomorrow when we can live for today?

Dreaming and planning your life can be rewarding itself. You will feel richly rewarded just thinking about what you want to own, what you want to accomplish in life, and who you want to be. Planning your life will be fun in this chapter.

To see the top remaining ten excuses people make for not setting goals, go to www.SixDayFinancialMakeover.com.

What Is an IMPACT-Goal?

The one objective in setting a personal goal is accomplishing it. Regardless of what the actual goal is, an IMPACT-Goal by design maximizes the chances of success. An IMPACT-Goal must be *I*nspiring, *M*easurable, *P*urposeful, *A*ctive, *C*ontrollable, *T*ime-specific. An IMPACT-Goal must contain all of these components:

Inspiring—Your personal goal must inspire and motivate you. Without this critical element, you will not have the fuel to overcome setbacks and challenges or to take continuous action to move the goal forward. Your goals don't need to be monumental—ending world hunger or curing cancer—to be inspiring. If it's inspiring, any goal, big or small, is enough. One of the ways to guarantee an *uninspiring* goal is to set a goal that someone else wants you to achieve. For goals to be personally inspiring, they must be personal.

Measurable—Your personal goal must be measurable. The goal should be drafted so that there is no room for confusion or misinterpretation about achievement. When creating a goal, ask yourself, "Can a stranger look at my goal and tell me—with 100 percent accuracy—if it has been accomplished?" The measurable element of your goal should have a number component—a dollar amount, a number of days, a number of times per week, and so on. By assigning a number or dollar amount to the goal, you will be able to clearly and objectively measure your success. See the worksheet on page 32 to make your Independence Factor "measurable."

Purposeful—A goal without a purpose is like a car without gas. The reason behind your goal must support your vision. If it doesn't, one of two things will happen. Either you won't be driven to accomplish the goal because it runs against your vision, or you will accomplish the goal and later realize that the "ladder was against the wrong building."

Active—Goal setting and goal attaining need to be active. A laminated list of your goals might look pretty, but that doesn't mean you're any closer to attaining them. For a goal to be an IMPACT-Goal, it must promote action. For each goal, list one or more tasks that will move you closer to realizing the goal.

Controllable—Don't fall into the trap of setting goals over which you have no control. This is a formula for failure. Set goals only where you have a substantial amount of control over the outcome.

Time-specific—A well-crafted vision should not have an ending, but a goal needs a specific deadline. An IMPACT-Goal should support that ongoing vision but it must have a concrete timeline. A realistic deadline for accomplishing your goal provides the invisible drive to complete it—a ticking clock gives most of us the determination to take action to realize our goal. A specific timeline allows you to prioritize your goals.

I Want to Increase My Independence Factor, but How Do I Make It "Measurable"?

To be an IMPACT-Goal, your goal must be measurable, but how do you know how much money you need in your investment account to produce a sufficient amount of passive income? If you took the Financial Independence Quiz in Chapter 1, this will be easy.
(You can also calculate this online at www.SixDayFinancialMakeover.com.)

Step 1—Enter your desired
Independence Factor   **Desired Independence Factor**   (A) _____

Step 2—Enter your current
Independence Factor   **Current Independence Factor**   (B) _____
("**I**" from the Independence Factor worksheet)

Step 3—Divide your Desired Independence Factor
by your Current Independence Factor
(A ÷ B)   **Independence Factor Multiple**   (C) _____

Step 4—Enter your current Total
Monthly Passive Income   **Total Monthly Passive Income**   (D) _____
("**G**" from the Independence Factor worksheet)

Step 5—Multiply your current Total
Monthly Passive Income by your
Independence Factor Multiple   **Desired Total Monthly**
(C × D)   **Passive Income**   (E) $_____

Step 6—Enter your Non-Investment Monthly
Passive Income   **Non-Investment Passive Income**   (F) $_____
("**F**" from the Independence Factor worksheet)

Step 7—Subtract Non-Investment Passive Income from
your Desired Total Monthly Passive Income
(E − F)   **Desired Monthly Investment Income**   (G) $_____

Step 8—Divide your Desired Monthly Investment Income by 0.33%*
(i.e., 0.0033):
(G ÷ 0.0033) = Enter total →   **Total Investments Required**   (H) $_____

Now that you know what an IMPACT-Goal is, it's your turn to create one for each of your Want List items!

Sally's Financial Want List

Sally came up with several pages of IMPACT-Goals. Here are two from her Financial Life Zone:

(1) I want to be debt-free within two years from today so I can feel better about myself and so I can start saving for my retirement. I will become debt-free by cutting up my credit cards, having $100 from my paycheck automatically sent to pay down my credit card bill, and by using 100 percent of my holiday bonus to pay off my debt.

(2) I want to have an Independence Factor of 35 by the time I am fifty years old. By having $725,000 in an investment account, I will have an Independence Factor of 35 and I will feel in control of my life! I will accomplish this goal by contributing the maximum to my 401(k) account, by saving and investing $300 per paycheck, and by investing all bonuses I receive.

---

* Why 0.33 percent? This calculation assumes you can withdraw 4 percent of your portfolio each year, a fairly conservative amount you should be able to take out, year after year, without depleting your assets.

At this point, you may have twenty, thirty, or more IMPACT-Goals. That's great! It can be daunting to look at this list, though. You may be wondering, "Where do I start?!"

Regardless of your background, upbringing, education, career, title, or bank account size, we all have the same number of hours in a week. How you choose to spend your 8,760 hours this year is your decision. Where you start entirely depends on what's most important to you. What do you want to accomplish first? Where do you want to focus your time and energy?

For each Life Zone, prioritize your IMPACT-Goals within that area. For example, if you have six IMPACT-Goals in your Relationships Life Zone, rank them in order of priority—which one do you want to accomplish first, second, third, and so on. Once you've done this for relationships, do it for physical health, financial health, family, etc. When you're done, you will have created several lists and several number one priorities.

It is important that you prioritize within each Life Zone rather than have one list where you list all of your IMPACT-Goals in order. By having multiple goals as a priority across each area, you minimize the risk of focusing all of your time on one area or goal. It's dangerous to focus all your time striving for one goal in one area of your life—you may eventually accomplish the goal, but at the expense of everything else. Live a balanced life by focusing on the most important goals across all areas of your life.

Prioritize your goals so you'll know exactly where to focus in each Life Zone.

Complete Power Exercise #3 Now!

Sally's Financial Want List Prioritized

Prioritizing Sally's want list across each Life Zone took some time, but she quickly determined what was most important when it came to her financial health. She put a big #1 and a star next to "become debt-free." For Sally, this was her number one financial priority.

Power Exercise #4—Calculate How *Money* Can Help

Annual income twenty pounds, annual expenditure nineteen six, result happiness. Annual income twenty

pounds, annual expenditure twenty pounds ought and six,
result misery.

—Charles Dickens

The importance of excellent financial health cannot be overemphasized. The lifestyle you desire and the goals you want to achieve either require or can be enhanced by an expense. This is pretty obvious for those dreams where we want something. For example, travel, better car, fishing boat, bigger house, vacation cottage, Rolex watch, and diamond earrings are expenses. It takes money to obtain each of these goals. Without the necessary finances, you will never accomplish these goals.

What about the vision of accomplishment? Regardless of what you want to accomplish, it requires money or can be enhanced with money. For example, working fewer hours, learning a new language, earning a master's degree, learning to play the piano, exploring the Amazon, diving the Great Barrier Reef, and so many other endeavors require you to open your purse or wallet.

For many, their number one goal is furthering their education. Yet if, for example, you want to earn your master's degree, unless you are one of those incredibly rare individuals who earn a full scholarship, tuition requires a substantial amount of money. Even if you take a loan, you must eventually repay it.

Let's examine a less obvious example. If your goal is to learn a new language, you could borrow a book from the library or buy an audio program and learn the basics. While learning a new language this way wouldn't cost you much, if you had money, it could shorten the time you needed to learn the new language. How? If you had money, you could spend time in the country of the language's origin, you could get a personal language tutor, and you could take group classes. Money, in this situation, would shorten the time it would take you to learn the language and would enhance your ability to speak the language. The difference is dramatic between reading a language book from the library and immersing yourself in the language and customs of a new country.

Finally, even many of those goals that support your vision of who you want to *be* can be *enhanced* with money, but it's important to first understand that shaping who you want to be doesn't *require* money. You can be generous, caring, good-natured, funny, optimistic, honest, loyal, courageous, wise, dependable, and so many other worthwhile characteristics without a dime to your name. I'm sure you've known countless people in your life who didn't have much money but who had become someone you admired, respected, and would like to emulate. My grandmother was one such person. She had every quality I could hope to obtain. She was rich in character but had very little financially. Money was not necessary for her to be that caliber of person.

Yet, you can use money as a tool to help enhance who you want to be. How? If your goal is to be more generous, excess money can certainly enhance your joy in accomplishing this goal. By having more, you are able to give more. If your goal is to be wiser, you can use money to take classes in subjects that interest you. If your goal is to be more dependable, you can use money to complete a time-management program. If your goal is to be funny, you can use money to take a stand-up comedy class. If your goal is to be more compassionate, you can use money to visit countries struck by famine or to learn about and visit Anne Frank's home in Amsterdam. If your goal is to be a great communicator, you can use money to hire a personal speech coach. Almost any goal that helps you become the person you desire can be enhanced with money.

Some people have a hard time thinking of money as a tool. Money has no value other than what it can buy. Don't be a slave to money. See it for what it really is—a way to enhance your goals. When you are on your deathbed, you won't ask yourself, "Why didn't I make more money?" Instead, you might ask yourself, "Why didn't I go on that African safari, donate to that charity, or help support my son's entrepreneurial spirit?"

The objective of this exercise is to assign a dollar amount to as many of your IMPACT-Goals as possible. This will be easy for many of your goals. If one of your goals is to own a new Mercedes SL 500, you can quickly determine how much this will cost. If your goal is to spend four weeks traveling throughout Europe, with a little research you can assign a price tag to this goal as well.

It may take some creativity to come up with a plan to support your goal. As an example, part of my career vision is to help as many people as I can to accomplish their goals. This is a vision that excites and inspires me. In order to turn this vision into a reality, I have created several IMPACT-Goals to support it. It wasn't easy to think of individual goals that would help me get closer to realizing this dream, but with a little creativity, I developed a few. I quickly realized that my time is limited—I can only work with a fixed number of clients individually. Yet, by writing a book, I could teach thousands of people how to accomplish their goals through better financial health.

Now it's your turn. For each of your IMPACT-Goals, think of as many things as you can to help you accomplish the goal. Some of these things won't cost you anything (for example, jogging three nights a week or read-ing to your children). For those that do cost money, assign a dollar amount to each of those strategies. For example, completing your bachelor's degree may cost $6,500 or taking time off from work may cost several hundred dol-lars in lost wages. Don't forget about your Independence Factor! One of your primary Financial Health IMPACT-Goals should be to increase your Independence Factor to at least 31.

Complete Power Exercise #4 Now!

Sally's Use of Money

Could Sally use money to help her pay off her debt? Yes, of course, but how much would she need? She calculated she would need to use $100 per pay-check and her $5,000 holiday bonus per year to pay off her credit card debt. In order not to get into credit card trouble again, she determined she could spend $119.50 and attend a local community college course on personal fi-nance and $29.99 to get a copy of her credit report from each reporting agency and to purchase a credit repair workbook. Additionally, she wanted an Inde-pendence Factor of 35! To achieve this, she would need to have $725,000 in an investment account. She calculated that it would take saving $300 per pay-check.

Power Exercise #5—Use *Pictures* for Motivation

When words become unclear, I shall focus with photographs.
—Ansel Adams

This next and final step is one of the most fun. We've done a lot of work put-ting our vision, purpose, and goals into words, but now it is time to trans-form the words into something more powerful—images. You are going to take the work you've done so far and create a picture scrapbook of your goals that will allow you to instantly reconnect with your goals.

Why pictures? Our mind thinks and remembers in pictures. We remem-ber faces but forget names. When we read a story, we create a visual image of the characters and the situation. The great communicators use language to create mental images. A picture can communicate much more quickly and efficiently than a word.

What is more effective, reading your goal about taking a trip to Fiji or looking at a picture of a Fijian beach with crystal clear water and palm trees? Which one gets you more excited? Which one will move you closer to accomplishing the goal? Which one will you remember longer?

So here's the exercise: For each of your goals, cut out two or three pictures that represent them. Take your time finding pictures that get your juices flowing. If one of your goals is to own a new Jaguar XJ8, buy a car magazine or visit your local dealership and pick up a brochure. If you are having trouble finding good pictures, the best place to find glossy pictures is in magazines, brochures, or on the Internet.

Remember, you've created goals not just for things you want to own, but also for things you want to accomplish and the person you want to be. While it is easier to find pictures representing tangible things you want to own, you can also locate pictures representing what you want to accomplish and who you want to be.

If you want to earn a Ph.D., cut out a picture of a diploma. If you want to learn how to play the piano, cut out a picture of a piano or of someone playing the piano. If you want to work fewer hours, take a picture of your office with a clock at 3:30 P.M. with you noticeably absent. You can find a picture for almost anything you want to accomplish. For example, one of the things I want to accomplish is to go on an African safari. There are a lot of places I could have gone to get pictures of Africa, but I chose to cut out pictures from a brochure created by Wilderness Travel—a company that offers guided adventures across the globe. Pictures that provide images more specific to my actual goal motivate me more strongly.

You can even find pictures representing the person you want to be. Do you want to be a better parent? Cut out a picture of your kids on vacation or doing their homework. Do you want to be a better communicator? Cut out a picture of Ronald Reagan. Bottom line, no matter what your goal, you can find a picture to capture or express it.

Have fun with this exercise—get creative. While it might sound slightly silly—like making a collage in elementary school—using pictures will bring life to your goals by making them real.

Once you've cut out all of the pictures, it is time to create your Dream Board™. There are a couple of options. You can either create a portable goal collage by using a three-ring binder or a poster board that you hang on a wall.

If you choose the binder, create several sections—each one representing a Life Zone. Within each section, write your IMPACT-Goals. You can tape the pictures next to each goal or you can have several pictures of goals on one page.

You could also create a poster board with pictures representing all of your goals. There is nothing more powerful than looking at a collection of pictures that represents your most important goals and dreams. Take a few minutes every day to review the destination you have set for yourself, and then spend the rest of the time pursuing it with vigor.

Complete Power Exercise #5 Now!

Sally's Use of Pictures

Sally was never much of an artist or arts and crafts person, but she really got into the collage exercise. She went through old magazines and cut out dozens of pictures. Her favorites? A credit card offer ad that she put a big "X" through. A photo of an Amish woman (they're known for paying cash for everything). And a photo of a big pile of cash she found to represent all the interest she was saving herself by paying off the debt quickly.

Congratulations! You've completed the first day of your financial makeover. Now that you have a clear vision for your future and a list of inspiring goals, you are ready to move to Day 2! If your financial makeover is going to have a long-lasting and positive effect on your life, we need to take a close look at our beliefs. Are they helping or hurting our financial success? Many of us are our own worst enemies. We talk ourselves out of success and set ourselves up for failure. By first recognizing and then changing our limiting beliefs we can transform our financial life from the inside out.

Action Steps

Every skyscraper you see today was first imagined in someone's head, but they didn't stop there. They took the next step and put their design on paper. Did you complete the exercises in this chapter yet? It's not easy to create the life of your dreams, but it should be fun!

Go through the Action Steps below and put a check mark in one of the following boxes for each one:

Create Your Online Financial Makeover Account

1. ☐ COMPLETED   ☐ NEED TO COMPLETE   ☐ DOES NOT APPLY

Did you create your free online account at www.SixDayFinancialMake over.com yet? If so, good for you! If you haven't, what are you waiting for? There are free tools, quizzes, and templates you'll have access to only if you have an account.

More important, you will have "someone" who will track your progress and help you take what you've learned and implement it in your life. If all you do is read this book, you won't transform your financial life. The only thing that will improve your finances and peace of mind is taking what you've learned and implementing it in your life. The free online assistant will guide you through the implementation process. It doesn't forget and doesn't take no for an answer, so go ahead and register right now at www.SixDayFinancialMakeover.com.

2. ☐ COMPLETED   ☐ NEED TO COMPLETE   ☐ DOES NOT APPLY

Log in to your account at www.SixDayFinancialMakeover.com and update it with your progress.

Design the Life of Your Dreams

1. ☐ COMPLETED   ☐ NEED TO COMPLETE   ☐ DOES NOT APPLY

Complete Power Exercise #1—Create the Perfect *Vision* for Your Future. You need to create a personal and compelling vision. This will drive your Financial Makeover and be the foundation for the rest of the work you'll do over the six days.

> *Where there is no vision, the people perish.*
>   —Proverbs 29:18

2. ☐ COMPLETED   ☐ NEED TO COMPLETE   ☐ DOES NOT APPLY

Complete Exercise #2—Define Your *Want* List. Determine what you want to own, what you want to accomplish, and who you want to be.

If one advances confidently in the direction of his dreams,
and endeavors to live the life which he has imagined, he
will meet with a success unexpected in common hours.

—Henry David Thoreau

3. ☐ COMPLETED   ☐ NEED TO COMPLETE   ☐ DOES NOT APPLY

Complete Power Exercise #3—Create and Prioritize *IMPACT-Goals.* Transform run-of-the-mill goals into Inspiring, Measurable, Purposeful, Active, Controllable, and Time-Specific IMPACT-Goals.

If you aim at nothing, you'll hit it every time.

—Author unknown

4. ☐ COMPLETED   ☐ NEED TO COMPLETE   ☐ DOES NOT APPLY

Complete Power Exercise #4—Calculate How *Money* Can Help. Turn your goals into dollar signs. Determine how money can help you accomplish your goals and set a dollar amount for each goal.

Annual income twenty pounds, annual expenditure
nineteen six, result happiness. Annual income twenty
pounds, annual expenditure twenty pounds ought and six,
result misery.

—Charles Dickens

5. ☐ COMPLETED   ☐ NEED TO COMPLETE   ☐ DOES NOT APPLY

Complete Power Exercise #5—Use *Pictures* for Motivation. Transform your vision, purpose, and goals from words to pictures!

When words become unclear, I shall focus with
photographs.

—Ansel Adams

Update Your Online Financial Makeover Account

1. ☐ COMPLETED   ☐ NEED TO COMPLETE   ☐ DOES NOT APPLY

Before you do anything else, update your Six-Day Financial Makeover account at www.SixDayFinancialMakeover.com.

CHAPTER 3

Eliminate Limiting Beliefs

Are you ready to stop your internal critic? Are you ready to break free from those limiting beliefs that have held you back from financial success? You have the passion, the vision, and the goals—but often, they are not enough. We may know what we should do, but for whatever reason, we don't do it. This chapter will help you stop being your own greatest barrier to success and will help you align your thoughts and actions for maximum achievement.

Should I read this chapter?

	TRUE	FALSE
1. I sometimes think that no matter what I do, I won't get ahead.	☐	☐
2. I don't think I'm smart enough or have what it takes to become financially successful.	☐	☐
3. Even though I'm "successful," I sometimes feel that getting by is good enough.	☐	☐
4. I've put off saving/investing because it's not worth it unless I have a few thousand to invest at once.	☐	☐
5. I'd like to learn how to eliminate limiting beliefs so they don't prevent me from living the life I created in Day 1.	☐	☐

If you answered any of these questions TRUE, you should read this chapter.

Chapter Toolbar			
Cost to Implement Advice	**Likelihood of Needing Strategies in Chapter**	**Need Professional Advice?**	**Website Tools**
$0	1 2 3 4 5 6 7 8 9 10 Not Likely Very Likely	👤 👤 👤 👤 👤 No Definitely	Yes

Congratulations! You've completed Day 1. You designed the life of your dreams by identifying your vision and destination. You know exactly what you want to own, accomplish, and be. Some of you may be excited and ready to get started making that vision a reality through good financial health and financial independence. Others may be hesitant or unconvinced. Is something holding you back?

Intellectually, I think we know that we *can* achieve our goals and feel financially secure, but emotionally, we may not believe it's possible. We think, "If I clarify my goals, save more, and invest wisely, I could 'theoretically' live the life of my dreams. If I got a good handle on my finances, protected my assets, and minimized my financial and personal risks, I could be more optimistic and confident about the future." In our hearts, we know it is true, but it may seem like financial success is for everyone else.

Day 2 will help you get out of your way. No matter how passionate you are about achieving the life you designed in Day 1, you won't maximize your finances and fully align yourself with your goals until you take a look within. Start by reviewing the most commonly held beliefs that undermine financial success and then take concrete steps to eliminate your limiting beliefs. In this chapter, we will review the common financial mental traps we set for ourselves, and discover ways to overcome those beliefs.

You can experience a financial transformation in six days—believe me, it *is* possible. In fact, you're already on your way. Before moving forward, take a moment to recognize the wonderful opportunity that lies before you. We live at a time and in a country where we are free to choose the life we want to live. Billions of others living right now do not have the exceptional free-dom that we take for granted.

How do we seize this opportunity? Unfortunately, as Henry David Thoreau wrote, we live lives of quiet desperation. We know there is more, but do not seek it. We create a perfect vision for our lives, but we don't go af-ter it. We get stuck in life. We wake in the morning, drive to work, put in our hours, and come home. We live for weekends, holidays, and our annual two-week vacation.

We race from one fire to the next—rushing by the smoldering ones to put out those that have already erupted into flames. We focus on the here and now, putting more thought and energy into planning our next vacation than in escaping the daily rut of our lives.

We seek change but continue to plod along doing the same things and wondering why nothing changes. Sometimes what we really need to change . . . is ourselves. This chapter will help you identify and overcome those beliefs that are holding you back. Those beliefs that have prevented you from achieving and living the life you've wanted.

Have you ever noticed how adult elephants are secured? You would ex-pect that such a large, strong animal would require several large, thick chains to prevent it from walking away. Instead, these thirteen-thousand-pound behemoths are secured by a thin rope tied around their foot. With very little effort, the elephant could easily break the rope and roam free, yet it doesn't.

How could such a large animal be rendered powerless with just a small rope? The answer lies in the elephant's early conditioning. Circus owners knew that it would have been nearly impossible to secure an adult ele-phant, but found that if they began restraining the baby elephant—when it was not yet strong enough to break free—it would learn, after repeated fail-ures, that it could never break free.

So a baby elephant is secured with a chain. At first, the young elephant struggles and struggles. Each unsuccessful attempt makes it more defiant to overcome. However, its defiance gradually lessens until its desire for freedom becomes lost forever. At this point, owners are free to replace the chain with a small rope. With its foot still "secured," the adult elephant doesn't bother to try to break free.

I'm sure you're thinking, "If I was an elephant, I would look down at that puny rope and snap it with a twitch of my leg. It can't keep me from doing what I want!" Perfect! That's the kind of attitude I want you to have. It may sound silly, but you need to become the elephant. Look down at your massive gray leg, see the little rope for what it is, and break free from your limiting beliefs.

Eliminate Limiting Beliefs

I've bought several used cars in my life, and I learned an important lesson early after making a big mistake. I did my research. I looked through the paper and auto magazines. When I saw an ad for the car I wanted at a local dealership, I called them and they invited me to look at the car that evening. With check in hand, I went to the dealership. The car looked and drove great.

After negotiating with the dealer, I purchased the car. The next afternoon, I came to pick it up. Much to my dismay, the car that looked so great at night looked terrible in the daylight. Don't make the same mistake. It's critically important to see things as they really are.

What are the thin ropes in your life that hold you back? What beliefs prevent you from moving forward and having the life you desire? Once you see the thin ropes for what they really are, you can easily break free from their hold on you; but you must first recognize them and see that they have no power over you.

The seven most common limiting financial beliefs are:

1. No matter what I do, I can't get ahead.

2. Getting by is good enough.

3. Small actions are insignificant and don't produce big rewards.

4. If I'm financially successful, I'll be working so much I won't have any time with my family or my hobbies.

5. You must lie, cheat, and take advantage of people to become successful.

6. I'm not smart enough to be financially successful.

7. I should be able to read a book or attend a conference and immediately become financially successful.

Read this section and determine which beliefs are holding you back. If you discover that one or more of these are keeping you from achieving financial success, take the necessary steps to break free and begin living the life you desire.

Limiting Belief #1: No matter what I do, I can't get ahead.

Warning: This belief is extremely dangerous to your wealth and is guaranteed to cause financial paralysis.

It would be easier to sprint to an Olympic gold medal while carrying a bag of groceries than it would be to succeed financially with this debilitating mind-set. Like the massive elephants secured by a tiny rope, people who have tried but failed to get ahead, gain control, or succeed can also give up and resign themselves to life on a tether.

Psychologists call this phenomenon "learned helplessness." Dr. Martin Seligman coined this term and has researched and written extensively on the subject. It comes down to one thing—control.

The cause of learned helplessness, according to Seligman, is being exposed repeatedly to an uncontrollable event. After many repeated and failed attempts to accomplish something while in an uncontrollable event, your brain "learns" that success is beyond your control; that you cannot affect the outcome. Once "conditioned" in this belief, the individual gives up hope and effort, even when later exposed to an event where control *is* possible. In effect, you've learned to become helpless.

This is one of the reasons why the rich get richer and the poor get poorer. Many poor people may have developed the belief that no matter how hard they work and how much education they get, they will never get out of the financial straitjacket they are in. It's no wonder why poor people play lotteries in greater numbers than any other income class. The middle class surely wants and needs the money, too. The difference is that some of the poor see the lottery as the *only* way they can get ahead. If you truly believe that regardless of what you do today, it won't positively impact tomorrow, you are destined to fall short of your potential.

In life, we all experience situations where we seem to lack control. It can be very easy for us to believe that we are powerless over certain aspects of our life. Worse yet, if we have this sense of defeat and powerlessness in certain areas of our life, it can bleed over into other areas—where we do have considerable control—and infect our success and happiness like a virus.

If there are areas in your life where you think your actions do not influence the future, chances are you *do* have some control and you need to break free from this limiting belief. Keep the following six concepts in mind to begin the process of eliminating this limiting belief:

- **Change is possible.** If you think your finances or life can't improve, you won't take any steps to make it better. You must first open your mind to the possibility that your current financial situation actually *can* improve. If you are still having a hard time accepting this, ask if it is possible for your life to get *worse* because of steps you take. If your life can get worse as a result of your actions, there's no reason to think it can't get better as a result of your actions!

- **Think big.** Think outside of your self-imposed restraints. If you think big enough, you will have the motivation to take the initial steps and the fuel to keep progressing even in the face of challenges and disappointment.

- **Get perspective.** If the elephant looked at his situation objectively, he would surely see the weakness in the small rope. If your friend were in your situation, wouldn't you encourage her to think about her situation objectively and to take whatever action that is appropriate? What would you tell her?

- **Set goals.** Just the act of setting goals will help you overcome the feeling that you have no control over your future. The energy and thought process required to set goals will get your mind thinking in a whole new way. Chapter 2 explained why goals are so important, why most of us don't set goals, and showed you, step by step, how to set motivating goals.

- **Achieving successes.** One of the best ways to overcome the belief that your actions don't affect your future is to start achieving small successes. While goals must be big and motivating, there should also be small and achievable goals along the way.

- **Consider a different viewpoint.** Seligman's research on learned helplessness inspired him to look at optimists and pessimists and examine how both types of people explain good and bad events. He writes in *Authentic Happiness*, "Optimistic people tend to interpret troubles as transient, controllable, and specific to one situation.

Pessimistic people, in contrast, believe that their troubles last forever, undermine everything they do and are uncontrollable."[1] In short, if we can change the way we explain the events that occur in our lives, we will be less likely to suffer from learned helplessness.

The conditioning of learned helplessness can take years to develop, so if the problem is severe enough, you should seek the advice of a licensed therapist or personal coach to help you break free from this paralyzing limiting belief.

> **TAKE AWAY** *You do have influence over your life. Even if you don't believe it right now, act as if you do. Start small so you can begin to see how your actions produce results.*

Limiting Belief #2: Getting by is good enough.

This is one of the most debilitating beliefs you can have. You get exactly what you are willing to accept. If you accept mediocrity, you will surely get it. Helen Keller once remarked, "Life is either a daring adventure or nothing at all."

It is easy to fall into the mental trap of mediocrity. Because it doesn't take much to get by, we grow complacent. We stop growing and seeking challenges. We don't push ourselves to succeed. We cultivate a lifestyle well below our potential, but one that is just good enough that it doesn't require much challenge or action.

Tolerance is critical for survival. It has allowed us to endure horrific conditions by helping us quickly adapt to the situation. Our ability to adapt to our surroundings is both a gift and a curse. There are some life forms that cannot survive unless their conditions are ideal. Vary their environment even a little and they perish. As humans, we don't have this problem. We can tolerate, and even flourish, in wild extremes.

In many situations, however, tolerance and adaptability are also a curse. We stay in poor relationships longer than we should because it is "comfortable enough" and requires so much more energy to make a change. We'll endure critical bosses who never have nice things to say about us because we tell ourselves that they're not "that bad." We'll live paycheck to paycheck for years because we fool ourselves into thinking it's the "best we can do."

---

1. Seligman, *Authentic Happiness*, 9–10.

If you place a frog in a pot of hot water, it will immediately jump out. However, if you place a frog in a pot of cold water and turn on the heat, it will stay in the pot and won't notice that it is slowly being boiled to death.[2] You and I tend to act like the frog, and don't notice incremental change.

It's amazing how much we can tolerate when our environment changes slowly. Incremental change is our worst enemy. It permits us to gradually accept living standards that we never would have accepted in the beginning.

The best way to determine if you have settled is to take an honest look at your present situation. Are you where you want to be? Have you forgotten once vivid dreams and aspirations? Success has been defined as the progressive realization of a worthy goal. Based on this definition, are you successful?

There is a dark side to not "settling." I'm sure there is at least one person in your life who suffers from the belief that nothing is ever good enough. No matter how successful he becomes or how much money he makes, he is never satisfied with his life. This mind-set is a guaranteed formula for frustration and unhappiness.

While it is healthy and motivating to work for and to dream about reaching your goals, it is imperative to be thankful for where you are and what you already have. Regardless of your situation, you have a thousand things for which to give thanks. Do not lose sight of these aspects of your life. Don't lose sight of how far you've come and of what you've already accomplished on your journey in life.

TAKE AWAY *The minute you realize getting by isn't good enough is the minute you will expect more for yourself. You can have more. The goals you set in Day 1 prove it.*

Limiting Belief #3: Small actions are insignificant and don't produce big rewards.

Have you ever thought the following? I won't go back to school until I can go full-time. I won't open that investment account until I have a few thousand dollars to invest. I won't start reading that book until I go on vacation and have a few days to finish it. I'm not going to start contributing to my

---

2. This often repeated frog story is actually a fable. *Fast Company* magazine debunked this urban legend in November 1995 in their humorous "Next Time, What Say We Boil a Consultant" article. It's still a great metaphor, though.

401(k) plan until I can defer at least 10 percent. It's not worth starting piano lessons until I have at least three afternoons free a week. I'm going to quit exercising because I can only make it twice a week. I'm not going to cut down on smoking until I can quit cold turkey. One doughnut a day isn't going to ruin my diet. When the kids move out and I retire, I will start writing my book.

If some of these statements hit close to home, you may be suffering from this debilitating belief. You're not alone. This is one of the most pervasive and limiting beliefs and is guaranteed to prevent you from reaching your goals and financial success.

It's easy to dismiss small actions as trivial and inconsequential for two reasons. First, we're impatient and expect immediate results. In the short-term, the results our small actions create really are unnoticeable. On the surface, these small actions don't appear to matter because you can't see any meaningful and immediate results. We want today's actions to produce visible and measurable results today, not tomorrow or a week or year from now. If we're putting in the effort now, we want the results now!

Second, we only expect big results from big effort. If you dedicate a lot of time or money to something, you expect the outcome to reflect your contribution. If I hire a tutor to teach me Spanish five days a week, I expect to learn Spanish quickly. If I bring a book with me on a plane, I know that I'll be able to get through most of it by the time I land. If I invest my entire bonus, I'll be able to make a lot of money on it. This kind of one-for-one tradeoff makes sense. Put in your time or money and get an equal result.

The problem in thinking that only big efforts produce big rewards is that it prevents you from taking small steps today. This kind of "big or nothing" thinking stops you from taking action that could, over time, lead to greatness. If you always stop yourself from taking action because "it's not worth it" or "it's not going to matter," then you may quit or never begin.

In 1997, I began taking classes in Brazilian Jiu-Jitsu—a type of martial art. I went three or four nights a week for almost a year, and enjoyed every minute of it, even when I was getting beat up by blue belts. Because of family and business interests, the time came when I couldn't go so many times a week. The first couple of weeks, I told myself I'd "make it up" and would be back to my regular schedule soon. Once I realized I would only be able to make it to class once or twice a week, I quit. I remember thinking that only one class a week wasn't worth it. "What's the point?" I thought. "I'd just be wasting my time."

Seven years later, I began taking classes again. Some things haven't changed—I'm still getting beat up by blue belts. Here's what shocked me— my fellow white belts in 1997 are now black belts! Some of them are world-class fighters and instructors. All of them who stuck with it—even if they could only make it once or twice a week—are experts now and I'm still a white belt!

Do Small Actions Matter?

While we expect big rewards from big effort, we don't expect big rewards from little effort. It goes against everything we are taught. You've heard the clichés . . . if you want something, do whatever it takes to get it. Pull out all of the stops. Make it happen. If at first you're not successful, try again. If you still fail, you're not trying hard enough. Work harder. Put in more time. Get behind it 100 percent. Focus all of your energy on achieving it. Don't stop until you succeed.

Sound familiar? What if you could put in a small amount of effort and get big results? It's not about getting something for nothing or about being lazy or winning the lottery. Your big dreams will require work, effort, and deliberate action, but probably a lot less than you've ever imagined.

If I asked you to go to your kitchen and walk in a straight line from your dishwasher to your stove, you'd reach your destination easily and successfully. If I asked you to do it again, but this time said to change your destination by one degree, would you still make it to the stove? Yes, of course. The one-degree change is so miniscule that you wouldn't even notice the difference. To miss your stove entirely, you would probably need to vary your destination by more than twenty degrees. Anything less than that, and you would still reach the stove successfully.

So far it doesn't seem like small changes matter. Certainly one degree didn't have any effect in your kitchen. Does such a small change ever amount to anything meaningful? Let's get out of your kitchen and put you on a plane. You've buckled in and are getting ready to embark on a summer vacation when the pilot casually mentions that because of high wind speeds, it will push the plane just one degree from your course. Who cares, right? Well, unless you packed warm clothes, you'd better care. That's right. A tiny, seemingly insignificant one-degree change has a dramatic effect over a long distance. In your kitchen, the impact was a few millimeters. In the plane, the difference is thousands of miles.

Archimedes' Principle—How Small Actions Produce Big Rewards

Thousands of years ago, a philosopher named Archimedes said, "Give me a lever long enough and a fulcrum on which to place it and I shall move the world." If Archimedes were alive today, he might say, "Give me consistent small actions and enough time on which to build them, and I shall accomplish anything."

We've all known people who, in their free time, produced a record, learned a new language, earned a master's degree, learned how to play the guitar, or started a small business. Or the friend who you know makes less than you but just became a millionaire. How did they do it and how can you do it?

Whether they know it or not, these people are using Archimedes' principle to achieve their goals and reach financial success. The difference lies in small consistent actions. Even if the most you can save right now is $100 a month (that's just a little over $3 a day!), *do it!* Doing this will accomplish three things:

1. **It will create momentum.** The biggest battle we all face is inertia. The fact that you are doing something will provide you with momentum to continue.

2. **It will motivate you to do more.** Even if you only start with $100 a month, you may find you want to save more and more as you see your account grow.

3. **You'll reach your goal.** That small contribution of just a little over $3 a day doesn't seem like much right now; but if you start young enough, it will grow into a million dollars.[3]

This same principle works just as well with nonfinancial goals as it does with savings and investing. Want to lose weight? Cutting out that seemingly insignificant breakfast doughnut each morning decreases your caloric intake by nearly twenty-one pounds per year! What seems like a harmless little pastry can wreak havoc on a diet over time. Want to learn a new language? If you've got twenty minutes a day to spare, you could be fluent in a

---

3. If you save $100 a month starting at age 20, by the time you retire at age sixty-five, your account will be worth $1,048,250 if it grows 10 percent per year.

new language in a few years. The average adult watches 4.5 hours of television per day. Just think what you could do with just a fraction of this time.

How has the limiting belief that small actions don't matter affected you over the years? Where could you be today if you took those small consistent actions a year ago? Five years ago? Twenty years ago? Better yet, how many of your personal goals could you reach in the future by taking minor and seemingly inconsequential actions today? With just a small commitment and enough time, what could you accomplish?

How One Little Sister Got Her Revenge

Sue had one of those older brothers that only a mother could love. For the first fifteen years of her life, she thought her purpose was to be the butt of Jack's practical jokes and teasing. Sue would have her revenge, though.

Once Jack graduated from business school, he began earning big bucks as a marketing executive—something he reminded her of at every occasion. Sue was never one for business or corporate life. She majored in English and poetry in college, and got a job as an editor of a book publishing company. Jack relentlessly teased her, "Why are you wasting your time in publishing? Anyone who's anyone is on Madison Avenue or Wall Street. Don't waste your time or money on poetry."

While Jack was busy spending his salary and being "somebody," Sue started saving a little every month. At first it was $50 a month, and then it turned into $100. After a few years, she was able to sock away $200 a month. When Jack would ridicule her for not making enough money, she'd calmly reply that she was diligently saving 10 percent of her $40,000-a-year salary. "What's the point, ten percent of squat is still squat," he'd say. "I make $400,000 a year and in a couple of years, I'm going to be able to save a ton of money."

The years passed and Sue was still saving $333 a month—10 percent of her monthly salary. At age fifty-three, her big brother made it known that he started saving as much as Sue made in a year—an incredible $40,000 a year! As Jack was closing in on sixty-three and seeing some of his friends retire, he got another retirement party invitation in the mail. This one came from Sue. "How in the world can my poor sister afford to retire when I can't?" He immediately called Sue and told her it was a stupid idea and that he wasn't going to support her financially. "Well," she said, "I don't have a business degree and I only make $40,000 a year, but I've been able to save $1,375,238. Based on my calculations, I'll be just fine," she replied. There was silence on the other end of the phone. "Hello? You there, Jack?" Jack cleared his throat, "Uh, yeah. We can talk later. I've got to go." "Okay, but I'm going to be on that Caribbean cruise for a couple of weeks, so call me when I get back," Sue said. Jack sheepishly looked down at the balance of his savings account, saw that it contained less than half of his little sister's, and said, "Enjoy your vacation and retirement."

SAVING AND INVESTING IN ACTION:

Sue
Age 21 to 22 = $50 a month for 1 year
Age 22 to 24 = $100 a month for 2 years
Age 24 to 27 = $200 a month for 3 years
Age 27 to 60 = $333 a month for 33 years → Retires Early!
TOTAL DOLLARS SAVED = $142,068
TOTAL IN ACCOUNT AFTER INVESTING = $1,375,237

Jack
Age 21 to 53 = Didn't Save Anything
Age 53 to 63 = $3,333 a month for 10 years → Keeps Working . . .
TOTAL DOLLARS SAVED = $400,000
TOTAL IN ACCOUNT AFTER INVESTING = $682,748

HIGHLIGHTS:

- Jack contributed more than twice as much as Sue ($400,000 versus $142,068)
- Jack saved $40,000 a year, as much as Sue made per year
- Jack ended up with half of Sue's savings ($682,748 versus $1,375,237)
- Sue retired at age 60
- Jack continues to work

SUMMARY:

Slow and steady wins the race. Start early, start small. Just start. And if you, like Jack, have waited to save, there's no time like right now to get started!

TAKE AWAY *A journey of a thousand miles begins with a single step. No matter how small or insignificant your actions, over time, they can have a tremendous impact on your financial* *and personal success. The most important step is just to get started.*

Limiting Belief #4: If I'm financially successful, I'll be working so much I won't have any time with my family or my hobbies.

We all know somebody who "has it all." He has the fancy job, the nice car, the big house, and the respect and power all of the trappings of success provide. He also has a cheating spouse, kids in rehab, a $1,000-a-week psychiatrist bill, and a bottle of sleeping pills next to his bed.

Is that how "financial success" looks to you? There are many financially successful people in this world who I would not consider successful in life. It's easy to point fingers and say, "See, that's what money does! It ruins marriages and your kids will hate you."

What's the point of working eighty hours a week and living with a spouse who doesn't love you and kids who don't respect you? Financial success doesn't have to look like this. You *can* be financially successful *and* have enough time for your family and your hobbies. That's the whole point in having a high Independence Factor—to give you the financial freedom to live the lifestyle you want with as much free time to spend with family, friends, and your hobbies as you want.

Money is a facilitator. It should be used to achieve other goals. People get into trouble when the pursuit of money becomes the goal. Suddenly their entire existence and life's purpose is to make more and more at the expense of everything else. Chapter 1 examined the importance of living a balanced life. If you strive for balance across all areas of your life—your Life Zones—you will have time for your friends, family, and yourself.

> **TAKE AWAY** *Financial success and happiness is not an either/or choice. As long as you keep your purpose and vision in mind, you won't get sucked into the rat race. Financial success shouldn't be a burden, but a tool to give you the freedom to pursue the other things in your life that are important to you.*

Limiting Belief #5: You must lie, cheat, and take advantage of people to become successful.

Remember that 1980s movie *Wall Street*, with Michael Douglas and Charlie Sheen? The tagline for the movie was, "Every dream has a price."

Michael Douglas played Gordon Gekko, a high-powered über-broker and investor who was ruthless, greedy, and would do whatever it took to make a buck. He lies, cheats, breaks the law, and uses anyone to become richer.

Unfortunately, Gordon Gekko is a lightweight compared to some of the executives who appear in today's headlines. Every time I turn on the TV or open a newspaper, there's another report of corporate accounting fraud and CEOs who are being investigated for cooking the books, deceiving investors, and lying to employees. It makes me sick to my stomach.

Take a guy like Dennis Kozlowski, the ex-CEO of Tyco International, who was convicted of massive corporate larceny and fraud. According to reports, he plundered corporate accounts, skimmed company profits, and threw a $1 million birthday party for his wife that featured, among other things, an ice sculpture of Michelangelo's *David*, which poured vodka from its penis. Greed may be good, but I don't think even Gordon Gekko would condone this behavior.

Do you have to lie, cheat, and take advantage of people to become successful? Isn't that how the world works now? If Gordon Gekko or Dennis Kozlowski are your idea of what it takes to become financially successful, you will resist and undermine your success at every turn.

The good news is that you don't have to be a slimy crook to get ahead. There will always be those willing to exploit others and break the law for their own gain, but there is an alternative. There are many more examples of good, honest, and caring people becoming financially successful, but their stories don't make the headlines. In fact, I believe you can become *more* successful by being honest and helping, not manipulating, others. My friend Tim Sanders feels the same way. He wrote a *New York Times* bestselling book about it called *Love is the Killer App*. Buy it, read it, and believe it.

It's true, money and power can be like a drug. Once addicted, your behavior and focus can radically change. Was Dennis Kozlowski born to loot hundreds of millions of dollars from those who trusted him? Probably not. Once he started down that slippery slope, things got more and more out of control.

Chances are you don't even want to be the CEO of a Fortune 500 company and will never be in the position to steal hundreds of millions of dollars from a company, so what's the point? People who are financially unsuccessful worry they'll have to lie, cheat, and steal to become successful. They use it as a crutch—an excuse. Whether they believe it or not, it is holding them back from success.

What's the solution? So many of these limiting beliefs come back to the dream life you envisioned on Day 1. During those exercises, you defined who you want to be. As long as you stay on course and remain true to the person you want to be, you will never turn into a Gordon Gekko or a Dennis Kozlowski.

TAKE AWAY *Although there are plenty of "rich people are bad people" examples today, a lot more rich people are good people. Don't let a few headlines influence your perception. You can be financially successful and be an honest, caring person at the same time.*

Limiting Belief #6: I'm not smart enough to be financially successful.

What does it take to become financially successful? Is there a proven formula that will provide us with the solution? If you look at those who are financially successful—not just the bigwig Fortune 500 executives and celebrities, but normal people (remember Sue?)—you will find they share one thing. It's not a fancy education and it's not a high I.Q. That one thing that they all share is diversity. They have each become successful for a thousand *different* reasons.

Some were born with a silver spoon and some with a plastic spoon. Some had loving and supportive parents and others had parents who abused them mentally and physically. Some went to Harvard and others didn't graduate from high school. Some are geniuses and others are just average.

No matter where you came from or what school you attended, if you're reading this book you have what it takes to become financially successful. Regardless of your childhood, your quirky traits, your sex or race, and your self-imposed "limitations," you can have the life you created in Day 1. For every one person who tells me it can't be done, I can show you a hundred who have succeeded against the worst odds.

We were not all given equal opportunities, but that doesn't mean we can't all succeed if we work at it. You don't have to be a genius, and you don't have to have a Ph.D. By developing a clear vision for your life, saving and investing wisely, and sticking to a plan, you can transform your financial life.

TAKE AWAY *Successful people come from all over the world and from different backgrounds. Some have college degrees from the best universities in the world and others don't have high school diplomas. If it didn't prevent them from achieving* *success, don't let this limiting belief stop you from going after the life you want.*

Limiting Belief #7: I should be able to read a book or attend a conference and immediately become financially successful.

When I was in high school, I'd lift weights twice a day, drink protein concoctions three or four times a day, and try just about anything to build muscle faster (only natural supplements, of course, no steroids!). My mother worked at a local health food store, so I had plenty of opportunities to try the latest and greatest pills and drinks. I'll never forget this one liquid "instant muscle" potion I tried. The idea was to fill up a liquid dropper and squirt the fluid under your tongue. Unfortunately, it was disgusting and, if that wasn't bad enough, it felt like you had a hive of angry wasps buzzing around your mouth. I felt like crying and puking at the same time. I wanted instant muscle, so I did this for *months*. I'm sure you can guess what happened. Nothing. Like all of the back-of-the-magazine ads promising big muscles with less effort, this one was no different.

Marketers haven't changed their tactics much since my high school days. They still prey on that part of us that wants something for nothing—a quick fix. New diets and get-rich-quick real estate and stock trading schemes flood the bookshelves and seem to monopolize our TVs after 11:00 P.M. The promises don't change—just the products and packaging.

Although I'm much better than I used to be about spotting scams now, I do get tempted. Wouldn't it be great to have abs of steel by exercising five minutes a day? Or a photographic memory in just two hours?

When it comes to financial success and realizing the life you designed in Day 1, there are no quick and easy solutions. There are only quicker and easier solutions. Reading this book will propel you light-years ahead from where you started, but it will require action on your part (that's why there are *Action* Steps at the end of each chapter!). Some of the tools, exercises, and Action Steps you'll have to do yourself while others you can put on autopilot or even outsource. For example, when it comes to saving, investing, and tracking your progress to your goals, you can do it yourself or you can outsource this burden to a firm to do it for you.

You wouldn't expect to speak fluently after reading a book on how to speak French, so don't expect miracles after simply reading this or any other book—you have to turn words into action. There's a popular commercial running that illustrates this perfectly. It shows a group of coworkers having lunch at a nice restaurant when one of them starts choking. Several of them begin discussing the Heimlich maneuver and debating how it should be done while their colleague and friend is dying before their eyes. The commercial ends when someone from another table calmly walks over and successfully performs the Heimlich maneuver. The company tagline, "Make it Happen."

The goal of this book is ACTION! If you spend all of your time and energy discussing, debating, theorizing, and pontificating on the finer intricacies of saving, investing, and protecting your hard-earned assets, you'll never get around to actually doing it. Take heed from another company's tagline and "Just do it!"

> **TAKE AWAY** *Your Six-Day Financial Makeover requires action. It doesn't matter how great and insightful this or any other book is, you've got to implement, implement, implement.*

Financial Success Attitude

What are the characteristics and behaviors that will propel you toward the life you designed in Day 1? The following thirteen elements make up your Financial Success Attitude and will help you achieve the life of your dreams:

1. **Strong feeling that you can influence your future.** Believe that your actions today *will* create results tomorrow.

2. **Desire for more out of life.** Be grateful for what you have, but not content to live a life of mediocrity.

3. **Have a "why not?" attitude.** Believe that anything is possible.

4. **Enjoy personal challenge.** Constantly challenge yourself. Don't think you "deserve" anything, but believe in working hard to get what you want.

5. **Constantly learning and improving.** Keep an open mind. Be willing to explore new possibilities. Don't think you have all the answers. Cultivate a thirst for learning and improving your life.

6. **Live a balanced life.** Do not overwork one area at the expense of others.

7. Optimistic. Be able to think beyond today's circumstances for a better tomorrow.

8. Action-oriented. Don't sit back, do things—however small—to realize your dreams. Understand that nothing gets done until you take action.

9. Willing to take risk. Analyze risk-reward tradeoff and take calculated risks.

10. Resilient. Do not be bothered by the thought of failing and starting over.

11. Persistent. Do not surrender easily. A hurdle is something to overcome, not to make you quit.

12. Willing to delay gratification. See the big picture and the reward at the end. Be willing to put in effort today for a payoff in the future.

13. Focused. Do not lose sight of what is important. Continue to review your vision, purpose, and goals.

Congratulations! You've completed Day 2. In order to transform your financial life from the inside out, complete the Action Steps below. Get ready for Day 3, where you'll take control of your finances!

Action Steps

How many psychologists does it take to change a lightbulb? Just one, but the lightbulb has to want to change. Limiting beliefs will strip you of your true potential. Your financial makeover won't be successful without first eliminating these weights that may be holding you back.

Go through the Action Steps below and put a check mark in one of the following boxes for each one.

Eliminate Limiting Beliefs

1. ☐ COMPLETED   ☐ NEED TO COMPLETE   ☐ DOES NOT APPLY

Eliminate Limiting Belief #1: No matter what I do, I can't get ahead.

2. ☐ COMPLETED   ☐ NEED TO COMPLETE   ☐ DOES NOT APPLY

Eliminate Limiting Belief #2: Getting by is good enough.

3. ☐ COMPLETED   ☐ NEED TO COMPLETE   ☐ DOES NOT APPLY

Eliminate Limiting Belief #3: Small actions are insignificant and don't produce big rewards.

4. ☐ COMPLETED   ☐ NEED TO COMPLETE   ☐ DOES NOT APPLY

Eliminate Limiting Belief #4: If I'm financially successful, I'll be working so much I won't have any time with my family or my hobbies.

5. ☐ COMPLETED   ☐ NEED TO COMPLETE   ☐ DOES NOT APPLY

Eliminate Limiting Belief #5: You must lie, cheat, and take advantage of people to become successful.

6. ☐ COMPLETED   ☐ NEED TO COMPLETE   ☐ DOES NOT APPLY

Eliminate Limiting Belief #6: I'm not smart enough to be financially successful.

7. ☐ COMPLETED   ☐ NEED TO COMPLETE   ☐ DOES NOT APPLY

Eliminate Limiting Belief #7: I should be able to read a book or attend a conference and immediately become financially successful.

Update Your Online Financial Makeover Account

1. ☐ COMPLETED   ☐ NEED TO COMPLETE   ☐ DOES NOT APPLY

Before you do anything else, update your Six-Day Financial Makeover account at www.SixDayFinancialMakeover.com.

CHAPTER 4

Take Control of Your Finances

You know what you want and understand what's holding you back, but how are you going to get from where you are to where you want to be? The answer lies in taking control of your finances. In this chapter you will learn how to quickly ascertain your overall financial health, maximize your income, get out of debt, and generate more income.

Should I read this chapter?

		TRUE	FALSE
1.	I'm not sure how much money I make a month.	☐	☐
2.	I don't know how much I spend every month.	☐	☐
3.	I don't know if I'm saving enough to reach my goals.	☐	☐
4.	I'm in debt and I want to get out of debt as soon as possible.	☐	☐
5.	I'd like to learn how to reach my goals by taking control of my finances.	☐	☐

If you answered any of these questions TRUE, you should read this chapter.

Chapter Toolbar			
Cost to Implement Advice	**Likelihood of Needing Strategies in Chapter**	**Need Professional Advice?**	**Website Tools**
$0	1 2 3 4 5 6 7 8 9 10 Not Likely Very Likely	☥ ☥ ☥ ☥ ☥ No Definitely	Yes

There are few things as important to your long-term financial success as your ability to take control of your finances. But what does it mean to "take control of your finances"? It means having a purpose and a strategy for how you spend money. Most of us tend to "go with the flow." While this philosophy can help us remain sane in bad traffic, it can be a disastrous strategy for our finances.

If you're like most people, you work hard for your money and will probably work hard for twenty, thirty, or forty years. Without a sound financial strategy, years can pass and you won't have anything to show for your hard work. This doesn't have to be your fate. You have a choice about whether you want to "get by" or thrive.

In Chapter 2 you thought long and hard about the kind of life you want. You discovered what you want to own, what you want to accomplish, and who you want to be. The driving force—the fuel—behind reaching the goals you set in Chapter 2 is your ability to save and invest.

How much do you save each month? Are you on track to reach your goals? Knowing what you want and setting goals is half the battle; taking control of your finances is the other half. If you aren't in control of them, they are in control of you. This chapter will help you get in the driver's seat and get closer to reaching your goals.

Taking control of your net worth and cash flow will help you measure and improve your financial health. Ultimately, it will help you obtain what you want to own, what you want to accomplish, and who you want to be. In addition to helping you reach your goals, taking control of your net worth and cash flow has several other real benefits:

- **It enables you to reach your goals much faster.** Many of your goals have price tags. Taking control of your finances means you will reach your goals faster because you will be able to save more.

- **It enables you to reach the goals that are most important to you.** Not all goals are created equal. In a perfect world you'd be able to reach all of your goals when you wanted to reach them, but for most of us, we must prioritize our goals. Often the goals that are most important—like a successful retirement or paying for your children's college education—are the ones that occur further in the future. If we are always trying to reach our more immediate, but less important goals, we may never have the resources to accomplish those more important long-term goals.

- **You worry less.** Anyone who has taken an important test and waited days or weeks for the results can appreciate this benefit. Worry comes from not knowing. Did I pass? Did I fail? Once you find out how you did, the worry disappears—even if you failed it is better to know. Once you understand your net worth and cash flow, you'll have a lot fewer sleepless nights because you'll know where you stand and you'll have a plan for improvement.

- **You can take advantage of opportunities.** If you have no idea how well you're doing, you won't be able to act quickly to take advantage of opportunities that come your way.

- **You can set realistic expectations.** Everyone wants it all, and they want it now. There's nothing wrong with wanting to reach your goals, but once you have control over your finances, you will be able to better manage your expectations.

- **It helps you keep score.** When it comes to your finances, you're either getting ahead, going nowhere, or falling behind. Taking control of your net worth and cash flow allows you to determine how well you are doing. If you discover you're falling behind, you can take the necessary steps to improve your situation.

- **It gives you a greater feeling of control.** Have you ever had to give a speech? There is an amazing difference between how you feel when you are prepared for the speech and when you are making it up on the spot. If you know little about the topic and you haven't rehearsed, public speaking is one of the most painful and nerve-racking experiences in the world. You just want it to end! If you're prepared, you stand taller. You are in control. It's a much better feeling. Taking control of your finances gives you knowledge and puts you in control.

Don't Let This Happen to You

Micah was a reasonably successful entrepreneur. He made enough to support a comfortable lifestyle for his wife and twin daughters. He had a college buddy who made millions in Silicon Valley during the late '90s. When his friend invited him to invest in a new venture he was starting, Micah jumped at the opportunity. Micah wrote him a check for $25,000. Although this check didn't bounce, six of Micah's other checks did—including his home mortgage. To make matters worse, he was planning on refinancing his mortgage to a lower rate, but because he missed a payment he was considered a "high-risk" applicant and was no longer qualified for the rate he wanted. Over the life of the loan, it will cost him over $150,000 more in interest. If Micah had been more in control of his net worth and cash flow, he would have known exactly how much he could afford to invest in the new opportunity.

Taking control of your finances means measuring, managing, and monitoring two very important issues:

1. **Net worth.** Your net worth is a measure of your overall financial health. Measuring your net worth is like getting a checkup to determine your physical health. Your net worth compares what you own to what you owe. If you own more than you owe, you have a positive net worth and are financially "healthy." If you owe more than you own, you have a negative net worth and are "unhealthy." You will learn how to measure your net worth and monitor it over time.

2. **Cash flow.** If net worth is a measure of your overall financial health, your cash flow is the daily exercise and nutrition that determines

your financial health. While your net worth tells you how financially healthy you are currently, it doesn't measure the health of your lifestyle. Cash flow is composed of the day-to-day actions and decisions that determine your net worth and long-term financial health. You will quickly and easily learn how to take control of your cash flow so it reflects your goals and improves your net worth.

Take Control of Your Net Worth

Your current financial health can be summed up with one number. This one number reflects all of the financial decisions you've ever made. That number is your net worth. For such a powerful number, you would expect a long and complicated calculation; however, it is easy to calculate your net worth.

Large well-known companies such as Microsoft and Disney constantly calculate and monitor their net worth, as do smaller, less-known companies. Companies list everything they own—from the company cars to the office equipment to their unsold products to their savings account balances. If they own it, they list it. Technically, this is how you calculate net worth, but you're going to calculate your net worth a little more easily.

Instead of listing everything you own—clothes, furniture, and electronics—list only things that you could sell easily without hosting a yard sale. There are three categories of things you can count as what you own:

1. **Savings/Investments.** Certainly include all of your savings, checking, certificates of deposit, emergency reserve (Don't have one? You will by the end of this book!), investment, IRA, and 401(k) account balances. Use the full account balance for each account. Also include any loans you've made to others if there is a good chance you'll get your money back.

2. **Large assets.** This category includes such assets as your home, rental property, automobiles, boats, expensive jewelry, etc. Value these items at their current market value—that is, list the price that you could get if you sold the item today. For example, if you bought a $25,000 car last year, don't list this asset at $25,000 because there's no way you could sell it for that today. Check the Kelley Blue Book (www.kbb.com) for a more accurate resale value. Likewise, if you bought a house five years ago for $325,000, don't list it at $325,000

since it hopefully has appreciated in those five years. List the amount that you could sell it for today (after closing costs). Check what houses like yours have sold for on the Internet or ask a real estate agent if you're not sure of the value of your house.

3. **Other appreciating or income-producing assets.** Chances are you won't have anything to list in this category, but if you have assets such as a coin or stamp collection or receive royalties or license fees, list these assets here.

Now it's your turn. Use the worksheet below or visit www.SixDayFinancial Makeover.com to help calculate your net worth. You will need to list everything you own that fits each of the "What I Own" categories and then list everything you owe (e.g., credit card debt, mortgage, home equity loan, car loan, etc.) in the "What I Owe" column. Total both columns and subtract what you *owe* from what you *own*. Voilà! The result is your net worth.

Net Worth Worksheet

What I Own (Assets)

SAVINGS/INVESTMENTS

Savings Accounts/CDs	$_____
Checking Accounts	$_____
Investment Accounts	$_____
401(k)/IRA Accounts	$_____
Misc. Savings/Investments	$_____

LARGE ASSETS

Home	$_____
Cars	$_____
Rental Property	$_____
Business Interest	$_____
Loans Payable to You	$_____
Boats	$_____
Jewelry	$_____
Art/Collectibles	$_____
Misc. Large Assets	$_____

What I Owe (Liabilities)

REAL ESTATE DEBT

1st Mortgage	$_____
2nd Mortgage	$_____
Home Equity Line	$_____

OTHER DEBT

Credit Card Balances	$_____
Auto Loans	$_____
401(k) Loans	$_____
Personal Loans	$_____
Misc. Debt/Loans	$_____

TOTAL LIABILITIES	**$_____**

OTHER ASSETS

Coin/Stamp Collection	$_____	**TOTAL ASSETS**	$_____
Royalties	$_____		**MINUS**
Misc. Other Assets	$_____	**TOTAL LIABILITIES**	$_____
TOTAL ASSETS	$_____	**NET WORTH**	$_____

Your net worth is a snapshot of your financial health. If you calculated it yesterday or tomorrow, it probably would be a different number—maybe better and maybe worse. The point is your net worth is constantly changing. If you own more than owe, you have a positive net worth and you are financially healthy. If, however, you owe more than you own, you have a negative net worth and are financially unhealthy. The good news is that you can become financially fit by increasing your net worth in one of three ways:

1. **Increase what you own.** This doesn't mean you should buy everything in sight. Remember, only savings/investment accounts, large assets, or assets that appreciate or produce an income are included in your net worth. Everything else is just stuff. When you buy an iPod or a new business suit, you are decreasing your net worth. Why? You are converting cash into something that isn't included in your net worth. If you go on a shopping spree and buy $300 worth of clothes, you have reduced your net worth by $300. You may be thinking, "If I buy the clothes on a credit card, it won't decrease my cash and I won't be decreasing my net worth." Nice try. Although you aren't decreasing what you own, you are *increasing* what you *owe* by $300.

2. **Decrease what you owe.** You can decrease what you owe by not borrowing money or using a credit card and by *paying off* your debt. Every dollar you're able to reduce what you owe is a dollar you are using to increase your net worth.

3. **Increase what you own *and* decrease what you owe.** Why do one or the other if you can invest in assets *and* pay off your debt? If you're serious about improving your financial health, this is exactly what you should do!

Because net worth changes over time and because your goal is to increase your net worth, you should monitor and track your progress on a regular basis. The best and easiest time to do this is during a monthly or quarterly meeting, which you will learn about in Chapter 6.

Take Control of Your Cash Flow

Now that you've got a handle on your current financial health, it's time to focus on what you're doing daily to improve or damage your financial health.

Getting control of your finances wouldn't be complete without understanding your personal cash flow. Cash flow is a fancy phrase that means the money coming into and out of your life. If you have an income and expenses, you have cash flow. This section will help you determine, manage, and improve your cash flow.

Most people automatically think "budget" when they hear "cash flow." For most people, budgets don't work. In fact, they don't even work for many businesses. When is the last time a Hollywood movie or a home-improvement project came in at or under budget? You can take control of your finances without a budget, and you'll learn how.

Taking control of your cash flow is at the center of your Six-Day Financial Makeover because it will allow you to save more. Your ability to save more of what you earn is going to be what drives your financial transformation. Our savings provide the fuel for investing and for achieving goals. Not having a handle on income and expenses causes unnecessary stress and aggravation and prevents us from achieving our goals.

Taking control of your cash flow isn't just for bigwig executives making six-figure incomes. If you are retired and on a fixed income, a young executive making a good salary, or a single mom working two part-time jobs, you need to know how much money is coming in and how much money is going out. Remember, it's not how much you make, but how much you save that is important.

As an example, imagine two friends about to depart on a long drive. They take separate cars. One of them has a vehicle with a sixty-gallon gas tank and the other has a compact with a little ten-gallon tank. It might seem obvious who is going to make it to their destination without stopping at a gas station. The person with the sixty-gallon tank has a lot more resources and won't need to refuel.

Would it surprise you to learn that the person with the small gas tank quickly and easily makes it to the destination but that the sixty-gallon vehicle arrives late after a long wait at the gas station? How can that be? The larger tank provides more fuel so it should take him farther than the car with the small tank. Does it make more sense when you learn that the vehicle with the large tank is a Hummer that gets thirteen miles per gallon and the car with the small tank is a Toyota Prius that gets more than fifty miles per gallon?

It doesn't matter how much fuel you have, it is how efficient you are at conserving, managing, and using it. In this case, the Hummer burns through its resources while the Prius uses what little it has efficiently.

Don't Let This Happen to You

Image was everything to Melinda. She had to have the latest business suits, shoes, and purses. She leased a new car every two years because after two years, she said, "they're relics." Although she made good money and could afford a nice house, she decided to rent because it allowed her to live in a bigger and nicer house than she could afford to buy. She was the epitome of "visual success." Anyone who met Melinda or spent much time with her could see she was successful. She had everything you could want. Although she had a lot of stuff, she couldn't afford to take time off or travel. She rationalized that she'd be able to do it when she retired because she'd have all the time in the world then. Right now, she had to work, work, work.

The years passed and Melinda continued to earn six-figure salaries. About a year before she was ready to retire, she decided it was time to get some professional financial help to prepare for her looming retirement. After thirty years of dedicating her life to her company and working fifty to sixty hours a week—sacrificing travel and time with her sisters and ailing mother—Melinda was first shocked, then angry, and then depressed at what she heard. With her company's pension, Social Security, and the $187,576 she had invested, she would have to move into a one-bedroom apartment and cut her lifestyle by 60 percent. Her retirement savings were paltry compared to the income she was used to making. No more fancy cars, fancy dinners, or fancy clothes. The retirement she had been dreaming of was turning into a nightmare.

When it comes to your finances, it doesn't matter how much or how little income you have as long as you use it efficiently. So don't worry that you can't reach your goals unless you make a lot of money. You can reach your destination if you manage your cash flow effectively.

The first step in taking control of your cash flow is to determine where you currently stand. When it comes to finances and cash flow, you are either swimming, treading water, or sinking.

Swim, Tread, or Sink? A Cash-Flow Quiz

Circle the letter that best describes where you are today or take the quiz online at www.SixDayFinancialMakeover.com.

1. I use a credit card but always pay off the balance every month.
   a. That's exactly right.
   b. Most of the time I do but there are months where I can't.
   c. It's rare when I don't have a credit balance.

2. I usually pay just the minimum on my credit card balance every month.
   a. No way. I always pay off the balance.
   b. It really depends on my other expenses that month.
   c. That sounds about right.

3. I contribute to my company's retirement plan.
   a. Absolutely.
   b. I'd like to soon but I don't think I can afford it.
   c. There's no way I have the extra money to invest.

4. I put as much money as I can in my company's retirement plan.
   a. I max out or am pretty close to maxing out the retirement plan.
   b. I put some money in but not as much as I would like.
   c. I couldn't afford to pay my rent if I maxed out my retirement plan.

5. I seem to run out of money at the end of the month.
   a. I sometimes have excess money that I can save each month.
   b. I have just enough to cover my expenses every month.
   c. That's exactly right.

6. I contribute to an investment or savings account every month.
   a. Of course.
   b. Once in a while I can save but then big expenses come up and wipe out my savings.
   c. I don't have enough to save or invest.

7. I make just enough money to pay the bills every month.
   a. I have money left over after I pay all of my bills.
   b. That's exactly right.
   c. On a good month I have enough, but I normally fall short.

8. Once I make more money or the kids move out I will be able to save for retirement.
   a. Why wait? I'm saving now.
   b. I either have to make more or spend less to be able to save for retirement.
   c. I should probably first pay off my debt before I save for retirement.

9. I use a credit card to support my lifestyle.
   a. No way.
   b. Once in a while I will use a credit card to buy something but usually my income supports my lifestyle.
   c. I will often use my credit card because I don't have the money to pay cash.

10. I work hard but don't seem to have anything to show for it.
    a. Not true. I have a growing savings and investment account to show for my hard work.
    b. What I make I seem to spend.
    c. The only thing I have to show for my hard work is loans and credit card bills.

Scoring the Quiz

Add up all of your As, Bs, and Cs.

If you scored highest in As—Congratulations! You're getting ahead every month—you're "swimming" to your goal. You are an active saver. All of your hard work is getting you ahead. Instead of waking every morning, driving to the office, and working forty or fifty hours a week with nothing to show for it, you are investing in yourself. With every month you are better off financially than the month before. You don't settle for "getting by" when you can get ahead. At the end of your journey, you will have made it to your destination. Don't relax yet, though. Even though you are above water, you might be able to optimize your income and savings even more. You can reach your destination quicker and more easily by learning the tools and implementing the Action Steps in this chapter.

If you scored highest in Bs—The good news is that you're not falling behind. The bad news is that you are not getting ahead. You are "treading water." You may work hard and you may put in sixty hours a week, but you are spinning your wheels. At the end of the day, the week, month, or the year, you are in no better shape than you were at the beginning. In fact, you are in worse shape. Even though you are paying your bills and aren't racking up credit card debt, you are getting no closer to your goals. Every day you are not getting closer to your goals you are creating more pressure because you have one less day to reach them. How long can you tread water without getting tired?

The ideas and Action Steps in this chapter will greatly benefit you. You'll be able to improve your financial health so you can do more than just survive. You will see tangible results from making a few changes in your finances. Rather than be at the mercy of your income and expenses, you will be able to take control of your cash flow.

If you scored highest in Cs—It probably doesn't come as a surprise to learn that you are "sinking." You are in worse financial shape at the end of every day. Your income isn't supporting your expenses. You may be incurring more debt every month or you may not be able to get out from under the debt you've already incurred. In either case, the debt and expenses are dragging you down and keeping you underwater. You won't be able to reach your goals if you continue down this path. You need ideas and tools you can immediately use. If you are in debt, you'll learn how to get out from under it and start getting ahead.

Don't Let This Happen to You

Ricardo was on the fast track. Everything he did was to get ahead. His parents were first-generation immigrants to the United States from El Salvador. Ricardo grew up in a two-bedroom apartment with his family of six. Although they didn't have much financially, Ricardo's parents made up for it with a lot of love and encouragement. They told Ricardo they were in the land of opportunity and that he could have anything and become anyone he wanted.

Like a good boy, Ricardo listened to his parents. He hated wearing shoes with holes in the bottom and jeans that were three inches too short. He hated that the other kids would make fun of him. He saw how the rich lived and he knew that someday he, too, would live like them.

Ricardo had the perfect combination of instinct, talent, and personality. He worked his way up in one of the largest talent agencies in the world—starting in the mail room and ending up becoming an agent to several television and B-movie actors in Hollywood. Ricardo was tasting the good life. He was making enough to drive a car and live in a house he could only dream of as a child, but he didn't think it was good enough. Other agents had faster cars and bigger houses. His clients ate at better restaurants and wore trendier clothes. He was making more money than he ever thought possible, but he still felt inadequate.

Ricardo began to relive the embarrassment of his youth. He took a home loan and started racking up thousands of dollars in credit card debt. He was living far beyond his means and had to rob Peter to pay Paul every month. This continued for five years until there was a prolonged writer's strike. His actor clients weren't working and, as a result, Ricardo wasn't making any money. He could only keep up the façade for so long. When the repo man took his car and the creditors started calling, he had no other choice but to file for bankruptcy.

Breakthrough Financial Formula Discovered!

Regardless of your score or current situation, you will be able to improve your financial health once you get a handle on your cash flow by following a never-before-seen breakthrough formula. After years of financial analysis by the top financial minds in the world, the following formula was discovered: $I > E$. Your Income must be greater than your Expenses. Okay, so it isn't a revolutionary formula, but it is the basis for your financial makeover. Short of winning the lottery, spending less than you make is the only sure way to achieve your life's goals.

Expense X-ray

While the advice to spend less than you make isn't new, you will learn how to see your expenses in a new way. You are going to X-ray your cash flow to look for hidden opportunities. What does this mean? It means you are going to take a close look at each expense to determine if it supports your overall vision for your life you created in Chapter 2.

Before you analyze your expenses and goals and develop a personalized

Common Spending Pyramid

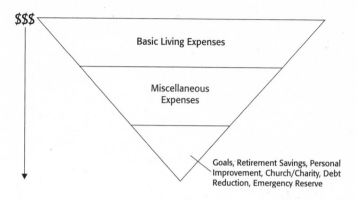

$$$

Basic Living Expenses

Miscellaneous
Expenses

Goals, Retirement Savings, Personal
Improvement, Church/Charity, Debt
Reduction, Emergency Reserve

cash-flow plan, let's look at a Spending Pyramid. A Spending Pyramid represents the order in which income is allocated (money flows from top to bottom, with more money going to those expenses at the top). A common Spending Pyramid of an average individual or family might look like the graph above.

You will notice most of the income is being spent on basic living expenses (e.g., rent, mortgage, food, transportation, utilities, etc.) and miscellaneous expenses (e.g., minimum credit card payments, entertainment, dining out, etc.). Only a small amount—usually what is left over—is used for retirement savings, goal achievement, debt reduction, charity, and establishing an emergency reserve account. Based on this fairly common spending pattern, it is easy to see the financial damage that can develop over time.

A more optimized Spending Pyramid would look like the graph on page 76.

For the average individual or family, the expenses that top the Spending Pyramid should be funded first and will most likely account for the majority of your income. Each layer of the Spending Pyramid should be funded from top to bottom. The bottom of the Spending Pyramid represents the expenses/goals that should be funded last and with whatever money is left over after funding the expenses/goals above it.

The Optimized Spending Pyramid has seven layers:

1. **Basic Living Expenses.** These include expenses such as rent or mortgage, food, clothing, insurance, day care, medication, car loans, school loans, and transportation costs and will probably take up most of your income.

Optimized Spending Pyramid

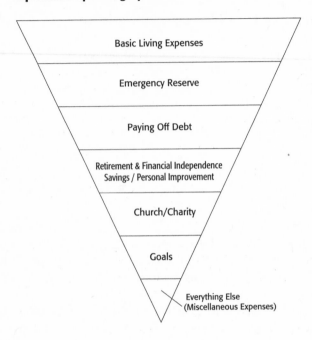

2. **Emergency Reserve.** Your emergency reserve is your financial cushion in case something goes wrong and you lose your job or you need access to money quickly. Your emergency reserve should consist of at least three months of basic living expenses in cash. Once you've saved enough for the cushion, you can move down to the other expenses/goals.

3. **Paying Off Debt.** Consumer debt such as credit card balances is like an anchor that weighs you down. Paying down this kind of debt is critical for long-term financial health. Once you have an emergency reserve, you should absolutely do what you can to reduce your debt as quickly as possible, which means you should allocate more of your income to this layer than to the layers below it. Non–credit card debt such as your home mortgage, school loans, and car loans do not have to be paid in full before you can start saving for other items farther down on the Spending Pyramid. The regularly scheduled payments are included above in the "Basic Living Expenses" category.

4. **Retirement and Financial Independence Savings/Personal Improvements.** Each of these categories are investments. Saving for retirement and saving to increase your Independence Factor are actual investments of dollars and cents. On the other hand, personal improvement is an investment in you. Personal improvement expenses include such things as college tuition, books, and gym membership. Retirement and financial independence savings as well as personal improvement are extremely important for your future success and happiness.

5. **Church/Charity.** I strongly believe that we should give regularly to charity/church. There are numerous financial and psychological benefits we receive when we give.

6. **Goals.** Remember those goals you set for yourself in Chapter 2? If your goals are like most people's goals, they require money or could be enhanced with money. If you are not actively and regularly saving for your goals you will not reach them, period.

7. **Everything Else.** This includes entertainment, dining out, and your Netflix account.

Of course, everyone's situation is unique, and you might not agree with the order of priorities suggested by the pyramid. For example, the two most common objections to the Optimized Spending Pyramid are:

1. **"You want me to contribute to church/charity before I spend money on entertainment?"** Yes. There are a lot of truly good causes that need our attention and money. Even if it's only a few dollars, I think it's our obligation and a privilege to help those who are less fortunate or to advance an important cause. You also get three bonuses when you contribute to church/charity—a nice tax break, your children learn the importance of giving from an early age, and it just feels good.

2. **"I'd rather save for my kids' college education than save for retirement."** While this impulse is understandable and certainly noble, I don't think this is a good idea. In a perfect world, you'd be able to pay for your children's college education and have enough for a

successful retirement, and if you have that luxury—congratulations! If you determine that you can't fund both, you must choose to save for retirement. Here's why. If you can't pay 100 percent of your children's college expenses it doesn't mean they won't go to college. There are a lot of alternatives such as student loans, financial aid, and scholarships. If you haven't saved enough for retirement, you won't have any options. They don't hand out scholarships or grants to pay for retirement. Take care of your retirement first. Your children will thank you.

The Expense X-Ray Process

The Expense X-ray Process is dynamic. It is not something you do once and forget about it. As you will see later in the chapter, you should monitor your income, expenses, and progress to ensure you are on track to reach each goal regularly. Once you get the system set up, it will be a snap to review and update.

Okay, let's get started!

Step 1—List regularly occurring sources of income.

You first need to get an accurate picture of how much money comes in every month. This will be the foundation of your plan and will help us determine how much you have for expenses and goals. The major categories of income include:

- **Earned income.** This is the money you earn from your job. List the net amount from your paycheck (the amount listed on your pay stub *after* taxes are taken out). If you are self-employed and/or do not get a paycheck, determine how much you earn per month after paying income taxes. Include commissions and bonuses if you are *sure* you will receive them. Make sure you divide the annual bonus by twelve since we're interested in calculating your income *per month.*

- **Rental income.** If you have rental properties, enter the amount of money you make after paying all expenses and taxes. For example, if you rent out a small house, be sure to subtract expenses and taxes that you pay on the property in order to calculate the actual profit per month.

- **Interest and dividend income.** This income is generated from your savings and investment accounts. While you may earn this income, most of us don't actually receive a check every month. Normally it stays in the savings or investment account and is reinvested; this is the power of compound interest. If you don't get a check, don't list any income here. If you actually receive this income, enter it in this category.

- **Other income.** Enter any other income you regularly receive.

Step 2—List all regularly occurring expenses and calculate the average monthly cost.

Now that you have documented your income, it's time to focus on your normally occurring monthly expenses: rent, groceries, gasoline, car payment, cable TV, and utilities. These expenses are easy to remember because you pay them every month. If you need help, your bank may let you download three to six months' worth of transactions into a spreadsheet or software program such as Quicken. The major categories of monthly expenses include:

- **Household expenses.** These expenses are probably one of your largest and include your mortgage or rent, homeowner's association dues, maintenance and upkeep, utilities, landscaping, pool service, housecleaning, etc.

- **Transportation expenses.** This includes most of the expenses related to your car: your lease, car payment, gas, toll charges, etc. Don't include your auto insurance here. We will include it in a separate category for insurance.

- **Taxes.** This includes various taxes such as property taxes that you are responsible for paying. It doesn't include income or payroll taxes since we used the "after tax" figure from your paycheck.

- **Groceries.** Enter your average monthly grocery and toiletry expense. Do not include the cost of eating out. These expenses will be listed in a separate category.

- **Personal care expenses.** These are things like haircuts, manicures, facials, massages, therapy, personal trainer, etc.

- **Dining out and entertainment expenses.** Enter the average monthly amount you spend eating out and on entertainment. This category includes everything from your daily Starbucks cappuccino, Friday night date with your spouse, Netflix, TiVo, cable TV, and Internet access.

- **Charitable.** Include any payments to nonprofit organizations.

- **Debt payments.** If you currently have credit card debt or outstanding loans other than your car or house, list the minimum payment due per month here.

- **Child care.** Enter the average monthly figure for day care and babysitting.

- **Miscellaneous.** Use this category for all regular expenses that don't fit within one of the other categories.

Step 3—List occasional expenses that are paid once a quarter, twice a year, or yearly and calculate their average monthly cost.

These expenses are easy to forget since they don't occur every month. In fact, some of these may occur only once a year. This is one area where people lose control of their finances. Here's what can happen. You may be going along smoothly—paying your monthly bills and saving for that vacation you promised your family. A month before the vacation you get six nonmonthly bills in the mail that wipe out your vacation savings fund. Hello, bills and good-bye, vacation. With a little planning, this doesn't have to happen. The major categories of occasional expenses include:

- **Transportation.** Tune-ups and oil changes need to be done on a consistent basis. Calculate the projected annual cost for these expenses and determine the average monthly cost. Monthly expenses such as lease payments and gas were already entered above, so don't duplicate them here.

- **Insurance premiums.** List all of the premiums you pay, including health, auto, homeowner's, life, disability, long-term care, etc. For insurance policies that you pay semiannually or quarterly, just figure out what you pay annually and divide by twelve to get the average monthly expense.

- **Taxes.** Include real estate taxes if you own a home and estimated tax withholding payments if you don't have taxes taken out of your paycheck automatically.

- **Gifts.** These include expenses related to birthdays, anniversaries, and holidays.

- **Education.** This includes tuition, books, and other education expenses for you and/or your children.

- **Clubs/Dues.** Include the cost of a health club or country club membership, and any personal or professional dues that are not reimbursed by your employer. Again, use an average monthly figure.

- **Hobbies.** List any costs associated with your hobbies.

- **Magazines/Newspapers/Books.** Enter subscription expenses for magazines, journals, or newspapers and the average monthly cost for books.

- **Medical/Dental.** Enter the cost of any medical or dental expenses that are not covered by your insurance policies (e.g., deductibles).

- **Clothing.** Although you might not buy clothes every month, calculate how much you spend throughout the year and enter the average monthly value.

- **Vacations.** Figure out how much you spend per year on vacations and getaways and divide by twelve to get the average monthly figure. Don't forget expenses such as transportation, lodging, dining out, and other expenses such as theme-park admission tickets.

Step 4—List all goals that cost money and calculate the monthly required savings rate to achieve them.

Remember back on Day 1 when you determined what you want to own, what you want to accomplish, and who you want to be? Many of your goals require money or can be achieved more easily with money. Take a look at Power Exercise #4 from Chapter 2. You've already calculated the total cost to achieve your goals. Now it's time to calculate how much you need to save per month to accomplish each of your goals.

For example, if you want to buy a house in three years (36 months) and you know that you will need a $30,000 down payment, you will need to save approximately $884 a month ($30,000 ÷ 36 months). For goals you want to achieve within a couple of years, this calculation will work just fine. For goals further out than three years, you need to consider inflation as well as an investment return. (Don't worry, I'll walk you step-by-step through how to invest on Day 4.) Go to www.SixDayFinancialMakeover.com to calculate how much you need to save each month for these longer-term goals. Do this calculation for each of your goals.

You've completed only four steps, but you've already discovered how much money comes in each month, how much your monthly expenses total, how much your nonmonthly expenses total, and how much it would cost per month to fund all of your goals. Keep up the good work, only a few more steps to go!

Step 5—Subtract income from your expenses and goals.

The moment of truth—subtract your income from your total expenses and from the cost of funding your goals. If you have money left over each month, congratulations! You can take that money and add it to your retirement or other goals. Most likely, though, you will find that your total expenses and goals exceed your monthly income. Don't panic! That's normal. Proceed to Step 6 to solve the problem.

Step 6—Go back over your expenses and goals and mark each one as a goal, need, or want.

As you discovered in the Cash-Flow Quiz, you are either swimming, treading water, or sinking. When it comes to cash outflows (i.e., money leaving your pocket), they help get you closer to your goals, help you survive, or move you away from your goals.

For each of your expenses, mark it as one of the following:

- **Goal.** This is an expense that gets you closer to a goal. Contributing money to a savings account is a goal, just as is investing for retirement or financial independence. Mark any cash outflow as a goal if you are saving money for a specific purpose.

- **Need.** A need is a cash outflow that is necessary to live and survive. Groceries, rent, and insurance are all needs. Dining out, although it is food, is not a need. You could survive by eating at home. Likewise, clothing is a need, but only to a point. That tenth pair of shoes or Prada bag is not a need (even though it may really feel like it!).

- **Want.** If money is leaving your hands and it is not getting you closer to a goal or is not helping you survive, it is a want. Dining out, entertainment, TiVo, CDs, and just about everything else you can think of is a want. Yes, many of these things are important. I'm not suggesting you sell everything and become a Buddhist monk. You just need to take a realistic look at each of your expenses.

Step 7—Determine which of your expenses and goals are negotiable.

What does it mean for an expense or goal to be negotiable? It means you are open to the possibility of eliminating, reducing, or postponing the expense. For example, maybe one of your short-term goals is to buy a used motorcycle. If you decide that this goal is not immediately necessary, mark it as negotiable. Likewise, if you come to a "DVD of the month" expense, you might also mark this as negotiable if you absolutely, positively do not have to have it. On the other hand, most of the expenses you marked as a need are probably not negotiable—but they could be. For example, if you rent a two-bedroom apartment for $1,400 a month and you could get by with a one-bedroom, this expense could be negotiable. You may have listed an expense as a want, but found it to be a nonnegotiable want. For me, my monthly TiVo expense is definitely a want (although it would be hard to imagine, I could theoretically survive without TiVo), but it is a nonnegotiable want. No matter what, I intend to keep my TiVo account, so I wouldn't mark this expense as "negotiable."

Step 8—Evaluate your list of negotiable items and mark the ones you would consider eliminating, reducing, postponing, or keeping.

Once you mark an expense or goal negotiable, you have four choices:

- **Eliminate.** If you determine that an expense/goal is no longer needed, you can remove it from your cash-flow form. For example, if you have season tickets to the opera but never go, you could eliminate the expense. The more expenses or goals you eliminate, the better your cash-flow situation.

- **Reduce.** If you are open to decreasing the cost or frequency of an expense/goal, mark the expense "reduce." For example, if you go out to lunch every day at work but are open to bringing a lunch twice a week, mark the expense "reduce." In this case, you are reducing the frequency of the expense. Likewise, you could continue to go out to lunch every day, but go to less expensive restaurants. Both situations reduce your expense.

- **Postpone.** If you have an expense or goal that is important to you and you don't want to eliminate or reduce it, consider postponing it. This will free up the cash now that can be used for more pressing expenses or goals. For example, if one of your goals is to learn how to play the piano and you have piano lessons as a near-term expense, you could consider postponing the lessons for another six months or year. Warning: Some goals such as saving for retirement should never be postponed. Since these goals often occur in the future, it is easy to put them on the back burner and concentrate all of your resources on more immediate but less important expenses or goals.

- **Keep.** Although you initially thought this expense/goal was negotiable, you can always change your mind. If you decide you don't want to eliminate, reduce, or postpone the expense or goal, keep it.

Step 9—For each negotiable expense or goal, recalculate the new cost depending on which action you marked.

Recalculate your new expenses. The more items you marked as eliminate, reduce, and postpone, the better your cash-flow situation.

Step 10—Retotal the new cost of your expenses and goals and go back to Step 5 to see if your income now supports all of your expenses and goals.

If you eliminated, reduced, or postponed enough, your income may now cover all of your expenses/goals. If so, congratulations!

If your income still doesn't support your expenses/goals, you need to go back over your list of negotiable items and eliminate, reduce, or postpone more of them. In a perfect world, you would have plenty of income to support all of your expenses and goals, but for most of us this isn't the case. The process of eliminating, reducing, or postponing your goals is certainly painful, but if you want to reach your most important goals, it is necessary. Continue to work with the negotiable expenses and goals until your income supports all of your expenses and goals.

Debt Demolition Program

Maybe the idea of a Six-Day Financial Makeover was attractive to you because you are in debt. How can you think about saving to reach your goals when you are plagued with overwhelming credit card debt? It will take discipline and hard work (see "Not for the Faint of Heart" in the next chapter for a tough-love approach for stopping credit card overspending), but you will be able to pay off your debt and start saving for your goals. The Debt Demolition Program is as easy as three steps:

1. **Destroy your credit cards.** Cut up all of your credit cards and tell each credit card company not to send you any "convenience checks." These convenience checks are a convenient way for you to stay in debt and avoid reaching your goals. Use a debit card tied to your checking account if you need to buy something online or over the phone. Ironically, canceling your credit cards could hurt your credit score, so just cut them and don't cancel them.

2. **Slash your expenses.** Eliminate, reduce, or postpone as many of your expenses and goals as you can. Go back over each expense and ask yourself if it is absolutely necessary. If it's not, get rid of it.

3. **Pay down your debt.** Use the extra cash to pay down your debt. After freeing up some extra cash in Step 2, you can use that money to pay off any of your loans or credit card balances. Pay down as much as you can.

If you've slashed your expenses as much as possible but your debt is not going down as fast as you want, you can take your Debt Demolition Program to the next level by focusing on the income side of the cash-flow equation. Think about it. You've done a great job cutting expenses, but what if you could cut expenses *and* increase your income? All of the extra income could go to wiping out your debt. If you want to ramp up your Debt Demolition Program or just want to make more money, the next section is for you.

Which Debt Should You Pay Down First?

Before you get caught up in which debt you should pay off first, make sure you have established an adequate emergency reserve. Once you have cash totaling three months of your expenses, you can start to pay down your debt. But which accounts should you pay down first? Normally it is best to go in this order:

1. Credit card debt. Start with the accounts that charge the greatest interest. Usually these are department store accounts. If you have several credit cards, see if you can transfer higher-interest-charging cards to lower-interest-charging accounts. If all of the cards have approximately the same interest rate, pay off the smaller accounts first. There's something psychologically powerful about paying off a credit card.

2. Student loans. Typically there are tax breaks for this kind of loan. You might be able to write off part of the interest you are charged. Tax break or not, it's still a debt. Once you pay off your credit card bills, go after your student loans with the same vigor!

3. Mortgage loan. The last debt you should pay off is your home loan. Typically this is the largest debt on everyone's net worth calculation. As long as you are paying the monthly balance, you should use your extra cash flow to fund your goals. If you get to the point where your goals are entirely funded, you can then consider paying down more of your mortgage.

Income Maximizing Program

I'm an advocate of living within your means. I don't believe in borrowing or using credit cards to fund a lifestyle that my income can't support. If you live a lifestyle beyond your means for too long, you dig an increasingly larger financial hole.

What should you do if the life you want—the one you envisioned in Chapter 2—is above your means? Unless you want to dig yourself into a hole of debt, you can either reduce your lifestyle to fit your income or you can increase your income to match your desired lifestyle.

How to Make Millions in Your Sleep!

Did you know that it would take 18.5 years to pay off a $2,000 balance if you just paid the minimum balance every month on a credit card with 18 percent interest? Did you know that you would pay $2,615 just in interest? If you want to make millions, start a credit card company. If you want to lose millions (that might be a stretch, but it's a lot of money!), pay only the minimum balance each month.

There are long-term and short-term strategies to increase your income. Long-term strategies include things such as your career choice and the level and type of education you receive. These decisions don't guarantee you'll be more financially fit, though. Remember, it's not how much you make that determines your financial health but how much you save and invest.

That said, there are definitely career choices that will provide you with a larger salary. If your career is one with small growth potential, you could change careers. It's been said that the average adult changes careers no less than six times throughout a lifetime. If you're going to change careers, you could select one with greater income potential. You might have to go back to school and you might even take a pay cut initially as you learn the ropes, but in the long run it might pay off.

What if you like your current career or don't want to go back to school? Do you have any options to increase your income? Absolutely! There are several short-term strategies that can temporarily or permanently boost your income.

The trick with the short-term strategies is that you shouldn't have to reinvent yourself. Start with what you know. Can you increase your income where you currently work? There are three ways to do just that.

1. **Get a raise.** Seems obvious but you'd be surprised how few people actually do it. A wise person once said, "You don't get paid what you're worth, you get paid what you ask for." What's the worst thing that could happen? They might say it's not in the budget right now, but at least they know you want and deserve it. Another wise person said, "The squeaky wheel gets the grease." You can be squeaky and tactful at the same time. Let them know you deserve a raise and tell them why. If they say no, ask again in a month. I can promise you that your coworkers aren't asking. So when there is extra money, who do you think will get it?

   If you really do deserve a raise and are not being paid what other people in your position are making at other companies, consider changing employers. This is especially true when you have been increasing your skills after hours by taking classes and expanding your knowledge. Sometimes companies only see their employees as they were and not who they have become. If this sounds familiar, talk to your boss and explain to her how you are not the same person they hired and that your new skills deserve a raise. If they don't agree, find a company that values you and pays you more fairly.

2. **Contribute to your retirement plan.** Many companies match part or all of an employee's contribution to their 401(k) plan up to a certain percentage. For example, your company might put in fifty cents for every dollar you contribute. This is free money! Take advantage of their generosity.

3. **Work more hours.** Tell your coworkers you are looking for more hours. If they want to take some time off or leave early, let them know you'll take their hours. Talk to your boss or HR department.

Let them know you want more hours. Is there a big project they need someone to tackle? Tell them you're interested. Look for opportunities to get time and a half or double time. Volunteer to work holidays or weekends. Again, these are short-term strategies. You shouldn't have to work extra hours, weekends, or holidays forever, but this extra income might be just what you need to reach one of your goals or to pay off your debt faster.

It's Only a Dollar

A dollar doesn't seem like much. There are few things you can buy with a buck, but don't underestimate what a dollar can do for you. If you can negotiate an extra dollar an hour raise, that's an extra $2,000 a year! If you worked thirty years and never got another raise, that $1 raise would turn into over $380,000 if you invested it and earned 10 percent a year! Every dollar you can negotiate today can turn into thousands of dollars in retirement.

What if they turned down your request for a raise, don't match retirement plan contributions, and don't have any more hours for you to work? All is not lost. If you have a job already, that means someone is paying you to do something eight hours a day. What are they paying you to do? Could you take your daily skills and use them at another company after hours?

There are many companies that would probably love to utilize your skills and knowledge and that need an extra hand for a few hours a week. A lot of companies are outsourcing non-key tasks and functions of their business. They are operating under the "do what you do best and outsource the rest" philosophy. This is a huge opportunity for extra work that you could do part-time after hours and/or on weekends.

For example, if you are a bookkeeper during the day, there are probably hundreds of small businesses in your local area that could use your book-keeping skills part-time. Do you live in a small town? The great thing about outsourcing is that your employer can be nearly anywhere. So instead of your small town, your job pool could be the hundreds of thousands of small businesses nationally that need a bookkeeper.

Again, since you have skills that someone already pays you to perform, start with what you know. Almost any "day job" can be turned into a night or weekend job. A word of caution—some industries or employers have strict rules regarding outside employment, especially if you are working for a competitor. If in doubt, talk to your HR department first.

Make Space for $1,000

One of the quickest and most rewarding ways to earn $1,000 is to have a yard sale. Sure it takes some work, but you accomplish two things at the same time. You get rid of a lot of "junk" and you make money. Could you pay off one of your credit card bills with $1,000?

What if you hate your day job? Does the idea of working nights and weekends doing what you do during the day make you ill? There are still a lot of other jobs you can do that have nothing to do with your day job. Great places to look for these jobs online are Monster.com and CraigsList.com.

Remember, you are not trying to establish a new career. You are just trying to earn a few extra bucks to save for a goal or to pay down your debt.

Congratulations! You finished another chapter. You are well on your way to experiencing a financial transformation. This was a tough chapter, but it is the foundation to your Six-Day Financial Makeover. You will accomplish your goals only if you can control your cash flow and monitor your net worth. The best financial plan in the world will come up short if you aren't regularly saving. If you were treading water or sinking, you should be swimming now. The next chapter will show you how to put your finances on autopilot!

Action Steps

Taking control of your net worth and cash flow is the foundation of your financial makeover. It's not easy, though. It takes work and time to complete these quizzes and the Expense X-ray Process. The time you invest now will absolutely pay off in more savings, more investments, and getting you closer to the life of your dreams. I'm probably starting to sound like a broken record, but just reading about improving your cash flow won't actually improve your cash flow. You've got to take the next step. . . .

Go through the Action Steps below and put a check mark in one of the following boxes for each one.

Take Control of Your Net Worth

1. ☐ COMPLETED   ☐ NEED TO COMPLETE   ☐ DOES NOT APPLY

Complete the net worth worksheet shown on page 67 or do it online at www.SixDayFinancialMakeover.com.

Take Control of Your Cash Flow

1. ☐ COMPLETED   ☐ NEED TO COMPLETE   ☐ DOES NOT APPLY

Take the Swim, Tread, or Sink Cash-Flow Quiz on page 71 or online at www.SixDayFinancialMakeover.com.

2. ☐ COMPLETED   ☐ NEED TO COMPLETE   ☐ DOES NOT APPLY

Go through the ten-step Expense X-ray Process starting on page 78 or online at www.SixDayFinancialMakeover.com.

3. ☐ COMPLETED   ☐ NEED TO COMPLETE   ☐ DOES NOT APPLY

Continue to eliminate, reduce, and postpone your expenses to fund your goals more quickly.

4. ☐ COMPLETED   ☐ NEED TO COMPLETE   ☐ DOES NOT APPLY

If you're currently in debt, go through the three-step Debt Demolition Program on page 85.

5. ☐ COMPLETED   ☐ NEED TO COMPLETE   ☐ DOES NOT APPLY

If you are serious about paying off your debt or just want to save more toward your goals, consider asking for a raise, requesting more hours, contributing to your retirement account, having a garage sale, or working after hours and/or on weekends for another company to make extra money.

Update Your Online Financial Makeover Account

1. ☐ COMPLETED   ☐ NEED TO COMPLETE   ☐ DOES NOT APPLY

Before you do anything else, update your Six-Day Financial Makeover account at www.SixDayFinancialMakeover.com.

CHAPTER 5

Goal-Oriented Saving and Investing™

The single greatest formula that will help you attain the life of your dreams is your ability to spend less than you earn, save consistently, and invest with a purpose. You've already identified the life of your dreams and aligned your income with your goals. This chapter will introduce you to Goal-Oriented Saving and Investing. (I call it GO! Saving and Investing™ for short.) If you think investing is confusing, complicated, and frustrating, it's not your fault. You'll learn what's wrong with how we've been told to save and invest, and more important, you'll learn a revolutionary solution that is both intuitive and effortless.

Should I read this chapter?

	TRUE	FALSE
1. I haven't started investing because it bores and/or intimidates me.	☐	☐
2. I'm not saving regularly and consistently.	☐	☐
3. I still feel confused and frustrated even though there's so much free investment information and research available.	☐	☐
4. I'd like to learn how to save for my goals effortlessly.	☐	☐
5. I'd like to learn how to reach all of my goals quickly and easily through goal-oriented saving and investing.	☐	☐

If you answered any of these questions TRUE, you should read this chapter.

Chapter Toolbar			
Cost to Implement Advice	**Likelihood of Needing Strategies in Chapter**	**Need Professional Advice?**	**Website Tools**
$0	1 2 3 4 5 6 7 8 9 10 Not Likely Very Likely	⬆ ⬆ ⬆ ⬆ ⬆ No Definitely	Yes

We've been duped. We've been misled, tricked, and hoodwinked. We've been led down a dead-end path. We've been told that more is better. The more information and choices you have—the better. If two is good, two hundred must be better. Right?

Information overload has permeated nearly every industry and market—including your local supermarket. Growing up, we had about four kinds of toothpaste. Have you seen how many different kinds of toothpaste your grocery store stocks today? It takes up nearly an entire aisle! At last count, my supermarket stocked more than eighty different types of toothpaste. Yes, eighty! And we're only talking about toothpaste!

I can honestly say my life (and my teeth!) are no better off because of these choices. In fact, buying toothpaste is a chore now. It actually causes me stress. I don't want to make the wrong decision. Is there a wrong decision? Should I get the teeth-whitening formula or the kind with baking soda? Do I want extra fluoride or should I go the natural route? Which brand do I get? Buying a tube of toothpaste shouldn't require this much thought.

We can't just pick on toothpaste manufacturers. We are overloaded with information everywhere we look. Do you remember when there were three television channels? Now there are three hundred. A dozen pain relievers a decade ago has morphed into six rows of pain relievers that all promise to be *the* cure.

While I'm not convinced having access to excess information and choices has worked with toothpaste, investing is a completely different animal. It's reasonable to assume that more information will make us less nervous and better investors. In fact, the unwritten promise of "more is better" has also been the rallying cry in the financial and investment industry. They claim that getting your hands on enough information is the cure to all of our investment anxiety and problems. It goes something like this:

> *Financial apathy and poor investment decisions are the result of a lack of information. The more information you have, the more involved you'll want to become and the better you will be as an investor. As an informed investor, you will be able to make investment decisions quickly, easily, and with less anxiety. If you are nervous or feel over-whelmed about investing, it's because you don't have enough informa-tion or options. Since the lack of information and options is what causes indecision, frustration, and anxiety, you should get as much in-formation and have as many choices as you can.*

The average investor has more data and information available at her fin-gertips today than entire investment departments had twenty years ago. The Internet and software have opened the floodgates and unleashed more investment information on you, the consumer, than you've ever had access to before in our history. Do you want to research a mutual fund? Do you want to know the gross revenue of a company? Do you want to compare the performance of all large cap mutual funds for the last twelve months? What about finding out what the top investment analysts think about Microsoft? How much did the economy grow last quarter? What was the most recent unemployment rate? The answers to all of these questions and thousands more can be answered within seconds for free.

In addition to the millions of pages of free financial information on the Internet, today there are multiple stock exchanges, dozens of electronic ex-changes, thousands of stocks and mutual funds, after-hours trading, inter-national trading, a never-ending assortment of new investment products, and more personal finance and investment books, magazines, and TV shows than ever.

Surely the availability of this free or inexpensive information means that we have become better investors. If information is power, we should be able to make smarter investment decisions in less time and feel less anxiety.

But what if the promise is wrong? What if all of this information doesn't make you a better investor? Worse yet, what if this supposed information elixir is actually making matters worse? What if all of this information is making you more nervous and apprehensive, and a worse investor?

Ask yourself if you feel less worry and doubt about your finances. Has your investment performance improved? Are you able to make investment decisions quickly, easily, and with less anxiety as a result of the information available? Or does it take you longer to make investment decisions? Do you sit on cash because you're not sure what to do with it? Are there too many choices? Do you feel overwhelmed? Don't feel bad if you do; it's not your fault.

Where Should I Park the Truck?

Imagine for a moment that you are an attorney and you represent a drug company. The company is being sued and it is up to you to defend them as best you can. Your opponents have requested documents and information related to a drug your client manufactures. By law, you have to give them what they request. But if you do, you will be providing them with incriminating information against your client. What do you do? You give them what they want—and more, so much more! When you've run out of things to send them, find more. Send them truckloads of boxes with documents and paperwork—the more the better. The strategy is to flood them with as much information as possible to paralyze their research efforts. The chance they will find what they're looking for decreases with each box you send them.

This is no different from the individual investor who has mountains of data and information in front of her. There's very little chance she'll find something worthwhile because to find it she must sort through all of the "noise" and she'll likely feel overwhelmed and frustrated and eventually quit.

Einstein was a pretty smart guy. Not only did he say compound interest was the most powerful force of the universe, he also said we should try to make things as simple as possible, but no simpler. Investing today is not as simple as it should be, though. We've made it more confusing and complicated than it needs to be. The way we invest today is both counterintuitive and counterproductive.

I don't believe in fixing something unless it's broken. Unfortunately, the traditional method of investing isn't intuitive and it just isn't effective.

What's Wrong with How We Currently Invest?

- **It's overwhelming.** We are programmed to think that more information is better, so when we feel overwhelmed and paralyzed, we seek more information. Unfortunately, the more informational "noise" we receive, the more overwhelmed we feel. Ultimately, many people give up and stop investing because it requires us to make too many complicated decisions.

- **It's confusing and complicated.** Even if we haven't gone through the process of putting our goals on paper, we know we have a number of different goals that our investments are supposed to meet. Even though we have multiple objectives, the traditional method of investing lumps all money into a single investment account. If all of your investments are in one or two investment accounts, it is very difficult to know if you are on track to meet your goals or if you need to make changes.

- **There is no rationale for investments or allocation.** Most people who review the investments in their account find that they have no overall investment strategy. Most are filled with a hodgepodge of mutual funds and stocks bought with good intentions or a recommendation, but are not part of a planned investment strategy.

- **There is too much risk.** The investments we choose and the investment allocations we create usually do not reflect both short-term and long-term goals. Investing for short-term goals requires more conservative investments, while we can invest more aggressively for long-term goals; but because all of our goals are lumped together in one or two investment accounts, we tend to take too much risk with our short-term investments and too little risk with our long-term investments. As a result, we can jeopardize reaching both our short-term and our long-term goals.

- **You waste time sitting on the sidelines.** Since we don't have a pre-planned investment strategy, anytime we have money to invest, we start from scratch. Not only is this frustrating and time-consuming, but you can miss out on opportunities while you are trying to figure out what do with your money.

- **It takes too much time to create and monitor investments.** The traditional method of investing takes a lot of time to develop an investment strategy and monitor since all investments are in one or two accounts.

- **All goals carry the same weight.** Your goal to take your family to Italy next year, your goal to send your kids to college in five years, and your goal to buy a new sports car all carry the same weight when your investments are lumped together.

Of Stocks and Cars

While the auto industry has made a lot of mistakes, the financial industry could learn a thing or two from them. Cars have become increasingly more complex and sophisticated under the hood, but at the same time, more user-friendly and easier to drive. On the other hand, investing has become increasingly more complex, but at the same time, more difficult and frustrating for the average investor.

If the auto industry operated like the financial industry, we'd all be taking the bus more often. Instead of turning the key and driving where we want to go, we'd have to be expert mechanics—knowing everything about the ignition, engine, fuel injection, electrical system, etc., just to get the car started!

We naturally think about what our investment success will help us achieve: it will help us send our kids to college, plan for a comfortable retirement, buy a vacation cottage, and buy a new car. But even though we have dozens of goals with different time frames, priorities, and risk characteristics, we often just have one or two investment accounts that are supposed to satisfy all of our goals. In addition, we make short-term decisions based on unimportant information and we don't stick to an investment plan. Or worse yet, we throw up our hands in frustration from too many choices and information overload and don't do anything.

The way we currently invest is broken, but we're going to fix it!

How We Achieved Our Goals As Kids

We can learn a lot from our youth. Do you remember what it was like to save for a goal when you were younger? The process was the same every time. I would get an idea for something I wanted, and then I'd figure out how I was going to make the money to pay for it. If it was a big purchase, it might take weeks or months to earn enough money to buy it. I'd write the goal in big red letters on an envelope and occasionally put money in it. Once I had earned enough money, I would take my savings from the envelope in my nightstand and head to the store.

Rarely did I have more than one goal at a time, but if I did I would have a clearly marked envelope for each goal. If I was saving for a large purchase, I would often change my mind and focus on saving for something else. Even though I changed my mind a lot, I always had a reason or a purpose for earning and saving money.

	AS A KID	MOST ADULTS TODAY	ADULTS AFTER THE SIX-DAY FINANCIAL MAKEOVER
Goals	Single goal	No goals	Multiple, clearly defined goals
Expenses competing for our money	Few, if any, expenses	Many competing expenses	Many competing expenses
Purpose of money	To achieve goals	To get by	To achieve goals
Amount of savings	As much as possible to achieve goals	Little to none	As much as possible to achieve goals
Purpose of saving	To achieve goals	Unsure	To achieve goals
Timing of saving	Before other expenses	After other expenses	Before miscellaneous expenses
Tracking of savings	Easily and regularly	None	Easily and regularly
Success or failure	Easy to determine	Unsure	Easy to determine

When we're young, we have a single focus and very few other expenses competing for our money. All of our earnings can be directed to our single goal. It was really pretty simple. We worked, earned money, and then put the money in a safe place until we had enough to achieve our goal. This was an effective way to save when we were young, but then we got older and our lives got more complex. Can we develop an equally effective and simplistic solution for saving, investing, and reaching our goals now?

Goal-Oriented Investing

Goal-Oriented Investing (GO! Investing) takes what worked for us as kids and updates it to work in a more complicated adult world. You'll be able to save and invest for your goals with laserlike focus. You will always know how close you are to reaching not just one or two of your goals, but all of them. The process will be very similar, but instead of using envelopes and nightstands, we will use a system that's more secure, effortless, and easier to save and invest for multiple goals.

We are outcome-focused, and we want to see immediate results. We need a purpose. There's nothing worse than action without a purpose. Traditionally, most people invest for various vague goals and lump all of their savings together in a single investment account. That's pretty boring. It's also not very inspiring or effective.

GO! Investing satisfies our need for a purpose *and* our need for instant gratification by thinking of each of our goals as a separate "basket." Each of our baskets represents a single goal with a clear purpose that we can see grow.

What does this mean in the real world? It means that we have a single investment account for every goal. For example, if one of your goals is to take the family on a European vacation, create a separate investment account called "Family European Vacation Fund." This account or basket contains all of your savings toward that one goal. Every penny in the account is for the European vacation—not for retirement, a new car, your emergency fund, your kids' college tuitions, or any other goal. What was once just a plain investment account is now a dream—a real goal you are committed to achieving. Account statements have been transformed from boring pieces of paper into exciting treasure maps!

GO! Investing simplifies investing so you don't feel confused or overwhelmed. It will help you develop an investment plan, help you stick to it, and help you achieve your goals—in order of importance—based on your level of sophistication and desire for involvement. GO! Investing is just a mature and more effortless version of the envelope system I used as a kid.

What's the Purpose of Goal-Oriented Investing?

GO! Investing simplifies the process, eliminates the information overload, and aligns how we naturally think with how we save and invest. It's not uncommon for someone to go from being bored or overwhelmed with investing to being excited. For example, a close friend of mine was never much of a saver. She never made a lot of money, but when she had extra, she'd always find a pair of shoes she just had to have. Intellectually, she understood why she should save and invest, but it never was important enough for her to make a commitment to it. That all changed when she began dreaming of owning a house. Instead of contributing to a savings and investment account (boring!), we set up a "My Dream House Fund." Now she gets so excited and can't wait to save and invest. When your vision is clear and your purpose real, saving and investing become fun, exciting, and something you look forward to!

Even though you may have never saved or invested like this before, it will immediately feel a lot more natural than what you've been doing because it recognizes that we may have dozens of goals at any one time, and that each of those goals has its own time frame and priority. The purpose is to help you reach your goals by becoming a better investor and taking fewer risks. You will make smarter investment decisions and you will feel less financial anxiety.

Does GO! Investing sound a little too touchy-feely for you? Don't worry, it has many real-world benefits.

Benefits of Goal-Oriented Investing

- **It fits your personality.** Trying to fit a square peg in a round hole usually ends in frustration and failure. Many investors have been trying to do just this. Not all of us have the time, skill, or even the desire to be actively involved in our investments. GO! Investing doesn't box you into a one-size-fits-all system. In the next chapter you will learn your Investment Personality and then an investment strategy based on your specific Investment Personality.

- **It is more intuitive.** It is more natural and in line with how we think about investing. Again, we are outcome-focused. We tend to compartmentalize things and think in terms of reaching individual goals. Buying a new plasma TV produces different emotions than paying for our children's college education. Not necessarily better or worse feelings, just different. Having separate investment accounts keeps these two very different goals mentally and physically separate.

- **It is easy to track progress.** Because each investment account is for a specific goal, you can instantly see how close you are to reaching each of your goals.

- **There are fewer risks.** Each account will be invested based on when you need the money and how close you are to having enough money to reach the goal for that specific account. You won't unknowingly take more risk than you need to for any of your goals.

- **You have a greater chance of reaching goals.** Accounts with short-term goals can be invested more conservatively and accounts with longer-term goals can be invested for growth. As a result, you have a much greater chance of reaching both short- and long-term goals.

- **You have the ability to prioritize goals based on importance.** Not all goals are created equal. Even though you may have eleven different goals you'd like to achieve, some are certainly more important than others. GO! Investing lets you easily add weight to more important goals. If you reach your more important goals, you can invest for your less important goals.

GO! Investing turns investing on its head. Rather than focus on the process, it focuses on the outcome—your goals. Do you want an investment with a low standard deviation, high alpha, and low P/E ratio or do you just want to put the kids through college, buy a house, and enjoy a nice retirement?

To invest successfully, you need not understand beta, efficient markets, modern portfolio theory, option pricing, or emerging markets. You may, in fact, be better off knowing nothing of these.

—Warren Buffett, Letter to Shareholders,
Berkshire Hathaway Annual Report, 1996

In order to achieve your goals as quickly and efficiently as possible, you must first save and then invest those savings effectively. How do you do that? Chapter 4 helped you identify how much you could afford to save for your goals each month. The Effortless Savings Program discussed below will show you how to put your savings plan on autopilot. And then get ready . . . the next chapter will show you a revolutionary investment strategy based on your Investment Personality that will transform your savings into achieving your goals.

Effortless Savings Program

A good savings plan is like a good diet: It's only going to work if you stick with it. When so many things compete for our time and attention, it's easy to push our finances to the back burner. While the consequences of ignoring your finances for a few months are not quickly apparent, it can have lasting repercussions for your future. They can be the difference between living the life of your dreams and barely getting by.

GO! Investing is worthless if we don't also save consistently and purposefully. This section will show you exactly how to set your savings program on autopilot so that, day after day, you'll have an effortless system working behind the scenes to ensure you stay on target to reach your goals.

The good news is there are several extremely easy solutions you can implement through your employer or on your own. Once it's set up, it will run smoothly and effortlessly. The bad news is you won't have any excuse not to do it! There are three ways to implement the Effortless Savings Program:

1. 401(k) or other employer-sponsored retirement account

2. Direct deposit

3. Automatic payments/transfers

1. Take advantage of your 401(k) account

The 401(k) is one of the best tools you have in your savings arsenal. It allows you to contribute money directly from your paycheck. Don't worry if your company doesn't offer a 401(k), they might offer a different type of retirement account that's just as good such as a SEP, SIMPLE, 403(b), or 457 account.

WHY YOU SHOULD CONTRIBUTE TO YOUR 401(K) ACCOUNT

- **Easy to set up.** If you are interested in participating in your company's 401(k) plan, just ask your HR department or talk to your boss. Enrollment only requires completion of a couple of forms. It couldn't be easier.

- **Automatic.** Once you have it set up, it runs itself. Every pay period, you will have money automatically taken out of your paycheck and contributed to your 401(k) account.

- **Tax savings.** Have you ever looked at all of the deductions on your pay stub? Federal income tax, state income tax, state disability, Social Security, Medicare, unemployment, etc. The list goes on and on. How would you like to pay less income tax? Contributing to a 401(k) gives you the chance to do just that. Every dollar you contribute to your 401(k) account escapes federal income tax and, in most states, state income tax!

- **Free money.** How would you like to benefit from an instant—and unsolicited—pay raise? Many companies with 401(k) retirement plans match part or all of their employees' contributions. For example, a company might contribute twenty-five cents for every dollar an employee contributes. If the employees' contributes a dollar every paycheck, the company will deposit twenty-five cents in that employee's account. The employee gets the extra twenty-five cents without having to work any harder or negotiate a raise. This can add up to hundreds of thousands of dollars in "free" money for your retirement. For example, under this scenario you'd have more than $1.1 million of *free money* if you contribute just $100 a week from your paycheck (assuming a 10 percent return and contributions for forty-five years).

- **It's easy.** Once you have contributed money to your 401(k) account, it is easy to invest that money. Once you have selected the investments you want to purchase, any additional money can be automatically invested for you.

- **Shielded from lawsuits.** Any money you have in your 401(k) account is protected from lawsuits and bankruptcies. In a litigious world, this is a huge benefit. In Chapter 10 you'll see just how important it is to shield your assets from flagrant lawsuits.

What If I'm Self-employed?

Not to worry! You have many retirement plan options available, and since you call the shots, you can select the one that's best for you! You can establish a 401(k) account, or if you don't have employees, you can easily establish a one-person 401(k). Traditional IRAs or Roth IRAs don't allow you to contribute very much per year, but for the self-employed, SEP and SIMPLE IRA retirement plans could be great solutions. If you're older and are looking for the biggest bang for your buck, you can create a defined benefit plan, which lets you defer more than any other plan (depending on a bunch of complicated calculations and actuarial assumptions). Work with a retirement plan specialist and your CPA to choose the best retirement plan for your situation.

It's hard to find a better or easier *retirement* savings vehicle than the 401(k), but that doesn't mean it's the only retirement savings vehicle or that it is appropriate for non-retirement goals.

PROBLEMS WITH 401(K) ACCOUNTS

- **Caps on annual contributions.** You can only contribute a maximum per year from your paycheck ($15,000 and then an additional $500 per year for future years). While this may be more than enough for a lot of people, you may want or need to contribute more annually to your retirement.

- **Eventually have to pay tax.** The good news is that your contributions to your 401(k) occur before your paycheck is taxed. The bad news is that you can't escape tax forever (unless you take advantage of the new Roth 401(k); see "A Retirement Account Blizzard," below). When you withdraw money from your 401(k), you have to pay income tax. What's the point of contributing? In addition to the many other benefits discussed above, your money has been able to grow tax-deferred all of this time.

A Retirement Account Blizzard

What happens when you combine the benefits of a 401(k) with the benefits of a Roth IRA? You get a Roth 401(k), of course! This hybrid retirement account is relatively new—it was born on January 1, 2006. If your employer offers this, you can contribute part of your paycheck to this account and you'll never have to pay tax on the growth, even when you withdraw from the account! Unlike a traditional 401(k), though, your contributions to the account are fully taxed. If you're in a relatively low tax bracket now and expect to build a nice retirement nest egg (and you should!), this could be a terrific option for you.

- **Only good for retirement savings.** Money you contribute to your 401(k) should be earmarked for retirement purposes only because if you take money out before you turn fifty-nine and a half you will be hit with a 10 percent penalty on the amount withdrawn—in addition to income tax (there are a few exceptions). As a result of the penalty, a 401(k) is not a good place to save for non-retirement goals such as an emergency fund, new car, or vacation.

If you are saving for your retirement (and you should be!), take full advantage of your company's 401(k) and/or Roth 401(k) plan. But how much should you contribute? The short answer is "as much as you can." The long answer is "it depends." There are no hard and fast rules, but here are a few tips you can use when you are calculating how much to contribute.

401(K) CONTRIBUTION TIPS

- Retirement savings should be your number one goal after having an emergency fund with three months of expenses in cash.

- Contribute at least as much as your company is willing to match. For example, your company may match a certain percentage of what you contribute up to a maximum amount. If your company will contribute fifty cents for every dollar you contribute up to 6 percent of your salary, you should contribute at least 6 percent of your salary in order to get as much free money from the company as possible.

- Make sure you save for your non-retirement goals as well. Just because you contribute to your 401(k) doesn't necessarily mean you shouldn't be saving in other accounts. Follow the Optimized Spending Pyramid and the cash-flow plan you created in the last chapter.

- When in doubt, save more than you think you'll need.

- If you get a raise, increase your contribution to your 401(k) by the same amount. If you were getting by without the raise, you won't even know notice that it's going to your 401(k).

- If you get a bonus, ask your HR department if they can deposit the whole amount in your 401(k).

You should definitely take advantage of your company's retirement account. Unfortunately, this is where most people stop. This is one of the best and easiest ways to save for your retirement, but it is a terrible way to save for your other goals.

2. Direct deposit your way to your dreams

How can you save for your other goals with the same ease as saving in your 401(k)? The answer is through direct deposit. Direct deposit is a slick way to save for multiple goals effortlessly. Instead of receiving a check that you have to bring to the bank to deposit, your check is automatically and directly deposited into a bank or investment account for you, and you get a printed pay voucher showing how much you earned, how much was taken out in taxes, etc.

If you work for a company that offers direct deposit—most companies do today—it saves you from having to go to the bank and more! You have complete control over how your paycheck is allocated. You can have a percentage of your paycheck directly deposited into one or more accounts automatically. It's your money. You get to decide where it goes and how much goes to each account.

Not for the Faint of Heart

This strategy works best if your finances are in complete disarray and you're spending too much on your credit cards every month. Drastic situations require drastic actions.

For individuals without a bank account, the larger payroll processing companies will direct deposit to a debit card. Even if you have a bank account you can still use this strategy. Tell your HR department to transfer what you need to pay your bills to your checking account and transfer only what you've allocated to credit card spending to the debit card.

For example, if you calculated that you can only spend $400 on clothes, entertainment, and dining out per month, you could have $400 (or $200 if you get paid twice a month) directly deposited on your debit card. When you run out of money on your debit card, you must stop spending. This automatically prevents you from spending too much. Of course, this only works if you cut up your credit cards!

You might be thinking, "Big deal. I can have my paycheck deposited into different bank or investment accounts. How does this help me achieve my goals?" The purpose of this chapter is to show you how to achieve your goals by putting your savings and investment plan on autopilot. The basket approach to saving aligns your hard work and salary with a purpose—your goals. Direct deposit is a tool that makes it effortless to save for each of your goals in a way that seems natural and intuitive.

Here's how you can direct deposit your way to wealth and success in the real world. You've already done all of the hard work in the last chapter. You should have a clear picture of your cash flow—what's coming in and what's going out to meet your expenses and to accomplish your goals. Every dollar that comes in the door has a purpose. The purpose might be to pay a bill or to reach a goal. Add up all of your expenses. This amount should be direct deposited into a checking account since you will need quick access to the cash.

What about your goals? For each of your goals, create a new investment account. Yes, that's right. For every goal that requires you to save money you will open an investment account. If you have six financial goals, you should have six separate accounts. You might be thinking, "This sounds more complicated and time-consuming than what I'm doing now!" If you give it a chance, you will find it is actually less complicated and a much more efficient use of your time than the traditional way of saving.

You've already calculated how much you need to save per month to achieve each of your goals, so now you can have that amount of your paycheck directly deposited for each goal.

For example, let's say after taxes and after contributing to her 401(k) account, Lisa takes home $3,000 a month. Based on the work she did in Chapter 4, here's what she found about her expenses and the cost to fund her goals:

Monthly Cash Outflows	Dollar Amount	% of Take-Home Pay
EXPENSES		
Regularly occurring expenses:	$1,525	51%
Occasional expenses:	$ 525	18%
DIRECT DEPOSIT TO CHECKING:	**$2,050**	**69%**
GOALS		
Emergency reserve:	$0 (already has enough in emergency account)	
Retirement/Financial Independence (outside of 401(k))	$ 300	10%
Accounting class tuition	$ 150	5%
French language class/trip	$ 125	4%
Caribbean cruise	$ 360	12%
DIRECT DEPOSIT TO INVESTMENT ACCOUNTS:	**$935**	**31%**

Lisa first had to calculate how much she needed to direct deposit into her checking account. Based on her monthly recurring expenses and more infrequent but predictable expenses, Lisa determined she needs to direct deposit $2,050 into her checking account.

Lisa knows that just paying her bills is like treading water. If she wants to get closer to reaching her goals she will have to save every month. Lisa has four goals: a fun retirement, an accounting class she'd like to take eight months from now that will cost $1,200 ($150 per month×8 months), a French language class in France she'd like to attend in three years that will cost $4,500 ($125 per month×36 months), and a Caribbean cruise she wants to take with her boyfriend in a year that will cost $4,320 ($360 per month×12 months).

Because she has four distinct goals, she needs four baskets—one for each goal. Of course, instead of a basket, Lisa is going to create four investment accounts. As long as Lisa doesn't lose her job (but if she does, her emergency reserve fund will help see her through such a problem) or change the direct deposit amount into each account, she will reach all of her goals effortlessly. Once the direct deposit accounts are set up and Lisa tells them how much to deposit into each account, her savings plan is on autopilot; she can forget about it.

Now it's your turn! Complete the worksheet below:

Monthly Cash Outflows	Dollar Amount	% of Take-Home Pay
EXPENSES		
Regularly occurring expenses:	$_____	_____%
Occasional expenses:	$_____	_____%
DIRECT DEPOSIT TO CHECKING:	**$_____**	_____**%**
GOALS		
Emergency reserve:	$_____	_____%
Retirement/Financial Independence	$_____	_____%
Goal #1:_____	$_____	_____%
Goal #2:_____	$_____	_____%
Goal #3:_____	$_____	_____%
Goal #4:_____	$_____	_____%
Goal #5:_____	$_____	_____%
Goal #6:_____	$_____	_____%
Goal #7:_____	$_____	_____%
DIRECT DEPOSIT TO INVESTMENT ACCOUNTS:	**$_____** **TOTAL**	_____**%** **TOTAL**

Once you know exactly how your paycheck should be divided, you can open investment accounts for each goal. Make sure they don't charge you any fees to open an account or high ongoing account fees. There are plenty of firms happy to work with you. If your brokerage firm gives you an attitude about opening so many accounts, open an account somewhere else. Remember, your goal is to reach your goals. Don't let a stodgy and uncreative firm get in your way!

Once you've opened the investment accounts, contact the human resources department at your work and tell them how you'd like your check split between the various accounts. After the accounts are set up and you have money flowing into them from each paycheck, you're done!

3. Use automatic transfers to reach your dreams easily

If your employer doesn't offer direct deposit, you can still put your savings on autopilot. Use automatic transfers through your bank. An automatic transfer is a transfer, or "payment," from your checking account to another account either at your bank or an investment account you've established.

For example, you can tell your bank that you want to schedule an automatic transfer of $100 on the third and eighteenth of every month from your checking account to your "Family Vacation" investment account and $125 to your child's college savings account.

With direct deposit, your employer transfers the money directly to these accounts—bypassing your checking account. If you don't have access to direct deposit, automatic bank transfers add another step, but once set up, they run seamlessly and automatically without any other effort or action on your part.

This is an example of "pushing" funds to another account. You are telling the bank, "Please send money to such and such account for me." Your communication and instructions are with your bank. You can also "pull" funds into an account. Many brokerage firms and college savings accounts allow you to schedule regular transfers from your bank. Here your communication and instructions are not with your bank, they are with the institution where you have your other account. Use whatever method is easiest for you.

How do you know how much and where to transfer funds? Complete the worksheet in Step 2 on page 109.

Action Steps

Wouldn't it be great to write a song and then get royalty checks in the mail every week? Although I can't help you write a song, if you complete the Action Steps below you will get maximum rewards for years to come with very little up-front effort. Again, it's not enough to read about putting your finances on autopilot . . . you actually have to do it!

Go through the Action Steps below and put a check mark in one of the following boxes for each one.

Emergency Reserve Account

1. ☐ COMPLETED   ☐ NEED TO COMPLETE   ☐ DOES NOT APPLY

An emergency reserve account should have cash equal to approximately three months of living expenses. Determine your monthly living expenses by completing the worksheet in Chapter 4.

2. ☐ COMPLETED   ☐ NEED TO COMPLETE   ☐ DOES NOT APPLY

Open an interest-bearing savings account at your bank. The interest rate the bank pays you should be competitive. If it's not, find another bank.

3. ☐ COMPLETED   ☐ NEED TO COMPLETE   ☐ DOES NOT APPLY

If you don't currently have an emergency reserve account but have investments or cash equal to or greater than three months of living expenses, open an emergency reserve savings account and fund it today.

Take Advantage of Your 401(k) Account

(Again, your company may not offer a 401(k), so talk to your HR department to see what retirement plan(s) you have access to.)

1. ☐ COMPLETED   ☐ NEED TO COMPLETE   ☐ DOES NOT APPLY

Get enrolled! Talk to your HR department and get all of the forms. Take them home and complete them. If you're having trouble, ask for help. Now's not the time to be shy.

2. ☐ COMPLETED   ☐ NEED TO COMPLETE   ☐ DOES NOT APPLY

Start deferring part of your paycheck. You'll probably have two options—a flat dollar amount per paycheck or a percentage of your paycheck. Select the percentage of paycheck option and enter the percentage you determined from Chapter 4.

3. ☐ COMPLETED   ☐ NEED TO COMPLETE   ☐ DOES NOT APPLY

If you're already contributing to your 401(k), adjust your contribution percentage based on the amount you determined from Chapter 4.

Direct Deposit Your Way to Your Dreams

(if your employer offers direct deposit)

1. ☐ COMPLETED   ☐ NEED TO COMPLETE   ☐ DOES NOT APPLY

Take out your list of goals.

2. ☐ COMPLETED   ☐ NEED TO COMPLETE   ☐ DOES NOT APPLY

Open an investment account for each goal.

3. ☐ COMPLETED   ☐ NEED TO COMPLETE   ☐ DOES NOT APPLY

Calculate how much you need to deposit into each account to reach all of your goals—you already did this in Chapter 2.

4. ☐ COMPLETED   ☐ NEED TO COMPLETE   ☐ DOES NOT APPLY

Tell your HR department exactly how much you want to direct deposit into each of the accounts.

Using Automatic Transfers to Reach Your Dreams

(if your employer doesn't offer direct deposit)

1. ☐ COMPLETED   ☐ NEED TO COMPLETE   ☐ DOES NOT APPLY

Take out your list of goals.

2. ☐ COMPLETED   ☐ NEED TO COMPLETE   ☐ DOES NOT APPLY

Open an investment account for each goal.

3. ☐ COMPLETED ☐ NEED TO COMPLETE ☐ DOES NOT APPLY

Calculate how much you need to deposit into each account to reach all of your goals—you already did this in Chapter 2.

4. ☐ COMPLETED ☐ NEED TO COMPLETE ☐ DOES NOT APPLY

Contact the firm where you opened your investment accounts and instruct them exactly how much you want to transfer from your checking account each paycheck or month.

Update Your Online Financial Makeover Account

1. ☐ COMPLETED ☐ NEED TO COMPLETE ☐ DOES NOT APPLY

Before you do anything else, update your Six-Day Financial Makeover account at www.SixDayFinancialMakeover.com.

CHAPTER 6

Six Steps to Investment Success

The financial world assumes that everyone wants to read the *Wall Street Journal* every morning, watch CNBC throughout the day, and be actively involved in their investments. While that may be true for some, you may not have the time, expertise, or desire to be actively involved in your investments.

This chapter will help you discover your unique Investment Personality and match it to an Investment Strategy made just for you. If you like to be hands-on, hands-off, or somewhere in between, you will learn a six-step investment solution that will work behind the scenes to ensure you reach your goals!

Should I read this chapter?

	TRUE	FALSE
1. I spend more time than I'd like researching my investments.	☐	☐
2. I want a simple and straightforward approach to investing that requires very little effort or time.	☐	☐
3. I get my investment statements in the mail, but I still don't know how I'm doing or if I should make a change.	☐	☐
4. I enjoy learning about investing, but I want a step-by-step action plan that I can easily implement.	☐	☐

TRUE   FALSE

5. I'd like to learn a six-step investment approach
    based on my Investment Personality that will
    help me reach my goals.   ☐   ☐

If you answered any of these questions TRUE, you should read this chapter.

Chapter Toolbar

Cost to Implement Advice	Likelihood of Needing Strategies in Chapter	Need Professional Advice?	Website Tools
$0	1 2 3 4 5 6 7 8 9 10 Not Likely Very Likely	↑ ↑ ↑ ↑ ↑ No Definitely	Yes

---

GO! Investing will help you reach your goals by making you a better investor. You will learn a simple and straightforward six-step process that will immediately feel more intuitive and be more productive than the investment strategy you've been using. You will learn how to invest with a purpose by following these six steps:

Step #1—Create Investment Accounts for Each of Your Goals

Step #2—Discover Your Investment Personality

Step #3—Match Your Investment Personality with the Corresponding Investment Strategy

Step #4—Determine the Initial Time Frame for Each Goal

Step #5—Invest Using the Investment Strategy That Best Matches Your Personality

Step #6—Monitor Your Investment Accounts

Without further ado, let's get right into the six steps!

Step #1—Create Investment Accounts for Each of Your Goals

If you've created your goals in Chapter 2, this step should be easy. You're just going to create separate investment accounts for each of your goals. There are dozens of account types to choose from. For most of your goals, you will want a plain vanilla taxable account or, if you have done any estate planning and have a living trust, make sure you open trust accounts for your goals. If you haven't created a living trust (or don't even know what one is), don't worry about this now—just open a regular individual account. For your retirement goals, you will probably want to open IRA or Roth IRA accounts in addition to regular taxable accounts. If you are saving for college tuition, definitely consider a 529 Plan. Money you put in these accounts grows tax-free if the money is used for college education. Since each state has its own 529 Plan with its own rules and regulations, make sure you do your own research or get help choosing the 529 Plan that's right for you. If you aren't sure what kind of account to open for each of your goals, just call your brokerage firm and they should be able to help you.

Get Off the Bus!

You might be thinking that it is overkill to have an investment account for each goal. Isn't that unnecessary? If the goal is to simplify investing, why go through the hassle of having so many different accounts? Remember, Einstein said to make things as simple as possible, but not simpler.

If you're having a hard time getting a handle on the purpose of GO! Investing, let's switch gears for a moment... literally. Pretend you are a bus driver. You've got a bus full of passengers, each trying to get to different locations at different times. A few passengers just need to go down the street while a few others need to get clear across town. If you drop off the passengers who need to go a few blocks, the passengers who need to go across town might be late. Of course, if you speed across town, you increase the risk of a ticket or an accident and the other passengers are going to be upset you didn't drop them off first.

How can you get all the passengers to their location safely and as fast as possible? Tell them to get off the bus! The only way everyone is going to get to their destination safely and quickly is if each passenger takes his own taxi.

Then the guy who needs to get across town for an important business meeting can get there quickly and the elderly woman who only needs to go a couple of blocks to the grocery store isn't stuck on the bus while you drive all over town. Each passenger can go directly where he wants to go as quickly as he wants to travel, and without taking any unnecessary risks.

The traditional approach to investing is like dumping all of our goals on a bus. It is very inefficient and counterintuitive. GO! Investing, however, provides each goal with its own car that goes directly to its destination.

Step #2—Discover Your Investment Personality

Do you read the *Wall Street Journal* every morning and actively monitor your investments throughout the day? Or do you want as little to do with your finances and investments as possible? Maybe you're somewhere in between these two extremes. . . .

One investment personality is no better than another. They each have their own advantages and disadvantages that we'll explore later in this chapter. If investing bores or intimidates you, you'll learn a strategy that is perfect for you. If you want to be more involved, you will learn a strategy custom-tailored for your personality that will put you on the fast track to reaching your goals.

The bottom line is that you don't have to dedicate hours and hours a week to your investments if you don't want to, but you do need to know and understand your investment personality to best maximize your return and keep yourself sane in the face of today's information overload.

There are three investment personalities:

1. **"Hands-off."** The Hands-off Investment Personality wants a simple and straightforward approach to investing that requires very little time and personal involvement.

2. **"Involved."** The Involved Investment Personality also wants a simple and straightforward approach to investing, but is comfortable taking a more active role in his investments.

3. **"Consumed."** The Consumed Investment Personality wants the greatest potential for investment return and needs to be in control and fully involved in all aspects of his investments.

Which type are you? If you don't immediately recognize your investment personality or are unsure, take the quiz below by circling the letter that best fits you or go to www.SixDayFinancialMakeover.com and take the online version. Don't dismiss the Investment Personality Quiz™ as a cute self-discovery tool. It is very important that you discover your Investment Personality because it determines your investment strategy and that strategy determines what and how you should invest to achieve your goals. If you don't have any investments yet, circle the letter you think *will* best describe your investing tendencies.

The Investment Personality Quiz

1. I check the performance of my investments
   a. Almost never between account statements
   b. Usually a few times a month
   c. Nearly every day

2. I read financial magazines such as *Fortune, Forbes,* or *BusinessWeek*
   a. Rarely or never
   b. Once in a while, if I have time
   c. Regularly

3. Do you enjoy researching various investments?
   a. About as much as I enjoy a headache
   b. Sometimes
   c. Absolutely

4. What describes you best?
   a. I'd be happy with an 8 percent annual return, if I didn't have to spend any time researching or paying attention to my investments.
   b. I'd be happy with a 10 percent annual return, if I spent a couple of hours a week on my investments.
   c. I'd gladly read and research 10 or more hours a week to get a 12 percent annual return.

5. Do you know what makes up the GDP and what it measures?
   a. I've never heard of GDP
   b. Not exactly
   c. Yes, of course

6. If you had to go back to college for one class, which class would you take?
   a. Short Stories
   b. Personal Finance 101
   c. Advanced Economics and Investing

7. What did the Dow Jones Index close at yesterday? (Pick a number and then check the actual figure in the newspaper or online.)
   a. I was off by more than 2,000 points
   b. I was off by 200 to 2,000 points
   c. I was correct within 200 points

8. What do you do with your investment statements when they arrive in the mail?
   a. I take a quick glance at them.
   b. I set them aside to look them over on the weekend.
   c. I go through them in detail that day to see how everything is doing and to make sure there are no mistakes.

9. If you were financially independent
   a. I'd be able to hire someone to deal with my investments.
   b. I'd spend about the same amount of time on my investments.
   c. I'd be able to spend even more time researching investments and monitoring the performance in my accounts.

10. I'd prefer to be
   a. As uninvolved in my investments as possible.
   b. Somewhat involved in my investments.
   c. As actively involved in my investments as possible.

Scoring the Investment Personality Quiz*

Count the number of answers you selected for each letter:

As_____   Bs_____   Cs_____

I scored highest in As: I have a Hands-off Investment Personality.

I scored highest in Bs: I have an Involved Investment Personality.

I scored highest in Cs: I have a Consumed Investment Personality.

---

* If you take the quiz and it still isn't clear which Investment Personality you have, read the descriptions on pages 120–21 and choose the one you identify with most.

Hands-off Investment Personality

If you have a Hands-off Investment Personality, you want as little to do with your investments as possible. You want the benefits of investing, but you don't have the desire, the time, or the expertise to take an active role in your investments. You're not opposed to saving or investing, you just don't want to be involved in the daily minutia.

Don't be disappointed or discouraged if you have a Hands-off Investment Personality. You don't have to be an investment guru to succeed as an investor. You do not need to dedicate hours to investment research and have a degree in finance and accounting to do well investing. I believe this myth is one of the reasons there are a lot of onlookers who would like to invest but who are too nervous or scared to begin.

I enjoy eating good food, but I don't want to be a farmer, a rancher, or a chef. I want to benefit from the fancy dinner, I just don't want to grow the vegetables, raise the livestock, or prepare the meal. As a Hands-off investor, you'll still benefit from investing in stocks and bonds just like the financial gurus, and you'll be saving and investing just as much as someone who has an Involved or Consumed Investment Personality. The only difference will be the degree of daily management.

Involved Investment Personality

If you have an Involved Investment Personality, you want to have more involvement than the Hands-off Personality, but not as much as the Consumed Investment Personality. You like to know what's going on, but you don't necessarily have the time, skill, or desire to be fully involved. You don't want to give up control of your investments, but you don't want to spend hours a week in the investment trenches, either.

You think you have a pretty good idea of how to invest and have a general sense of what works and what doesn't. Although you can talk the talk, you don't have enough time or desire to know everything going on in the economy or stock market. It's hard enough keeping track of how your own investments are performing.

You may read the business section of your local newspaper, keep current on what's happening with the economy, and track the performance of your investments. You choose investments by reading magazines or talking to others. It's a reactive approach—any research you do is a result of reading or hearing it somewhere first.

If you had more time, you might get more involved, but you'd never want to do as much research or have as much control as the Consumed Investment Personality. It's not a matter of time or skill—it's a matter of choice and desire.

Consumed Investment Personality

If you have a Consumed Investment Personality, you probably already knew it. You love the stock market and want to be as involved as you can. You, quite literally, are consumed with investing: you research, monitor the economy, and check your accounts. The Consumed Investment Personality probably represents less than 5 percent of the population.

You need as much control as possible. It's worth spending several hours a week reading the *Wall Street Journal* and other financial publications because you enjoy it. You wouldn't want it any other way. If you quit your day job, you'd consider entering the financial services field if you're not in it already!

You select investments after you've done your research and you make adjustments to your portfolio to take advantage of any changes you've identified in the economy. Control, flexibility, and involvement are very important to you and worth the extra time it takes to generate a better investment return.

Step #3—Match Your Investment Personality with the Corresponding Investment Strategy

Each investment personality requires a specific investment strategy. If you have a Hands-off Investment Personality, you aren't going to want to read the *Wall Street Journal* every morning, track the Federal Reserve's decisions, and perform regular research on your investments. Likewise, if you have a Consumed Investment Personality, there's no way you're going to be comfortable reviewing your investments once a quarter or content making an investment decision without doing a sizable amount of research.

Each investment personality has a corresponding investment strategy. You've got to do what's right for you and what feels most comfortable for you. If your investment strategy is inconsistent with your investment personality, you will experience anxiety and discomfort and may ultimately feel so frustrated that you quit investing.

Hands-off Investment Strategy

Summary

If you have a Hands-off Investment Personality, you need a strategy that provides a simple and straightforward approach to investing. The Hands-off investment strategy uses only Lifecycle mutual funds. These kinds of funds are offered by almost all fund companies including Fidelity, Vanguard, and many others and can also be called Lifecycle, Target Date, or Target Retirement funds (throughout the book, they will be referred to as Lifecycle funds).

A single mutual fund purchase is all that is required for immediate diversification across bonds, stocks, and the sub-asset classes. Lifecycle funds have target dates that can be closely matched to your desired goal date. As your goal gets closer, these funds automatically allocate to a more conservative portfolio. The Hands-off Investment Strategy takes all of the guesswork and research out of investing.

Advantages

- **It's simple.** If you think investing is confusing and overwhelming, and you want little to do with it, you are going to be pleasantly surprised at just how easy it can be with the Hands-off Investment Strategy.

- **It's easy to create.** Not sure where to start or what to do? The Hands-off Investment Strategy is truly that—hands-off! All you need to do is buy a Lifecycle fund with a target date that most closely matches your goal. That's it!

- **It's easy to monitor.** Forget about asset allocation, the economy, studying the stock market, rebalancing your account, diversifying, and learning which funds to buy. Setting up and monitoring your investments will take about as much time as it takes you to read this sentence.

- **It's good enough for many investors.** At the end of the day, the Hands-off Investment Strategy is good enough for most investors, who don't have the time, skill, or desire to be more involved in their investments. In fact, even if you want to be more involved, once you learn how easy and straightforward this strategy is you might be hooked!

Disadvantages

- **It's more expensive.** The Hands-off Investment Strategy is not the most cost effective investment strategy. Most Lifecycle funds charge at least 1 percent of the amount you have invested per year in investment management fees and some charge additional fees.

- **You may see the lowest possible return.** If you use this strategy, there is a good chance that you won't do as well compared to the Involved or Consumed investor. This doesn't mean that you won't have a good return over time, it simply means you might not do as well as the others. However, you'll still probably do better than the average investor.

- **It's tax inefficient.** Because of the nature of the Hands-off Investment Strategy, this approach is the least tax efficient. That doesn't matter in a tax-deferred account, but it can make a difference in a taxable account.

- **It's the least flexible of the strategies.** This strategy offers virtually no investment flexibility. You buy one diversified mutual fund and hang on to it. There aren't any choices.

If you know deep down you are a Hands-off Investor but aren't happy with the list of disadvantages to this investment strategy, you have a couple of choices. One, you can disregard your investment personality and try to use the Involved or Consumed strategies. This is what most investors do and it is a mistake. Not only will you be frustrated and overwhelmed, your investment performance will suffer because your heart (and head!) will not be in it. A much better alternative is to take advantage of the benefits of the Involved or Consumed strategies by "outsourcing" the work to an objective investment planning firm.

Involved Investment Strategy

Summary

This strategy provides a great deal of control over the investment allocation, but no control over the investments that make up the allocation. Only

The Rich Get Richer and the Poor Get Screwed

I have the privilege of providing financial and investment advice to some of America's wealthiest families. I've found that regardless of net worth, individuals with $200 million have the same financial concerns and fears as someone with $2,000. I've had clients worth nearly $100 million tell me they just want to make sure they won't have to work again. The difference between someone with $50 million and someone with $50,000 (other than a few more zeroes!) is that the person with $50 million can afford to hire the best financial and investment consultants available. The person with $5,000 doesn't have this luxury. The rich get richer and the poor get screwed.

While I've worked with the very affluent, I also have a personal passion to help the "average" guy or gal struggling to get by. I know what it's like to struggle. When I was a child, we shopped at the Goodwill, stood in line for government cheese, went without heat in the winter, and occasionally sold our furniture to buy food. I know firsthand what it's like to struggle. I also know there aren't many good resources and solutions for the average person trying to raise a family and save for retirement.

GO! Investing is the solution for those who can't afford to hire an advisor, for those who don't want to work with an advisor, or for those who are frustrated by the current method of investing and want a simple, fun, and rewarding alternative.

low-cost index funds are used to build a portfolio. Instead of buying one fund and having no control over the allocation as in the Hands-off Investment Strategy, the Involved Investment Strategy has the flexibility to create a customized allocation by purchasing a blend of index funds. You are responsible for creating the right mix of stocks, bonds, and cash in your account for each of your goals. As you get closer to achieving your goals, it is your responsibility to reallocate to make the accounts more conservative.

> *Most investors, both institutional and individual, will find that the best way to own common stocks is through an index fund that charges minimal fees.*
> —Warren Buffett, letter to shareholders,
> Berkshire Hathaway Annual Report, 1996

This approach requires some initial involvement to create the individual allocations for each account and ongoing participation as you reallocate over time, but is much less time consuming than the Consumed Investment Strategy because you don't have to research or compare individual stocks, bonds, or mutual funds since all you will be using are low-cost index funds.

Advantages

- **It is low cost.** Because you are only using low-cost index funds, this approach is the least expensive. Most index funds charge an annual expense ratio of less than 0.50 percent.

- **It gives you more flexibility.** This strategy lets you have complete control over the investment allocation for each of your accounts. You can overweight small-cap stocks if you think they are going to do well and underweight international bonds if you think they are overvalued (see "What the Heck Is an 'Asset Class'?" on page 134 for a discussion of the different types of investments).

- **It's tax efficient.** The Involved Investment Strategy is tax efficient for two reasons. First, index funds naturally have a low turnover ratio (percentage of investments in the fund that are bought and sold in year). This helps limit short-term and long-term gains. Second, you are able to tax-loss harvest throughout the year.

- **It's easy to compare performance.** Since you are using index funds that aim to match an investment benchmark, the performance for each asset class should be the same investment return as the "market."

Disadvantages

- **It's more time-consuming to create.** Greater control requires a greater time commitment from you. To create individual allocations for each of your investment accounts, you need to determine an appropriate blend of stocks, bonds, and cash.

- **More ongoing work is required.** This is not a buy and hold strategy—it requires regular rebalancing and reallocating to a more conservative mix of stocks, bonds, and cash as you get closer to achieving your goal. If you neglect the ongoing work, it can derail your chance of achieving your goals.

- **It's impossible to beat the market.** Since you are only using index funds that match a benchmark, you can't, by definition, do better than the benchmark in each asset class. In other words, when you're buying the "market," you can't do better than the market.

Like the Hands-off approach, if you are not happy with the disadvantages of the Involved investment strategy or just don't have the time to dedicate, you really only have two options. One, you can disregard your investment personality and try to use the Consumed strategy. This is what most investors do and it is a mistake. Not only will you be frustrated and overwhelmed, your investment performance will suffer because your heart (and head!) will not be in it.

A much better alternative is to take advantage of the benefits of the Involved or Consumed Strategies by outsourcing the work to an objective investment planning firm.

Consumed Investment Strategy

Summary

This strategy provides the greatest amount of control over the entire investment process. Not only do you control the investment allocation, but you also control the specific investments that make up the allocation.

Like the Involved Investment Strategy, you are responsible for choosing an appropriate mix of stocks, bonds, and cash for each of the accounts initially and for reallocating the accounts as you get closer to reaching your goals. Unlike the Involved Investment Strategy, where the only investment options are index funds, the Consumed Investment Strategy uses both low-cost index funds and actively managed mutual funds.

The use of actively managed funds adds a whole new level of commitment and responsibility. There are thousands of actively managed mutual funds from which to choose. Where do you start? For the Consumed Investment Personality, this is what it's all about. It takes a significant time commitment, but you have the ability to do better than the Hands-off or Involved Investment Strategy.

Advantages

- **It's possible to beat the market.** This strategy has the ability to outperform the benchmarks because it uses actively managed funds. This advantage is what drives the Consumed Investment Personality.

- **It provides the greatest flexibility.** The Consumed Investment Strategy provides the greatest degree of control—both the investment allocation and the investments are under your complete control.

- **It's tax efficient.** Like the Involved Investment Strategy, this approach can be highly tax efficient for the same two reasons. You're using index funds with low turnover ratios (percentage of investments in the fund that are bought and sold in a year), which helps limit short-term and long-term gains and you're able to harvest losses throughout the year to offset gains.

Disadvantages

- **It's the most difficult to create.** You can't get something for nothing. The high amount of control and flexibility comes with a price. This strategy is the most time-consuming because you have to create the overall allocation among stocks, bonds, and cash for each account and have to select the individual investments for each asset class.

- **It's the most time-consuming to monitor.** The "buy it and forget it" approach that works so well with the Hands-off Investment Strategy does not work with the Consumed Investment Strategy. To do this well, you must continuously monitor the actively managed mutual funds against dozens of criteria. In addition, you have to rebalance and reallocate each account as you get closer to reaching your goals.

- **It's not the most cost-effective.** This strategy is not the cheapest. Using actively managed mutual funds increases the overall cost because they charge a higher investment expense fee. According to Morningstar, the average actively managed stock mutual fund costs 1.40 percent of the amount invested per year compared to the average stock index fund of 0.85 percent. Of course, if you choose good actively managed mutual funds, you can make up for the higher fees with better performance.

- **Bad habits may affect your investment return.** The more control you have over your investments, the greater the potential for problems such as trying to chase hot asset classes or funds, trying to time the market, overtrading, or making investment decisions based on emotional reactions.

What do you do if you really want to be involved but just don't have the time? I suggest reading the Hands-off and/or Involved Investment Strategy, which might be better for someone who is as time-constrained as you, or outsource the work to an objective investment planning firm.

Again, one strategy isn't better or worse than another. The best strategy is the strategy that most closely matches your investment personality. Don't get caught up in the advantages or disadvantages of each strategy, just focus on the strategy that applies to you.

Step #4—Determine the Initial Time Frame for Each Goal

You've heard the saying, "Time is money," right? When it comes to investing, it's absolutely true! The more time you have to reach your goal, the more your investments can help you. But before you can create an asset allocation and start investing, you need to determine the initial time frame for each goal. In other words, you need to know when you want to accomplish each goal and when you'll need to start withdrawing money from each investment account. Select the initial time frame from the options below for each goal:

- Immediate—Less than one year

- Close—One to two years

- Approaching—Two to four years

- Intermediate—Four to eight years

- Distant—Over eight years

This step is very important because it will determine how conservatively or aggressively each of your investment accounts is allocated, the projected investment return, and how much growth you'll get from your investments. The more time you have to reach your goal, the less money you need to save and the more the dividends, interest, and growth from your investments will propel you to your goal. This is the power of compound investing.

To better understand the value of time and compound investing, meet Bernie and Cynthia. They're both twenty-five years old. Cynthia begins saving for retirement early. She saves $1,000 per year for the first ten years and then stops. Bernie doesn't start saving for retirement until he's thirty-five. He's a late bloomer but tries to make up for it by saving $1,000 a year for thirty years (twenty years longer than Cynthia!). Assuming they both earn 10 percent per year, look at what happens:

Cynthia was out of pocket only $10,000 and ends up with over $300,000 at age sixty-five. Bernie, on the other hand, was out of pocket $30,000 and ends up with barely $180,000 at age sixty-five. Cynthia started early and used the power of compound investing to her advantage!

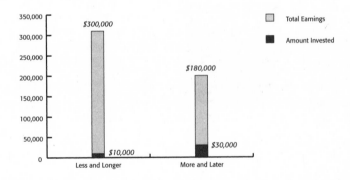

Immediate Time Frame (Less Than 1 Year Away)

If your goal is less than a year away, you will want to invest in something very conservative. You do not want to risk investing in anything aggressive because you will need access to the money soon. Instead of trying to hit a home run with your investments, your greatest objective should be protecting them. Because you have very little time for compound investing to work and because you are investing conservatively, the final account value will come almost entirely from your contributions.

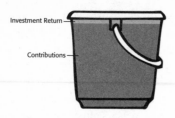

- *Time Frame:* Less than a year away
- *Type of Account:* Savings account or investment account
- *Objective:* Don't lose money
- *Investment:* High interest savings or money market account
- *Anticipated Average Annual Return:* 3%–4%

Close Time Frame (1 to 2 Years Away)

If your goal is between one and two years away, be careful. Although the time frame to reach your goal is far enough away to warrant investing, you still must invest very conservatively. Because of the conservative investments, most of the final account value will come from your contributions and only a small part will result from dividends, interest, and the growth of your investments.

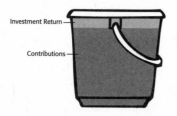

- *Time Frame:* 1–2 years away
- *Type of Account:* Investment account
- *Objective:* A little growth
- *Investment:* Money market/bond portfolio
- *Anticipated Average Annual Return:* 5%–6%

Approaching Time Frame (2 to 4 Years Away)

If your goal is between two and four years away, your money can be invested a little more aggressively. While the majority of your bucket will be

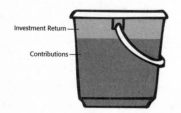

- *Time Frame:* 2–4 years away
- *Type of Account:* Investment account
- *Objective:* Some growth
- *Investment:* Diversified stock/bond portfolio
- *Anticipated Average Annual Return:* 6%–8%

from your contributions, a good part of it should also be from dividends, interest, and the growth of your investments.

Intermediate Time Frame (4 to 8 Years Away)

If your goal is between four and eight years away, you have even more investment flexibility. You can invest more aggressively, especially if your goal is seven or eight years away. Depending on your investment allocation, the dividends, interest, and growth of your investments should be a big help in reaching your goal.

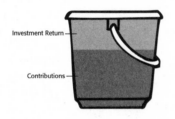

- *Time Frame:* 4–8 years away
- *Type of Account:* Investment account
- *Objective:* Growth
- *Investment:* Diversified stock/bond portfolio
- *Expected Average Annual Return:* 8%–10%

Distant Time Frame (8+ Years Away)

The bad news is that you won't be able to enjoy accomplishing your goal for a number of years, but the good news is that you'll be able to invest your savings and will get a lot of help from compound investing.

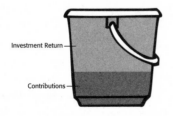

- *Time Frame:* 8+ years away
- *Type of Account:* Investment account
- *Objective:* Maximum growth
- *Investment:* Diversified stock/bond portfolio
- *Anticipated Average Annual Return:* 10+%

Step #5—Invest Using the Investment Strategy That Best Matches Your Personality

Now that you've created separate investment accounts for each of your major goals, identified the best investment strategy based on your investment personality, and classified your goals based on their time frame, it's time to get down to business. It's time to invest!

To help you reach your goals as quickly and safely as possible, first find the investment strategy that matches your investment personality below and then answer two questions for each account.

What Is Asset Allocation?

The goal of asset allocation is diversification. Even if you've never heard of asset allocation, if you've played roulette, you are already an expert. Would you put your entire stack of chips on just one number? Probably not. Since it is impossible to predict which number will win, you would most likely go bankrupt with this strategy. To avoid this, we spread our chips around. We may place a few chips on the month of our birthday, our anniversary date, and our birth year. We try to increase our chances of winning and decrease the chances of losing by placing bets across several numbers. At the same time, though, we decrease the potential payoff. It is a juggle between risk and reward. It is no different with investing. Asset allocation is simply spreading your dollars across several assets since you can't know which one will perform the best.

Hands-off Investment Strategy

- **What is an appropriate asset allocation for this goal?** For the Hands-off Investor, select a Lifecycle fund with a target date that is closest to your goal's date. For example, if you are investing for a cruise you want to take in 2008, select a Lifecycle fund with a 2008 target date. If you are saving for your son's college tuition and he starts his freshman year in 2025, select a fund with a 2025 target date. The Lifecycle fund automatically creates an appropriate asset allocation based on the target date so you don't have to!

- **What specific investments should I buy for each asset class?** You have a lot of options. Nearly every mutual fund company has its own Lifecycle fund, including Fidelity, Vanguard, T. Rowe Price, and others.

Just match your goal date with the Lifecycle fund's target date (as closely as possible) for each goal. That's it! That's all you have to do for instant allocation and diversification.

You Talking to Me?

Not all Lifecycle funds are created equal. There can be huge differences in how these funds are invested for the same target date. For example, the Fidelity Freedom 2025 fund has over 17 percent more invested in stocks compared to the same 2025 target date fund at Vanguard. This doesn't mean Lifecycle funds are not good. In a perfect world, you'd want to take a look at how each Lifecycle fund is allocated and select the fund company that offered the Lifecycle fund with the allocation that most closely capitalizes on your economic and investment outlook (e.g., more allocated to international stocks if you thought the international market was poised for growth).

I know, I know! You're a Hands-off investor. The last thing you want to do is think about coming economic and investment influences and research and compare allocation differences. Don't worry. You'll probably do a lot better by selecting any fund company's Lifecycle fund than if you haphazardly selected a bunch of different mutual funds (which is what most people do) or if you did nothing (which is also far too common).

Involved Investment Strategy

1. **Determine if your goal is a Sprint Goal or a Marathon Goal.** A Sprint Goal is a goal that requires a specific amount of money on a particular date. On that date, you need to withdraw all of the money from that goal's investment account. It's called a Sprint Goal because you're using a burst of energy (money, in this case) and then the goal is complete and you can close your account for that goal. For example, needing $10,000 for a vacation in Venice in two years is an example of a Sprint Goal because you'll take the $10,000

out of the account, take the trip, and spend the $10,000 almost immediately.

A Marathon Goal, on the other hand, is a goal that requires you to withdraw money slowly over a number of months or years, instead of all up front. A marathon, like a sprint, has a specific beginning and a finish line, but, unlike a sprint, you need to conserve your energy for a much longer period. Likewise, a Marathon Goal has a specific starting date and requires the money to last a lot longer than that first initial withdrawal.

Retirement is a perfect example. You may know the year, month, and even day you want to retire, but unlike buying a new car or paying for a cruise, you're not going to spend 100 percent of your retirement money on the day you retire (at least I hope you're not!). You'll need part of your investment account on day one, but your retirement assets will need to pay for your retirement for years and even decades.

What the Heck Is an "Asset Class"?

An investment portfolio can be divided into parts, just as a meal can be classified as carbohydrates, fats, and proteins. The following is a list of the major asset classes:

- **Cash.** Highly liquid investments with little or no risk of losing your original investment. Examples include checking and saving accounts, CDs, money market accounts, and T-bills.

- **Bonds.** Bonds are an I.O.U. The borrower pays you occasional interest and ultimately returns the original amount lent.
  - ▸ **High Quality U.S. Bonds.** Loans made to established and trustworthy borrowers in the United States including our government (e.g., Treasury bonds) and large secure corporations (e.g., GE).
  - ▸ **Municipal Bonds.** These are bonds issued by local cities and state entities. These bonds are special because the income you earn is both federal and state tax-free if you lend money to a municipality in your resident state.
  - ▸ **High Yield Bonds.** These are loans to companies that have a greater chance of not repaying the original investment (also called "junk" bonds). To compensate the borrower for this added risk, the company pays a higher interest rate.

> **International Bonds.** These are loans made to governments and corporations outside of the United States.

• **Stocks.** Also referred to as equities, stocks provide direct ownership in a company. Unlike a bond, a stock is not an IOU. As a stockholder, you own a piece of a company.

> **Large Cap Stocks.** "Cap" refers to capitalization. The capitalization of a company is a measure of how much the company is worth. Large cap stocks are very large companies such as Microsoft, Ford, and Intel. Large cap stocks can be further classified as growth or value. Growth companies tend to have smaller earnings, grow faster than their peers, reinvest their capital to stimulate additional growth, and provide no dividends. On the other hand, value companies tend to have greater earnings and pay higher dividends.

> **Small Cap Stocks.** Small cap stocks are smaller companies—usually valued at less than $1 billion. Because the company is smaller and usually younger, there is greater risk that the company will fail and for your investment to become worthless. Because they are small companies now, though, they have the potential to grow into large and profitable organizations. Like their more financially secure large cap cousins, small cap stocks can also be categorized as growth or value.

> **International Stocks.** These are investments in companies outside of the United States and as a result, are subject to regulation and political changes in other countries that could affect your investment.

Are these the only asset classes? Nope. There are many other asset classes including mid cap stocks, private equity, timberland, hedge funds, emerging markets, and sector investments such as technology and health care, to name just a few. Remember, more doesn't necessarily mean better. Keep it simple and stick to the basics!

2. **What is an appropriate asset allocation for a Sprint Goal?** For Sprint Goals, where you will need to withdraw the entire amount from the account on the initial start date (e.g., buying a car, making a down payment on a house, going on a family vacation), you can use the following charts as general sample allocations if you're doing it yourself. Keep in mind that these sample allocations are a snapshot in time. The specific allocation you choose should depend on many factors including the current and predicted economic and financial climate.

Goals Less Than 1 Year Away

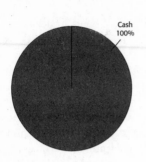

Cash
100%

Goals 1–2 Years Away

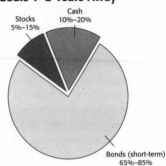

Stocks
5%–15%

Cash
10%–20%

Bonds (short-term)
65%–85%

Goals 2–4 Years Away

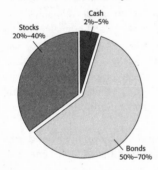

Stocks
20%–40%

Cash
2%–5%

Bonds
50%–70%

Goals 4–8 Years Away

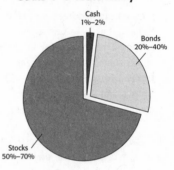

Cash
1%–2%

Bonds
20%–40%

Stocks
50%–70%

Goals More Than 8 Years Away

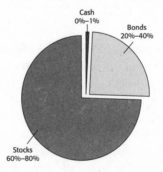

Cash
0%–1%

Bonds
20%–40%

Stocks
60%–80%

3. **What is an appropriate asset allocation for a Marathon Goal?** The most appropriate allocation for a Marathon Goal depends on how close you are to reaching the goal *and* how long you will need to withdraw money from the account to fund your goal. Marathon Goals require a conservative asset allocation that reflects the beginning withdrawal date, but that is also growth-oriented to reflect your ongoing need for the money. Even if you have a Marathon Goal, if you're not going to need to withdraw funds from the account earlier than eight years, you can simply use the sample recommended allocation for a Sprint Goal. If you have a Marathon Goal and you will need to start withdrawing funds from the account within eight years, you need to create a "weighted average" or blended time frame based on the number of years until you begin withdrawing to fund the goal and the goal's duration. The quickest and easiest way to calculate the blended time frame is to go to www.SixDayFinancialMakeover.com and use the online calculator.

Oh Yeah, You Blend!

Why go through the hassle of creating a blended time frame? The only reason to think about the time frame, whether it's the initial time frame or the blended one, is to create an appropriate asset allocation based on when you will first need to withdraw money and how long you need to continue to withdraw money to support the goal. If you don't create a blended time frame, you may invest too conservatively. For example, let's say you are retiring in eight months. If you didn't create a blended asset allocation based on the blended time frame, you would invest 100 percent of your retirement account in cash. Does that seem like a reasonable allocation? Investing your entire retirement account in cash is a recipe for disaster because your retirement account will need to last for twenty, thirty, or more years. By calculating the correct blended time frame, you can create a much more appropriate asset allocation for those goals that continue for years.

4. **For Sprint and Marathon Goals, what specific investments should I buy for each asset class?** This question is easy to answer since all you will be using are index funds. There are many index fund companies to choose from, including Vanguard, T. Rowe Price, Fidelity, Russell i-Shares, and others.

Consumed Investment Strategy

1. **Determine if your goal is a Sprint Goal or a Marathon Goal.** See page 133 for a detailed description of Sprint versus Marathon Goals.

2. **What is an appropriate asset allocation for a Sprint Goal?** See page 136 to view sample allocations for Sprint Goals with different target dates.

3. **What is an appropriate asset allocation for a Marathon Goal?** Calculate a blended time frame at www.SixDayFinancialMakeover .com.

4. **What specific investments should I buy for each asset class?** While the Involved Investment Strategy only uses index mutual funds, the Consumed investment strategy makes the most of "efficient" and "inefficient" asset classes by utilizing index mutual funds and *actively managed* mutual funds.

Efficient asset classes are those where the overall market responds so quickly to new information that it is nearly impossible for an individual investor or fund manager to have information unavailable to everyone else or to take advantage of news first.

For example, large cap stocks are an efficient asset class (see "What the Heck Is an 'Asset Class'?" on page 134 for a discussion of the different types of asset classes). Most large cap stocks are analyzed by hundreds of mutual fund managers with sophisticated computer programs and intricate networks of people around the world that quickly share information. With so many people and institutions intensely focused on the same investments, it is unlikely that you will know anything that somebody—probably thousands— don't already know. Your "secret" information or "hot tip" is almost certainly known by hundreds of other investment firms and thousands of investors. "Efficient" in an efficient asset class refers to the immediacy of information shared and its near-immediate reflection in the price of a security.

Inefficient asset classes, however, do not quickly reflect market changes based on new information. There are not as many fund managers and investors analyzing the securities. For example, small cap stocks are considered inefficient. While Microsoft, a large-cap stock, may have hundreds of analysts covering it, smaller and lesser-known companies may only have a handful or none at all. As a result, it is possible to have information not as quickly reflected in the market price of small cap stocks.

You should use passively managed index mutual funds for the following efficient asset classes because active managers will probably not be able to beat the market after their higher expenses:

- Use index funds in these *efficient* asset classes:
  - ‣ Large cap stocks
  - ‣ Municipal bonds
  - ‣ Government and corporate bonds

You should use actively managed mutual funds for the following inefficient asset classes because it is possible for active mutual fund managers to do better than the index:

- Use active mutual fund managers in these *inefficient* asset classes:‘
  - ‣ Small cap stocks
  - ‣ International stocks
  - ‣ High yield bonds
  - ‣ International bonds

Remember, as you get closer to reaching each of your goals, you need to reallocate the accounts to a more conservative portfolio. It's okay to have a more aggressive, growth-oriented portfolio for goals that are five or more years away, but as they turn into four-year, three-year, two-year, and one-year goals, you need to ratchet down the account's risk to create a more conservative portfolio. For example, you'll want to shift your retirement account to a more conservative portfolio as you near retirement age. Use the sample allocations for each time frame above as a starting point.

Step #6—Monitor Your Investment Accounts

In a typical cross-country flight, the plane is on autopilot 98 percent of the time. Does this mean the pilots are unnecessary? I don't know about you, but I want an experienced pilot in the cockpit to fly the remaining 2 percent of the time and to immediately take over if there's a problem.

Managing your finances is no different. Do as much as you can on autopilot, but check in occasionally to make sure you're still on course and there are no problems. Paperwork is inherently boring, but you don't need a

The Secret to Finding the Best Actively Managed Mutual Funds

17,913! That's how many mutual funds are available to individual investors, according to Morningstar. With so many mutual funds available it's enough to make even the Consumed Investor's head spin! How can you possibly know how to evaluate each of these and, ultimately, know which ones to buy?

This is a question that has plagued individual investors and professional investment advisors forever. There have been entire chapters, books, classes, and even degrees that have attempted to answer this question. To date, there is no "right" way or system . . . and there is no answer to this question.

That said, here are a few tips that should help you eliminate 95 percent of the inferior funds out there. Finding the right funds among the remaining 5 percent is up to you.

- Look for mutual funds where the fund manager has been with the fund for at least five years.

- Look for mutual funds that have beaten their benchmark over a three-, five-, and ten-year period.

- Look for mutual funds that have received at least four stars from Morningstar .com.

- Invest in no-load mutual funds (loads are sales charges added to the purchase and/or sale price of some mutual funds).

- Look for mutual funds with an investment expense ratio of less than 1.50 percent.

Ph.D. in finance to track your progress. Although there are a hundred things I'm sure you'd rather do than sort through your account statements, if you want to get control of your finances, you will have to spend a little time in this area. You just need a workable system that takes the guesswork and frustration out of monitoring your accounts. Say hello to that system.

Step 1—Buy supplies

Three-inch, three-ring binder

Three-hole punch

A box of three-hole punched plastic protector sheets

Three-hole punch divider tabs

Step 2—Create your Goal Tracker binder

Label the tab on one of the dividers "Financial Health: Net Worth," and put it in front of the three-ring binder. You will insert a new net worth report behind this tab every quarter. Keep the newest net worth report in front of the old ones.

Now, for each goal, create dividers (see sample Goal Tracker Binder below) The accounts should be put in order of importance. Keep your more important goals in front of less critical goals.

Step 3—Complete a Goal Tracker Report Card

Download a copy of the "Goal Tracker Report Card" (see page 142) from www.SixDayFinancialMakeover.com. Complete this template for each

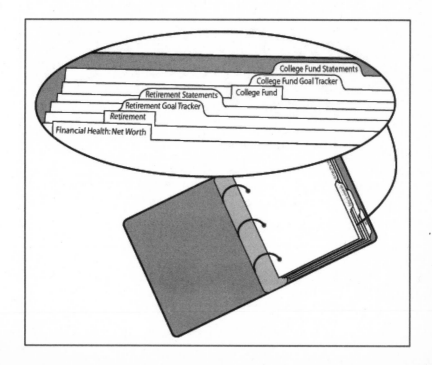

account, insert it in a plastic protective sheet, and put it immediately behind the divider tab for each account. (See example of completed Goal Tracker Report Card below.) You can quickly and easily look at your Goal Tracker Report Cards for each account to see how much you've saved, how much you've earned, and if you're on track to reaching your goals.

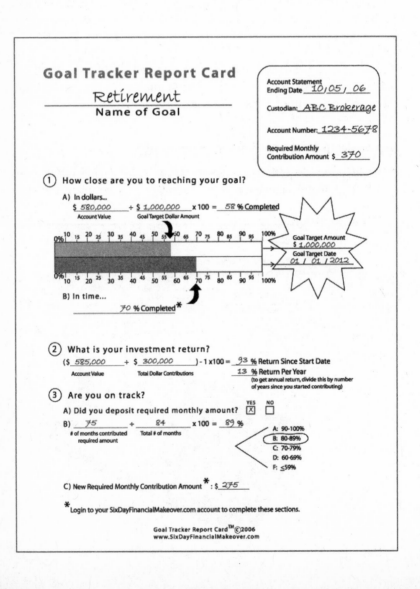

Step 4—Insert account statements

Every time you get an account statement from your bank or brokerage firm (usually monthly), insert it behind the Goal Tracker Report Card for that account. This ensures you have all of your account statements in chronological order and in one place.

Step 5—Update the Goal Tracker Report Card every month/quarter

Every month (or every quarter if you're a Hands-off Investor) after you get your account statement, complete a new Goal Tracker Report Card. Update how much you've contributed, the value of the account, and how close you are to reaching your goal. Verify any transactions that occurred or that should have occurred. For example, if you have a direct deposit payment scheduled to occur twice a month, look at your statement and make sure it was processed.

It's been said that to err is human. To *really* err is your bank or brokerage firm! Mistakes happen all of the time and can cost you hundreds or thousands of dollars. If you are cash-flow clueless, you won't even know it. Don't leave it up to them to make sure your money is making it to the right place.

Step 6—Make a financial date with yourself

Whether you use the old-fashioned binder system or one of the off-the-shelf computer programs discussed below, you should make a date with yourself at the same time every month or quarter to complete a new net worth report and Goal Tracker Report Card for each account. Although it might sound like a lot of work now, you'll probably begin to look forward to this monthly date. It should take less than twenty minutes and it will give you the opportunity to see how well you're doing and how close you're coming to reaching your goals.

If you're really fancy and are computer savvy, there are some pretty neat software programs that can help you keep track of your goals and accounts electronically. The two most popular are Quicken (www.intuit.com) and Microsoft Money (www.microsoft.com). They can download transactions from your bank and investment accounts directly into the program. These programs make running a net worth statement and tracking your accounts a breeze for the right person. The only problem with them is that they require an investment of time to learn well. If you have the aptitude and the patience, they can help you sort out and track your finances.

Action Steps

A journey of a thousand miles begins with what? That's right, a single step. There are a lot of Action Steps in this chapter, but don't let them overwhelm you. The important thing is to get started. The work you do in this chapter will help transform your financial life!

Go through the Action Steps below and put a check mark in one of the following boxes for each one.

Step 1: Create Separate Investment Accounts for Each Goal

1. ☐ COMPLETED   ☐ NEED TO COMPLETE   ☐ DOES NOT APPLY

Create separate investment accounts for each of your goals.

Step 2: Discover Your Investment Personality

1. ☐ COMPLETED   ☐ NEED TO COMPLETE   ☐ DOES NOT APPLY

Take the short Investment Personality Quiz on page 118 or take the online version at www.SixDayFinancialMakeover.com and determine your investment personality: Hands-off, Involved, or Consumed.

Step 3: Match Your Investment Personality with an Investment Strategy

1. ☐ COMPLETED   ☐ NEED TO COMPLETE   ☐ DOES NOT APPLY

Read the overview and advantages/disadvantages for the investment strategy that matches your Investment Personality.

Step 4: Determine Each Goal's Time Frame

1. ☐ COMPLETED   ☐ NEED TO COMPLETE   ☐ DOES NOT APPLY

Take a look at the goals you listed in Chapter 2. Separate each of them into the following categories:

Immediate: Less than 1 year
Close: 1–2 years
Approaching: 2–4 years
Intermediate: 4–8 years
Distant: Over 8 years

Step 5A: How to Invest If You Have a Hands-off Investment Personality

1. ☐ COMPLETED   ☐ NEED TO COMPLETE   ☐ DOES NOT APPLY

    Read the specific investment approach for the Hands-off Investment Strategy.

2. ☐ COMPLETED   ☐ NEED TO COMPLETE   ☐ DOES NOT APPLY

    Simply buy a Lifecycle fund with a target date closest to your goal date.

Step 5B: How to Invest If You Have an Involved Investment Personality

1. ☐ COMPLETED   ☐ NEED TO COMPLETE   ☐ DOES NOT APPLY

    Read the specific investment approach for the Involved Investment Strategy.

2. ☐ COMPLETED   ☐ NEED TO COMPLETE   ☐ DOES NOT APPLY

    For each goal, determine if it is a Sprint or a Marathon Goal.

3. ☐ COMPLETED   ☐ NEED TO COMPLETE   ☐ DOES NOT APPLY

    For Sprint Goals where you plan to withdraw 100 percent of the money on the first day, create an investment allocation based on your goal's initial time frame. Use the sample allocation on page 136 as a starting point.

4. ☐ COMPLETED   ☐ NEED TO COMPLETE   ☐ DOES NOT APPLY

    For Marathon Goals—those goals that will require you to withdraw money over a number of years—you need to create a blended time frame to create a blended asset allocation. Use the online calculator at www.SixDayFinancialMakeover.com to help you create an appropriate allocation for these special goals.

5. ☐ COMPLETED   ☐ NEED TO COMPLETE   ☐ DOES NOT APPLY

    Buy passively managed index funds in each asset class.

6. ☐ COMPLETED   ☐ NEED TO COMPLETE   ☐ DOES NOT APPLY

    As you get closer to reaching each of your goals, reallocate the accounts to a more conservative portfolio.

Step 5C: How to Invest If You Have a Consumed Investment Personality

1. ☐ COMPLETED   ☐ NEED TO COMPLETE   ☐ DOES NOT APPLY

   Read the specific investment approach for the Consumed Investment Strategy.

2. ☐ COMPLETED   ☐ NEED TO COMPLETE   ☐ DOES NOT APPLY

   For each goal, determine if it is a Sprint or a Marathon Goal.

3. ☐ COMPLETED   ☐ NEED TO COMPLETE   ☐ DOES NOT APPLY

   For Sprint Goals where you plan to withdraw 100 percent of the money on the first day, create an investment allocation based on your goal's initial time frame. Use the sample allocation on page 136 as a starting point.

4. ☐ COMPLETED   ☐ NEED TO COMPLETE   ☐ DOES NOT APPLY

   For Marathon Goals—those goals that will require you to withdraw money over a number of years—you need to create a blended time frame to create a blended asset allocation. Use the online calculator at www.SixDayFinancialMakeover.com to help you create an appropriate allocation for these special goals.

5. ☐ COMPLETED   ☐ NEED TO COMPLETE   ☐ DOES NOT APPLY

   Buy passively managed index funds for each efficient asset class.

6. ☐ COMPLETED   ☐ NEED TO COMPLETE   ☐ DOES NOT APPLY

   Buy actively managed funds for each inefficient asset class.

7. ☐ COMPLETED   ☐ NEED TO COMPLETE   ☐ DOES NOT APPLY

   As you get closer to reaching each of your goals, reallocate the accounts to a more conservative portfolio.

Step 6: Monitor Your Investment Accounts

(Turn to page 140 for a more detailed step-by-step description)

1. ☐ COMPLETED   ☐ NEED TO COMPLETE   ☐ DOES NOT APPLY

   Go to an office supply store and buy the supplies listed on pages 140–41.

2. ☐ COMPLETED   ☐ NEED TO COMPLETE   ☐ DOES NOT APPLY

Create your Goal Tracker Binder.

3. ☐ COMPLETED   ☐ NEED TO COMPLETE   ☐ DOES NOT APPLY

Complete a Goal Tracker Report Card.

4. ☐ COMPLETED   ☐ NEED TO COMPLETE   ☐ DOES NOT APPLY

Insert account statements.

5. ☐ COMPLETED   ☐ NEED TO COMPLETE   ☐ DOES NOT APPLY

Update the Goal Tracker Report Cards every month/quarter.

6. ☐ COMPLETED   ☐ NEED TO COMPLETE   ☐ DOES NOT APPLY

Make a financial date with yourself.

Update Your Online Financial Makeover Account

1. ☐ COMPLETED   ☐ NEED TO COMPLETE   ☐ DOES NOT APPLY

Before you do anything else, update your Six-Day Financial Makeover account at www.SixDayFinancialMakeover.com.

CHAPTER 7

Survive . . . Accidents, Sickness, Disability, and Death (Insurance Essentials)

The best financial plans can go up in smoke (sometimes literally) in a matter of seconds. Insurance provides the best defense for situations that are impossible to predict, control, and prevent. But what insurance do you need? And how much should you have? The answers to these questions can have serious consequences for you and your family. This chapter will show you how to survive *when,* and not *if,* disaster strikes.

Should I read this chapter?

	TRUE	FALSE
1. I don't remember the details of my auto insurance policy.	☐	☐
2. I'm not sure how I would pay my bills if I couldn't work.	☐	☐
3. I'm not sure if my insurance company would pay to replace my home or not.	☐	☐
4. I've never calculated how much life insurance I really need.	☐	☐
5. I'd like to learn how to survive when disaster strikes.	☐	☐

If you answered any of these questions TRUE, you should read this chapter.

Chapter Toolbar			
Cost to Implement Advice	Likelihood of Needing Strategies in Chapter	Need Professional Advice?	Website Tools
$500–$2,500	1 2 3 4 5 6 7 8 9 10 Not Likely Very Likely	↑ ↑ ↑ ↑ ↑ No Definitely	Yes

I've been there, too, and it's not fun. Once something bad has happened the first response is shock, which is quickly followed by panic and then a deep, hollow, sick feeling you get in your stomach. The questions start flying by and it's hard to think straight. Did I do everything I could to protect myself? Did I renew my insurance policy? Will this be covered or did I need some sort of special supplement for this? Moments earlier, an insurance policy was the last thing you wanted to think about, but now it's one of the only things you can think about.

When disaster strikes, I want you to have a sense of absolute certainty that you've done everything you possibly could to protect yourself and your family. No panic. No questions. No second-guessing. This is a critical chapter in your Six-Day Financial Makeover. It will give you a sense of peace and will help you survive when disaster strikes.

The chapter is divided into five sections:

- Auto Insurance

- Homeowner's Insurance

- Health Insurance

- Disability Insurance

- Life Insurance

You'll get the inside track on what each of these policies are, whether you need them, and how much insurance you need for your individual situation. No more guesswork. No more slick insurance salesmen. Just the facts you need to transform your financial life.

Automobile Insurance

Don't Let This Happen to You

"Can I borrow twenty bucks, Mom?" Ethan asked. "No, but I'll let you borrow the car," Mary replied. Ethan was graduating high school with honors and getting ready to go away to college. Mary was very proud of him and wanted to help him enjoy his last summer at home. Ethan gladly accepted his mother's counteroffer.

Ethan was a good driver. He went through his school's driver education program and missed only two points on his driver's license exam. But on this night, a momentary lapse of concentration was all it took for disaster to strike.

On his way home from his friend's house, as he was fumbling to find a CD, he ran a poorly marked stop sign and struck a much smaller car. Ethan walked away from the accident with a few bruises and a cracked rib. The driver of the other car wasn't as lucky. He required an extended hospital stay and months of rehabilitative therapy. The medical bills kept adding up—one after the other.

Fortunately Mary had auto insurance and Ethan was a covered driver, but their coverage was woefully inadequate. It paid only a fraction of the overall cost. Mary got frequent calls from the other driver's attorney and insurance company. She had to come up with $176,000 for medical bills, loss of income, and pain and suffering. Without any other options, she had to liquidate Ethan's college education fund.

Now Ethan goes to a local community college. Thinking about it now, she wished she had let him borrow the twenty bucks instead.

What is it?

You probably think you have a pretty good idea about auto insurance, but little-known tips and tricks can have a dramatic impact on your financial plan. Most auto policies automatically provide both property liability and bodily injury liability for accidents where you are legally responsible. Auto policies also offer medical payments, collision, comprehensive, uninsured/ underinsured coverage, and other optional coverages (e.g., towing, rental).

STANDARD COVERAGE

Property damage liability. This part of your auto coverage will pay for the damage your car causes to someone else's property. This coverage applies only if you are considered legally responsible for the damage. Like any other type of insurance, it will pay up to the policy's property liability limits. For example, if you rear-end a car because you were searching for your CD of *Cher's Greatest Hits*, the damage to the other person's car will be covered up to the limits on your policy. You are responsible for paying any damage over that limit.

Keep in mind that property liability doesn't just cover damage to another person's vehicle. Your policy will cover any property damaged by your vehicle. If you slide around a corner and crash into your neighbor's front porch, your policy should cover it.

Bodily injury liability. Standard auto insurance policies will also pay medical expenses for anyone injured in an accident that you caused. Again, the insurance company will only pay up to the limits of your policy—and not a penny more. For example, if you are legally responsible for an accident that results in medical expenses of $250,000 and your policy has a liability limit of $50,000, you are responsible for paying the additional $200,000.

OPTIONAL COVERAGE

Medical payments. Medical payment insurance covers the cost of medical treatment resulting from an auto accident—regardless of fault—for you and your passengers. Depending on the state, this can also be called Personal Injury Protection. Regardless of the name, this coverage will protect you in any accident involving an automobile; it will cover you if you are in an accident while you are driving a friend's car (with permission), riding in a friend's car, etc. Medical payment coverage generally doesn't have a deductible.

If you already have a comprehensive medical insurance policy, you may think this coverage is unnecessary. Unless you live in a "no-fault" state, medical payment insurance is not required, but even so, it should be a part of your financial plan. For example, if you're driving your friend to the movies and are involved in an accident that causes your friend to incur thousands of dollars in medical expenses, you are responsible for paying your friend's medical expenses if she doesn't have insurance and if no one is found at fault in the accident. If you are found at fault in the accident, your bodily injury liability coverage would pay for your friend's medical bills up to the limits of your policy.

Collision. This optional coverage pays for damage to your vehicle that results from colliding with another vehicle or object, whether you caused the accident or not. If you back out of your driveway, hit your cement mailbox, and cause thousands of dollars of damage to your new convertible sports car, collision coverage would pay for these damages after you've satisfied the deductible. Without it, you would be responsible for the entire bill.

Comprehensive. Although comprehensive coverage also pays for damages caused to your vehicle, it only pays if the damage was by something other than a collision with another vehicle—such as theft, vandalism, fire, flood, hail, or hitting an animal. In other words, the damage has to be caused by a nonautomotive accident. If your car window is broken in an attempt to steal your stereo, the comprehensive part of your auto policy covers these damages above the deductible.

Uninsured/Underinsured. Uninsured or underinsured auto insurance covers you if you are injured in an accident caused by uninsured or underinsured drivers. If you get hit by a driver without insurance, your uninsured/underinsured coverage pays for any property and bodily injury damage up to the limits of the policy. Should you worry about uninsured drivers? Yes! According to the Insurance Research Council, there is a 14 percent chance that an uninsured driver is responsible when an insured driver is injured in an auto accident. Depending on the state you live in, your odds may be significantly worse.

STATES WITH THE HIGHEST PERCENTAGE OF UNINSURED MOTORISTS

STATE	PERCENT UNINSURED
New Mexico	30%
South Carolina	28%

Alabama	25%
Mississippi	25%
California	22%
District of Columbia	21%
Florida	20%
Texas	18%
Tennessee	18%
Nevada	15%

An auto policy's liability limits are composed of three numbers. For example, 30/50/20. What do these numbers mean?

30 = The first number represents the maximum bodily injury liability limit per person per accident (in thousands). In this example, you would have a maximum of $30,000 in bodily injury coverage per person in any given accident. You would be responsible for paying the medical bills above $30,000 for any one person.

50 = The second number represents the maximum bodily injury liability limit for all persons per accident (in thousands). In this example, you would have a maximum of $50,000 in bodily injury coverage for all persons in one accident. If your accident injured several people, your policy would pay a maximum of $50,000 of medical costs. Any amount over $50,000 would be your responsibility.

20 = The third number represents the maximum property liability limit for a single accident (in thousands). In this example, you would have a maximum of $20,000 in property damage coverage in one accident. If your accident results in property damage exceeding $20,000, you will have to pay out of your own pocket.

For example, on his way home from a long day at work, George runs a red light and hits an SUV with two passengers. One of the passengers wasn't wearing a seatbelt and suffered serious but not life-threatening injuries. Luckily, George had some auto insurance (15/30/20). The total financial impact of the accident was as follows:

Passenger A—$15,000 medical costs

Passenger B—$35,000 medical costs

Totaled SUV—$56,000 property damage

Here's what George's insurance would cover and what George had to pay out of his own pocket:

	INSURANCE PAYS	GEORGE PAYS
Passenger A	$15,000 fully paid by insurance.	$0
Passenger B	$30,000 is the limit per person, per accident for his policy.	$5,000
Totaled SUV	$20,000 is the maximum property limit per accident for his policy.	$36,000
TOTAL		**$41,000 out of pocket**

If you think $41,000 is a lot, can you imagine if there were more serious injuries or a death? A single distraction while driving can immediately destroy your financial health. This is exactly why it is important to have a proper amount of auto insurance.

Do I need auto insurance?

If you drive, you need auto insurance. In fact, every state requires a minimum amount of auto liability insurance. Minimum amounts vary by state, but you will definitely want more protection than is required by law.

How much do I need?

BODILY INJURY AND PROPERTY LIABILITY

Forget the minimum amount required by law in your state. It is severely inadequate. Although there are no hard and fast rules for how much auto insurance you need, I recommend *at least* 100/300/100 in protection. With medical costs soaring, you can't walk out of a hospital without spending $20,000 or $30,000—even for relatively minor injuries. If the injuries are serious and require surgery or a prolonged stay, the bill can easily top $100,000.

Also, there are a lot more $30,000, $50,000, and $70,000 cars on the road.

If you cause an accident with multiple vehicles or one luxury vehicle, it can easily top $100,000. I live in Southern California, where it seems like almost every other car is a Porsche, Mercedes, BMW, Jaguar, Ferrari, Maserati, or other luxury automobile. Chances are that any car I hit will cost $75,000 or more to replace. I want to make sure I'm covered. If you can't afford $100,000 in property liability, get at least $50,000. Unless you drive a bumper car, don't go any lower.

If you purchase an umbrella liability policy (discussed in Chapter 10) and I strongly suggest you do, make sure that your auto liability limits are high enough that there is no gap in coverage between your auto and umbrella policies. (Many insurance companies will require adequate liability limits on your auto and homeowner's before they will give you umbrella protection.)

Of course, the more liability protection you want, the more the policy will cost. If you have sufficient assets, the minimum I would recommend is 100/300/100. If the premiums are too high, don't go any lower than 100/300/50. Your chances of causing an accident and of jeopardizing your assets are too high for less auto liability insurance. Don't be penny smart and pound foolish with your auto coverage.

Don't Let This Happen to You

Howard thought auto insurance was a necessary evil, so when he got his policy he told his agent that he only wanted the minimum required by law. His agent, not wanting to lose his business, sold Howard exactly what he wanted.

Howard would brag to his friends that he paid less for his car insurance than anyone he knew. He called his friends with more auto insurance "suckers" and told his friends they were getting "worked by the man." Howard saw conspiracy in everything, and auto insurance was just one more thing created to take advantage of the little guy.

In a bittersweet kind of karmic revenge, while ranting about the evil of excess while driving through Beverly Hills, he rear-ended a Ferrari. Luckily for Howard, no one was hurt. The damage to the Ferrari was quoted at $84,725, though. Howard's auto policy happily paid the policy's property damage maximum of $5,000. The additional $79,725 owed to fix the Ferrari came out of Howard's pocket. Now his friends joke about how Howard "bought" a Ferrari, except Howard isn't laughing.

MEDICAL PAYMENTS/PERSONAL INJURY PROTECTION

I recommend at least $5,000 in medical payment coverage. Remember, if you're driving someone who does not have health insurance and you get in an accident where there is no fault, you will be entirely responsible for your passenger's medical expenses.

COLLISION

If you can't afford to replace your vehicle, buy a collision policy on the full value of your vehicle. Of course, if you lease it or have a loan on the vehicle, your bank will require full collision coverage to protect their collateral until you pay off the loan or your lease ends. Collision insurance is often expensive. One way to reduce the premium is to increase the deductible for collision. Instead of a $500 deductible, try a $1,500, $2,000, or higher deductible to decrease the premium.

COMPREHENSIVE

Again, if you can't afford to replace your vehicle, buy a comprehensive policy for its full value. Even if you can afford to replace your car, your leasing company or bank may still require it.

Comprehensive insurance isn't cheap. The more expensive your vehicle is and the smaller the deductible, the higher the premium. To reduce your monthly insurance premium, increase your deductible to an amount you could afford to pay in damages.

UNINSURED/UNDERINSURED

Uninsured/underinsured coverage should be purchased at the same limits and coverage amounts as your regular property and bodily injury policy. For example, if your regular coverage is 100/300/100, you would want uninsured/underinsured at 100/300/100.

If you can't afford the same limits, don't just pass on this coverage. Work with your insurance agent to find a reasonable amount of coverage at a premium you can afford.

Use the auto insurance worksheet found in the Action Steps section at the end of this chapter or online at www.SixDayFinancialMakeover.com to quickly calculate how much insurance you need.

Homeowner's Insurance

Don't Let This Happen to You

Terrel and Latanya had done well in Los Angeles but just couldn't afford the kind of home they wanted. They talked about quitting their jobs and moving to "Stuckeyville," the fictional town featured in the television show *Ed*. The tranquillity and small-town feel of the fictional town appealed to them.

After nearly being sideswiped in a high-speed police pursuit, Latanya convinced Terrel it was time to move. They sold their small home—making several hundred thousand dollars—and packed up their belongings. Their family told them that they'd get bored living in a small town, but it didn't faze them. They both knew they wanted a big house with a creek in their backyard.

Within a few weeks they found their dream home in an idyllic town in Florida. They paid cash for the house and couldn't move in fast enough. They settled in and made friends quickly.

Everything went smoothly during that first year until hurricane season began. At first there were a handful of tropical storms that began to hit the area they lived in. It rained and rained and rained. The stream that went through their backyard began to rise. Terrel thought it was a lot of fun initially. He joked, "When's the last time you saw rain like this in Los Angeles?" That's when Hurricane Helena was announced. This wasn't "just" another tropical storm, this was a huge hurricane headed straight at them! They were forced to evacuate their new house. The hurricane wiped out their entire home. All of their belongings were ruined and the house, once the water dissipated, was "red tagged," which meant it was unsafe to live in.

If that wasn't bad enough, in their haste to leave Los Angeles and get into their dream house, they neglected to get the appropriate type and amount of homeowner's insurance. Without a home and any belongings, the only thing they could do was to move in with family back in Los Angeles and start saving for their next dream house and the insurance to protect it.

What is it?

A homeowner's policy covers your residence, but you already knew that. What you might not know is that not all homeowner's policies are created equal. The biggest challenge with homeowner's (and auto) policies is that the policies are familiar—everyone already has one and thinks they know everything they need to know about it already. Yet, with insurance, it's what you don't know that can hurt you the most. Let's start with the basics.

Homeowner's policies have two parts—the first part covers your property and the second part provides liability protection.

PART 1—PROPERTY COVERAGE

Your home. Depending on the type of homeowner's policy, your home will be protected against various perils such as fire, windstorm, hail, vandalism, etc. Land is not insured.

Your property. The contents of your home are also protected. Most homeowner's policies will automatically cover the contents up to a maximum of one-half of what you insured the structure for. For example, if your home is insured for $500,000, you will automatically have $250,000 in content protection. Not all of your contents are automatically protected. Homeowners routinely overlook certain limitations on property coverage.

Policies usually restrict the amount of coverage on jewelry, furs, gun collections, and flatware. Automobile coverage, business-related claims, and credit card losses are almost always excluded. In addition, property that belongs to someone else—even if it is in your home—is generally excluded unless the property belongs to a relative who lives in your home.

PART 2—LIABILITY COVERAGE

Liability insurance. Homeowner's policies also provide liability protection for damage or injury incurred inside or outside of your home. This is usually the first line of defense if you are involved in a lawsuit that wasn't the result of an automobile accident. For example, if a guest in your home slips and falls on the patio, the liability protection from your homeowner's policy will pay the judgment up to the policy's limit. If the judgment is greater than your policy's limit, your umbrella liability policy (discussed in Chapter 10) will provide additional coverage.

Liability protection is not limited to lawsuits caused on your property. If your son is involved in a basketball game at his school's playground and accidentally elbows another player and breaks his nose, your homeowner's policy may pay his medical payments and any judgment up to the limits of the policy.

Liability protection is not limited to injury claims. If you leave your sprinkler system running while you're on vacation and the water floods your neighbor's basement, your homeowner's liability policy may pay for the property damage to your neighbor's home up to your policy's limit.

Unlike content coverage, the amount of liability protection varies considerably and is not set by a formula based on the amount of dwelling coverage.

There are three different types of homeowner's insurance coverage.

- **House.** An HO-3 insurance policy is a comprehensive policy you can buy for a house—that is, it covers against most perils. Even though this is the "Rolls Royce" of policies, it won't typically cover your home from damage as a result of earthquakes, floods, tidal waves, war, termites, or nuclear accidents.

- **Condominium.** An HO-6 policy is for condominiums and co-ops. Since the common areas, exterior walls, and structure are covered by the homeowner's association's insurance policy, condo/co-op owners need coverage only for their internal walls, personal property, and liability.

- **Apartment.** As a renter, the only coverage you need is for your personal property and liability. The apartment owner is responsible for buying insurance for the building. An HO-4 policy provides renters the protection they need.

Do I need homeowner's insurance?

A home is the single largest asset for many people. A comprehensive financial plan would not be complete if you failed to ensure adequate protection for your home and your personal property. If you could buy an inexpensive insurance policy protecting the value of your investment accounts from a market crash, would you? Of course! The question is not *do* you need it, but *what kind* do you need.

There are two types of coverage and most homeowners do not know the difference until it is too late.

- **Actual cash value.** This type of homeowner's policy will reimburse you the actual cost of the dwelling or property at its fair market value immediately before it was damaged. If you purchased a dresser for $1,500 eight years ago, it may be worth only $300 today. If it was destroyed by a fire, an actual cash value policy would reimburse you only $300. This kind of policy has obvious problems. Insurance should be like a childhood "do over" or the computer's "undo" function. The purpose of insurance is to make you whole again—to replace what you lost. If your dresser is destroyed, you need to buy a new one. Can you buy a new dresser for $300? If the dresser you owned was $1,500 eight years ago, it will probably cost a lot more than $300 if you needed to replace it today. This is the problem with cash value insurance. It will only pay you what the property is worth, not what it will cost to replace it.

- **Replacement-cost.** Although it will cost more, this is the type of coverage you should try to have. A replacement-cost policy will reimburse you for the actual cost of replacing the damaged dwelling or contents—regardless of the property's age or condition. If a similar dresser is now worth $2,300, the insurance company would pay you this amount so you could replace the dresser that was destroyed. Replacement-cost coverage actually does make you whole. It provides that childhood "do-over" as much as it is possible after a loss.

  A little known caveat with replacement-cost coverage is that the policy should rebuild your home based on current building codes in the event of a loss. For example, if new homes being built require double-pane windows in order to be up to code, you want to make sure that your replacement-cost insurance policy will pay to have double-pane windows installed in your home if your home is destroyed. Not all policies cover this. If your home is destroyed, you want to make sure that you won't be out-of-pocket for any costs, even those as a result of new building specifications that were not required when your original home was built.

  For additional protection, I highly recommend obtaining extended replacement coverage. This is a special feature that provides additional coverage (usually 25 percent) over and above the base amount of dwelling coverage. With the cost of materials and construction increasing steadily, if you can afford it, you should have this kind of protection.

Be careful. Some homeowner's policies will have replacement-cost coverage for the dwelling but not for the contents or vice versa. Make sure that both your residence and its contents are covered by replacement-cost.

INSURING AGAINST THINGS THAT TYPICALLY AREN'T INCLUDED IN A STANDARD POLICY

Although most homeowner's policies protect against many perils, they do not protect against them all. Even the Rolls Royces of policies specifically exclude earthquakes and floods. Depending on your location, some of these excluded perils may be real and all too often threats to your greatest asset. To remedy the situation, you must obtain a separate policy specific to the excluded perils.

Certain agencies offer up to $250,000 of basic flood insurance through the federal government's National Flood Insurance program. You must purchase any additional protection through a private insurance company. If you live in an area prone to flooding or where there is even a slight chance of flooding, purchase a flood policy.

You may also need earthquake insurance. Finding an insurer that will cover earthquake damage may be difficult. Fewer companies are providing this protection, and of those that do, most have a high deductible (10 to 15 percent) and may put restrictions on content coverage. California homeowners can purchase insurance through the California Earthquake Authority—a state agency providing limited earthquake policies—but these policies have a high deductible and only cover a limited amount of content protection.

When deciding on these additional policies, remember that homeowner's insurance is to cover the one time out of a million that something will happen to your home. However, don't neglect coverage just because it is unlikely you will need the protection. If there is any chance, weigh the costs of insurance against the costs of a potential claim. If you can afford the premium but cannot afford the cost of replacing your home, get the additional policies.

INSURING CONTENTS

Personal content protection is usually set at 50 to 70 percent of the value of your dwelling's limit. While this may be more than enough for your personal property, if you own jewelry, furs, antiques, or artwork, you will need additional coverage—even if these items are valued within your policy limits. Why? These items have specific limitations on most homeowner's policies. For example, jewelry has a cap of $1,000. If you lose your wedding ring worth $4,500, your standard homeowner's policy will only pay $1,000. If you own valuable art or antiques, these will be significantly underinsured unless you separately schedule them under your policy.

To schedule jewelry or other items on your policy, ask your insurance company specifically what they require. Typically, they will need a detailed description of the property with pictures and receipts to substantiate their value.

Don't Let This Happen to You

Michelle and Andy were young and in love. They waited until they married before they moved into their first apartment together. Andy saved for six months and borrowed what was for him a substantial amount of money so he could buy the perfect engagement ring for Michelle. Andy joked that after he proposed with the ring, he wasn't sure if Michelle was crying because she was so overcome with joy or because she loved the ring so much.

Unfortunately, Michelle has recently been crying in despair. As fate would have it, exactly one year after Andy proposed, Michelle lost her precious ring during their anniversary celebration at Disneyland. Andy felt like crying, too. Even though he had renter's insurance, he didn't go the extra step to schedule the ring and his insurance company covered only $1,000. This wasn't even enough to cover the debt he still owed on the ring, let alone enough to buy Michelle a new one.

How much homeowner's insurance do I need?

According to Marshall & Swift/Boeckh, 64 percent of homes were underinsured by an average of 27 percent in 2003! They cite that one of the reasons for this huge amount of underinsurance is that construction costs have been increasing dramatically.

With any insurance policy, the more coverage you want, the more you have to pay. The easy answer is that you need enough to make you financially whole and no more. How much it takes to make someone financially whole varies considerably based on the type of coverage.

- **Dwelling coverage.** Work with your insurance company to determine the appropriate coverage for your home.

- **Personal content protection.** Again, this coverage is typically set at 50 to 70 percent of the value of your dwelling's limit. Calculate the cost to replace all of your personal contents. If it is less than one-half of the value of your dwelling coverage, this coverage probably protects you. If your contents are worth more, contact your insurance company and increase the limit for personal contents.

- **Restricted personal items.** Remember, if you have antiques, artwork, or jewelry valued at more than your policy's limits, get them scheduled on your policy immediately for their replacement cost.

- **Liability protection.** I strongly recommend an umbrella liability policy that sits on top of your automobile and homeowner's policy (discussed in Chapter 10). Increase your homeowner's liability so there is no gap in liability coverage between your homeowner's policy and the umbrella policy. Most umbrella policies start coverage at $500,000, so your homeowner's policy would need liability protection up to $500,000. Check with your insurance company to make sure there is no gap in liability coverage.

Health Insurance

Don't Let This Happen to You

Sara always said she had an identity problem. Her older sister was always in charge and her younger brother could get away with anything. That left Sara right in the middle and, as she'd say, neglected.

From a very young age Sara tried to assert her independence. When she was seven she told her parents that she was going to live in the tree house she built and that she didn't need her room anymore (her plan lasted until 10:30 that night when she heard a scary noise). At nine she got her first job and vowed she was going to buy her own food from then on. At eighteen she graduated high school and went to college. She took out loans and got a small scholarship. Life was good. She was on her own and she didn't need help from anyone.

After graduating college she moved to Manhattan to start her own company. "Why start out in the mailroom when you can instantly be the CEO?" she asked her family. The city was tough. Everything was more expensive. The bills started to come in, but she swore she could do it and that she didn't need any help. She cut back on a lot of things and moved into an even smaller studio in an even more questionable part of the city. She also dropped her health insurance, rationalizing that because she was young and in good health she didn't need it. Besides, her company was going to take off any day, and she'd get it then.

Things were starting to turn around for Sara when she got mugged after walking home from a late night business party. She doesn't remember anything from that night, but the doctors think she hit her head on steps after the mugger threw her down. Sara was in a coma for two days. She suffered serious injuries, but the doctors took very good care of her. After two surgeries and several months of rehabilitative work, Sara's health was as good as new.

Unfortunately, her financial situation did not recover as quickly. Her medical bills totaled $124,345.65, and because she didn't have any health insurance, she owed the whole amount. With all of the phone calls she gets about the bills and payment, she doesn't feel neglected anymore.

What is it?

Health insurance provides coverage for medicine, visits to the doctor or emergency room, hospital stays, and other medical expenses if you are injured or sick.

There are several different types of health insurance plans, but the most common are the following three:

1. **HMO**—HMOs provide a wide variety of services ranging from preventative care to office visits to surgery. HMOs typically require you to receive medical treatment from providers in their network and make you see your primary doctor to get a referral to another doctor. Generally speaking, HMOs are the least flexible and the least expensive option.

2. **PPO**—PPOs provide greater flexibility, but cost more. They allow you to visit any doctor, but encourage you to visit doctors within the PPO network by reimbursing you at a higher rate when you do so. PPOs also allow you to call any doctor within the network and make an appointment without obtaining permission from your primary doctor.

3. **POS**—A POS is a hybrid of an HMO and a PPO. Like an HMO, you can use the doctors in network, but unlike an HMO, you're not stuck with just the doctors in the HMO network. Like a PPO, a POS plan allows you to choose doctors outside of your plan. So if you find a doctor you really like but she's not in the network, you can still see her. One caveat, though: Like a traditional HMO, you are still required to get permission from your primary doctor.

Each of these plans has advantages and disadvantages. The greater the flexibility the greater the cost. If you want a plan where you can go to any doctor without obtaining permission, a PPO might be right for you. On the other hand, if you're watching your budget and don't mind going through a few hoops, an HMO or a POS plan might be appropriate.

Common Health Insurance Terms

Deductible: This is a set dollar amount per year that you must first pay before the health plan begins paying claims.

Co-Insurance: A percentage of the bill the patient is responsible for paying on an insurance claim. For example, most insurance companies pay only a percentage of a claim, such as 80 percent. The remaining 20 percent is the "co-insurance" amount the patient must pay.

Co-Payment: This is a specified dollar amount the patient must pay the medical provider at the time of an office visit. Typically it is between $10 and $30.

Formulary: A listing of drugs the insurance policy covers.

Stop Loss Clause: This is the maximum dollar amount per year the patient must pay. Once the stop loss clause is met, the insurance policy pays 100 percent of all charges up to the policy limits.

Lifetime Benefit Cap: This is the maximum amount of coverage your health insurance plan must pay over the course of your life—typically $1 million.

Superman Wants Superbenefits!

After actor Christopher Reeve became paralyzed from the neck down during a 1995 riding accident, it only took about two and a half years to burn through the $1 million lifetime benefit cap on his health insurance plan (thankfully, he had two other insurance plans that kicked in). As a result and after hearing about others who maxed their insurance caps, Christopher Reeve became a proponent for increasing the lifetime benefit cap from $1 million to $10 million. Legislation called the Christopher Reeve Health Insurance Reform Act is now making its way through Congress.

Do I need health insurance?

Absolutely. Regardless of your age or health, you need health insurance. Without it, you are putting yourself and your family in financial jeopardy. With medical costs soaring, all it takes is a trip to the emergency room or a surgery to be in debt thousands and sometimes hundreds of thousands of dollars.

How much health insurance do I need?

At the very least, you need a comprehensive policy that will pay your medical bills if you get seriously ill or injured. These plans are called catastrophic health plans because they only kick in after you've paid a high deductible—sometimes as much as $5,000 per year. They're much cheaper than a traditional health insurance plan because of the high annual deductible. The objective with this type of plan is to have coverage if something really bad happens and you need costly medical care.

Catastrophic plans are plans of last resort. Choose them only when you must choose between no insurance and catastrophic health insurance. Of course, if you can afford a traditional health plan, you should buy one. Since many Americans get their health insurance through their employers, the choice of an HMO, PPO, or POS will depend not only on your own needs and budget, but also on what choice of plans your employer gives you.

Disability Insurance

Don't Let This Happen to You

Eric enjoyed his job, but still didn't mind a three-day weekend once in a while. He liked spending time with his wife and two children. Fridays were "family night." They'd rent movies and order a pizza. On most Saturdays, they'd plan an event—nothing too outlandish, but something that they could do as a family.

During one of the family's Saturday adventures, Eric tumbled down a steep ravine and suffered several serious injuries: eight broken ribs, a fractured clavicle, a shattered fibula, a concussion, a broken neck, and memory loss. After four weeks in intensive care, he spent another eight weeks in traction. He was sent home to spend another three months in bed. It took another two months before he could move without significant pain. Much to the surprise of his doctors, Eric was able to return to work after recovering for just thirteen and a half months.

He'll tell you that the physical pain was excruciating, but that wasn't what kept him up at night. All he could think of was how he was going to provide for his family. The agony of his debilitating injuries was less painful than his financial anxiety.

Even though Eric couldn't work, he didn't stop receiving bills. Their checking and savings accounts were depleted first. Next, Eric's wife, Shawna, cashed out their investments and lived off the proceeds for about four months. Once these funds were used, Eric told her to take a complete distribution from his 401(k) and IRA accounts—paying income tax on the entire amount. Eric hadn't been able to save much, so his retirement accounts didn't provide much relief. The bills kept coming, month after month. Shawna started charging as much as she could on her credit cards because they didn't have the cash. Soon the credit card bills weren't getting paid and they froze her accounts.

Eric was a fighter and was dedicated to providing for his family. Although he wasn't ready to return to work—he couldn't move well and he still had severe headaches—he knew it was the only way to get his family out of the mess he put them in by not having a disability policy.

What is it?

While our homes may be the greatest financial asset on our balance sheet, until we become financially independent, our ability to produce an income is a much greater financial asset. Once we have enough asset-producing income, our ability to produce earned income becomes less important. Until you become financially independent and do not need to work to produce an income, your ability to get up every morning and go to work is extremely valuable and needs to be protected. Disability insurance provides this protection.

Disability insurance could be called income protection insurance—it replaces part of your income if you become seriously ill or injured and cannot work. While the basic concept behind disability insurance is really pretty simple, there are a lot of "moving parts" that can make analyzing and comparing a disability policy difficult.

- **How much will the policy pay?** Insurance is supposed to make you whole, but when it comes to disability insurance, these policies fall short. Insurance companies do not want to encourage policyholders to fake a disability or to remain disabled, so they will never pay 100 percent of your pre-disability income. Policies pay a set dollar amount a month (e.g., $3,000 per month) typically up to 60 percent of your base salary. For example, if you earn a $60,000 salary, you would be able to get a disability policy that pays $36,000 per year (60 percent of $60,000). Not all policies have the same percentage limit, so it is important get all the facts on a policy when comparing premiums.

- **What is the maximum a policy will pay per month?** Although a policy will replace a certain percentage of income—say 60 percent—all policies have a maximum monthly payout. The maximum monthly payout varies by insurance company, but generally it is between $5,000 and $10,000. For example, if you earn $225,000 a year and you have a policy that covers 60 percent of your salary with a maximum monthly cap of $6,000, the policy would only pay $72,000 a year ($6,000 cap times 12 months) and not $135,000 (60 percent of $225,000).

- **How long will the policy pay?** Policies can pay out for as short a time as a year or until age sixty-five. Because disability insurance is intended to replace earned income, policies stop paying when a policyholder reaches retirement age.

- **What is the definition of "disability"?** A disability is a physical or mental condition that limits your ability to work as a result of sickness or injury. Each policy has its own definition of disability:
  ‣ *Any occupation*—The inability to perform the duties of any occupation. This definition is also known as the Burger King disability policy because if you're capable of flipping burgers this policy won't pay out.
  ‣ *Modified own occupation*—The inability to perform duties of your occupation, or any occupation for which you are deemed reasonably qualified by education, training, or experience. This is a common definition of disability on many policies issued today.
  ‣ *Own occupation*—The inability to perform the material and substantial duties of your regular occupation. This is the best definition of disability you can have but is more expensive and fewer insurance companies offer this kind of protection.

- **How quickly will benefits start?** This is another option that you are able to modify when creating your income protection plan. You can choose a waiting period as short as 30 days or you can extend it to 60, 90, or more days. Think of this feature as a deductible. The longer you extend the waiting period, the larger the "deductible."

- **Will the policy payout increase with inflation?** Again, this is another "moving part" where you have some control in designing a disability policy. A policy with inflation protection will cost more than one that does not increase with inflation.

- **Does the policy offer income protection if I return to work but make less?** This feature is typically called residual disability, and it will pay a benefit to a policyholder who returns to work and makes less money during the recovery process.

- **Will benefits be reduced if I received benefits from other sources?** Some policies will pay out a monthly benefit but will reduce it dollar for dollar from any other benefit sources (e.g., Social Security, other disability policies). This kind of policy is inferior to one that will pay out regardless of other benefits sources.

- **Can the insurance company cancel my policy or increase my rates?** If you have a guaranteed renewable policy, they cannot cancel your policy if you pay the premiums. The insurance company can increase your premiums if they also increase other policyholders' premiums. In other words, the insurance company can't single you out and increase your rates, but it can increase them for a whole class of policyholders. A guaranteed renewable policy is good, but a non-cancelable policy is better because the insurance company can't ever cancel your policy or increase your premiums so long as you pay your premiums.

Disability insurance is offered through two sources. The most common source of disability insurance is through a group plan provided by an employer. The second source of disability insurance is from private insurance contracts. Both sources have disadvantages and advantages, and for many people, a combination of the two is best.

GROUP DISABILITY INSURANCE

A lot of companies offer disability insurance to their employees as part of their employee benefits plans. The good news is that most of the time these plans are automatically provided without any cost to the employee. However, while these group plans offer a great place to start your income protection plan, most of them have serious limitations:

- **Low payout percentage of income.** The maximum percentage of income the standard group plan will pay is 60 percent of an employee's base salary. For example, if you earn $100,000 a year, the group plan will only pay $60,000.

Problem—Individuals used to receiving a certain salary may find that their disability income benefits that pay 60 percent do not cover their expenses, especially at a time when there are added costs to treat the disability.

- **Payout percentage restricted to salary only.** Most group disability plans calculate an employee's income on base salary only and do not include commissions or bonuses.

    Problem—Executives and salespeople who earn a relatively small base salary supplemented by significant bonuses or commissions may find their group disability insurance policy nearly worthless.

- **Low maximum payout caps.** Almost all policies have a maximum monthly cap they pay policyholders. This maximum payout is usually $5,000 to $6,000 per month, even if this amount is much less than 60 percent of the employee's base income.

    Problem—High-income earners expecting to fully replace their income if they become disabled may be caught off guard when they learn of the maximum payout caps on their group policies.

- **Benefits are taxable.** If your employer pays the premiums for your disability insurance, you will be taxed on any payout. Some group plans allow you to pay disability premiums on an after-tax basis. If you choose this option, any disability benefits you receive will not be taxed.

    Problem—Federal and state tax rates can further erode an employee's income protection plan.

- **Weak definition of disability.** Rarely do group plans provide for an "own occupation" definition of disability. Good group plans may have a "modified own occupation" definition, but even these are becoming more difficult to find.

    Problem—Unless the plan has an "own occupation" or "modified own occupation" definition of disability, if you can perform the tasks of any position you are no longer considered disabled and may not receive income from the disability plan.

Don't Let This Happen to You

Her parents will tell you that Shelly was a tomboy. Growing up with four brothers and a free-spirited father, Shelly was more interested in fishing and football than tea parties and Barbie dolls. Her father used to say he had five boys—and Shelly was proud to hear it.

After studying economics and receiving a degree in finance, she accepted a position at a large Wall Street financial and investment bank in Manhattan. Quickly she became "one of the boys" at the firm. Her natural flair for business, her beauty, and her easy understanding of men helped her rise to the top of the company. She worked on some of the biggest mergers and acquisitions in the country, earning seven figures a year.

On a deer hunting trip with her father and four brothers during Thanksgiving, Shelly was struck in the spine by a stray bullet. The accident left her paralyzed from the waist down. She remained strong after she found out— never shedding a tear. She vowed she wasn't going to let it get her down, but she couldn't help but break down when her entire office made a surprise visit to her hospital room.

The second time she cried was when the head of human resources at her company told her that her group disability plan was going to generate only $5,000 a month—significantly less than the $100,000+ a month Shelly was used to bringing home before the accident. She was told that the company's group plan only considers a base salary in its calculation and not commissions or bonuses. Shelly's base salary was a little over $120,000, but she'd been making over a million a year in commissions and bonuses. Furthermore, the plan had a maximum payout of $5,000 per month. If this wasn't bad enough, Shelly was told that all income paid by the disability plan would be taxable since the company paid the premiums. Shelly told her family that she felt like an idiot. She had a finance degree from a top school and worked for one of the biggest financial services firms in the world, yet she didn't know enough to ask these questions before it was too late.

Because of the limitations of group disability plans offered by employers, nearly everyone should at least consider supplementing their group disability plan with an individual disability insurance plan.

INDIVIDUAL DISABILITY INSURANCE PLANS

Individual disability plans are often more generous and flexible than group disability plans. Individual plans can be used to fill in the gaps of a group plan or can be the primary source of income protection because of their numerous advantages.

- **Higher percentage of income payout.** While group plans typically limit their maximum percentage payout at 60 percent, individual plans can be purchased that will pay out a greater percentage of an individual's pre-disability income.

- **Payout includes bonuses and commissions.** Not all individual plans include bonuses and commissions, but there are some that do. Try to find one with this feature if this is a big part of your annual compensation.

- **Payout is not taxable.** The disability income paid to a policyholder is not taxable if the premiums for the individual disability plan are paid by the policyholder.

- **The "own occupation" definition is available.** Own occupation coverage is provided by some insurance companies.

- **Higher maximum payout caps.** Maximum annual payout caps can be as high as $180,000.

Of course, all of these benefits and this flexibility come at a cost. Unlike group plans, individual disability plans are paid by individuals and almost always require a medical exam. Even with these limitations, individual plans can be a critical part of your income protection plan.

Do I need disability insurance?

The statistics on disability are shocking. You are three times more likely to need disability insurance by the time you are sixty-five than you are life insurance. According to a Hartford study, one-third of Americans will find themselves disabled for at least ninety days during their working years.

A long-term disability can destroy a family's finances very quickly. What would happen if you couldn't work for six months? Nine months? Two years? Would your company continue to pay you? Can you count on it? If not, how will you pay your bills? Will you have to sell your investment accounts? Will you have to sell your home?

Your ability to generate an income is your greatest asset and its significance cannot be overemphasized. Unless you are financially independent, the money you generate not only pays your expenses but also funds your retirement. If you want to accomplish 100 percent of your goals, the ability to generate sufficient assets is crucial.

Even with the compelling statistics on disability, most people don't think they need disability insurance. Disability, it seems, is something that happens to anybody but them. We all suffer from Superman Syndrome; we think we are invincible. When I sense this, I remind uninsured and skeptical clients that the Man of Steel, Superman himself—Christopher Reeve—became disabled. There is a greater frequency of disability in higher-risk occupations—such as Superhero—but anybody in any occupation can suffer a disability.

Unlike death, disability has two unique problems. Not only are you not earning an income or saving for retirement, you still have a mortgage, utilities, clothing, and food costs and additional expenses as a result of your disability such as transportation, medication, therapy, etc. It is a double whammy—no income and more expenses—that can quickly decimate a family's finances. If your goal is to insure your family's future, an appropriate amount and type of disability insurance is absolutely critical.

Reasons why you wouldn't need disability insurance.

There are no precise formulas that can determine when disability insurance isn't necessary, but there are several situations where there may be little need. Consult an independent financial advisor who does not earn a commission on insurance if you are not sure if a disability policy is right for your situation.

- **Retired.** Disability insurance is to replace earned income during working years. If you are retired, you don't have any earned income to replace.

- **Almost retired.** If you are near retirement and have the resources to cover a year or two of living expenses, you might not need a disability policy. You can invest the premiums you save on a disability policy in your retirement.

- **Financially independent.** Regardless of your age, if you don't require earned income to support your lifestyle, you may not need a disability policy. However, if you have passive income that requires your participation, you might consider a disability policy to hire a part-time employee to take over your involvement. For example, if you have rental real estate that you actively manage, consider an individual disability policy that would provide an income for you to pay someone to manage your properties while you are disabled.

- **No income.** If you don't currently have an income or expect to have one in the immediate future, a disability policy will not be helpful since a policy will only pay a percentage of your current salary.

When is an individual disability plan necessary?

Unless you fall within one of the categories listed above, you need an income protection plan. For many people, this need begins and ends with a group disability plan. For others without group disability coverage or for those who need additional protection, an individual plan may be necessary.

- **No group disability coverage.** If you don't currently have any source of income protection if you become disabled, you need an individual disability insurance policy.

- **Maximum percentage of income not enough.** If your expenses are greater than 60 percent of your income (remember that you will pay tax on the 60 percent payout from your group disability policy), you will need an individual policy to increase the percentage to 70 percent or 80 percent.

- **Earn $120,000 or more a year.** Since most group plans pay out 60 percent of income or a maximum of $6,000 a month, if you earn $120,000 or more your group plan will be capped out at the maximum benefit of $6,000 a month. If your fixed expenses are more than $4,000 or so a month (this is approximately what you'd take home after taxes), an individual disability policy that increases the nontaxable income payout percentage to 70 percent or 80 percent with higher monthly caps may be necessary.

- **Small salary with large bonuses/commissions.** Most group plans do not consider bonuses and commissions when calculating benefits. If these represent a large part of your compensation, you should look for an individual policy that specifically includes these sources of income.

- **Highly specialized occupation or business owner.** If your compensation is based on performing highly specialized work such as a surgeon or attorney, or if you own a business, an individual disability policy with "own occupation" is critical. With just a group plan, your new career may be the fry guy at your local McDonald's.

How much disability insurance do I need?

The short answer is—as much as you can get. For most people, an income protection plan revolves around disability insurance—this is the only way to "insure your future" if you become disabled.

Calculating how much disability insurance you need is straightforward. You will need as much disability insurance protection as you have expenses (see Chapter 3) that you are responsible for paying. If you become disabled, chances are that most of these expenses will not change—they are fixed. A few expenses will decrease or be eliminated such as gasoline, dining out, business lunches, expensive business clothes, certain hobby expenses, and disability insurance premiums (once you become disabled, you won't have to pay the premiums if you get the right rider), but there will be new expenses such as transportation, health care, medication, and special nursing or therapy. Just like retirement, don't assume that if you become disabled your expenses will decrease. Chances are they will stay the same or even increase.

Minimum Amount of Disability Insurance Calculation

Step 1. Enter total monthly expenses for your family. $_____

Step 2. Enter total after-tax income your spouse or partner generates. $_____ (if single, enter $0).

Step 3. Enter total after-tax income from sources other than you or your spouse (e.g., group disability, investment, rental real estate). $_____

Step 4. Add Step 2 + Step 3 to get total monthly income. $_____

Step 5. Subtract Step 4 from Step 1. $_____

→ This is the minimum amount of tax-free disability insurance you need to cover your or your family's expenses. Now perform the same calculation for your spouse or partner to determine how much insurance he needs. You can go to www.SixDayFinancialMakeover.com for the online version of this worksheet.

For example, Brent and Denise have monthly expenses of $6,500. Brent earns $5,800 a month and Denise earns $2,800 a month. Brent must have at least $3,700 in disability insurance ($6,500 expenses = $2,800 from Denise's job + $3,700 from Brent's disability insurance) and Denise must have at least $700 a month in disability insurance ($6,500 expenses = $5,800 from Brent's job + $700 from Denise's disability insurance) to cover their expenses. Here's how it would look:

	MONTHLY EXPENSES	DENISE EARNED INCOME	DENISE DISABILITY INCOME	BRENT EARNED INCOME	BRENT DISABILITY INCOME	MONEY LEFT OVER
Neither Disabled	$6,500	$2,800	$0	$5,800	$0	$2,100
Denise Disabled	$6,500	$0	$700	$5,800	$0	$0
Brent Disabled	$6,500	$2,800	$0	$0	$3,700	$0
Both Disabled	$6,500	$0	$700	$0	$3,700	–$2,100

For Brent and Denise, this represents the minimum amount of disability insurance they need to just pay their bills if *one* of them becomes disabled. They may want more disability insurance to cover them if they both become disabled, have unexpected expenses, or want to save for retirement when their disability policy terminates, but this provides a snapshot of precisely how much insurance they need to stay afloat during a disability.

In a perfect world, you could afford as much disability insurance as you need, but most of us have other expenses—retirement savings, college education, braces, mortgages, alimony—vying for our paychecks. The formula above calculates the minimum amount of disability insurance you need to cover your expenses. If you can afford additional insurance, it may make sense to increase the monthly benefit amount to a level that will allow you to save and invest.

Life Insurance

Don't Let This Happen to You

Jackson was a tax guy. He loved getting knee-deep in numbers and helping his clients save money. His friends called him "Action Jackson" (just as a big man is called "Tiny"). You see, Jackson was a bit of a prude. He was not a risk taker. He did not live life on the edge. His idea of excitement was playing air hockey with his kids.

Jackson was slowly building his tax and accounting practice. He worked six or seven days a week—sometimes for more than twelve hours a day. He wanted to be the good husband who could provide for his wife and kids. He was so wrapped up in his job and making money for his family that he often didn't take the time to manage his own finances. He assumed he had enough life insurance through his company's group plan.

At forty-two, Jackson was content with his life. He had a great family and he was developing the reputation as the man to see if you needed to fight the IRS. Everything was going smoothly until he went to see his doctor for a headache that wouldn't go away. Jackson figured he was going to get the same prescription he always got from his doctor—take a day off once in a while and try to relax. His doctor's advice was different this time. He suggested Jackson see a neurologist for an MRI.

Jackson scheduled the MRI and didn't think much of it. He complained that it was going to take him away from the office for three hours, but he reluctantly went anyway. A day later, he got the news. The MRI showed an unremovable tumor logged in his frontal cortex. His doctor gave him four months to live.

Jackson lived another twenty-two weeks—a little over five and a half months. He spent those weeks as he spent his previous twenty years, getting everything situated and trying to provide a better life for his family. Unfortunately for Jackson's family, he had only $50,000 in life insurance through his company. With the insurance check, their savings account, and Jackson's 401(k), his family had a total of $224,875. In addition to the emotional torture his family endured, they also had to deal with the financial disaster that resulted from Jackson's death.

What is it?

Do you know the quickest way to silence the chattiest neighbor on a plane? Tell him you sell life insurance. You're guaranteed to be left alone for the rest of the flight. Is it fair that life insurance salespeople have such a bad reputation? Sure, there are a lot of bad apples who have tainted the industry, but there are also a lot of honest and caring individuals who want nothing but the best for their clients.

How can you protect yourself and not be scammed by the bad apples in the business? After you read this section, it won't matter because you are going to walk in the door and tell the insurance agent exactly how much life insurance you need, the type of insurance you want, and how long you want it. Get ready to be in the driver's seat!

All of the other types of insurance we've discussed so far are pretty easy to understand. Once you know the basics, you can easily compare one auto insurance policy with another or one disability insurance policy with another. When you start talking about life insurance, people's eyes tend to glaze over.

Just what is life insurance? At its very basic, life insurance is a simple agreement. It's an agreement between you and a life insurance company. The agreement says that if you die, the life insurance company pays money to your beneficiaries. It's that simple.

In fact, life insurance is even simpler than auto or disability insurance because there is no ambiguity. If you become disabled, your disability has to be examined and approved by the insurance company before they will pay you. If you get in an auto accident, you usually have to prove who was at fault before the policy will pay to fix your car. With life insurance, there is no guesswork. If you die, the insurance company pays—it's a simple situation.

As straightforward as it sounds, life insurance can be one of the most complicated and confusing forms of insurance available—even for those selling it. Truckloads of books have been written about life insurance. If you think Hollywood is creative, you haven't seen anything. The insurance industry has some of the most ingenious and creative people in the world who continuously create a dizzying array of new types of life insurance.

Before I discuss the various types of life insurance, it's important to get a handle on a few definitions:

Owner (or Policy Owner)—The owner is a person who owns a life insurance policy and who is responsible for paying for the life insurance. Owners are in the driver's seat. They determine who is insured and who is the beneficiary. The owner and the insured are usually the same person, but they don't have to be. For example, if Mike is required to pay Cheryl alimony for ten years, Cheryl might own a life insurance policy on Mike's life in case he dies before the end of the ten years. In this case, Cheryl owns the policy, but the life insurance policy covers Mike's life.

Insured—The insured is the person whose life is covered by the life insurance policy. Stated another way, the insured is the "life" in the life insurance policy agreement. As soon as the insured passes away, the insurance company is required to pay the death benefit to the beneficiary. In the example above, Mike is the insured.

Beneficiary—This is the person named in the policy to receive the life insurance proceeds upon the death of the insured. The beneficiary can be a spouse, child, or business partner. The proceeds can also be split between several people. Using the example above, Cheryl is the owner and also the beneficiary. If Mike dies, she wants to receive the death benefit. The owner can name multiple beneficiaries—a spouse and a charity, for example. Also, beneficiaries don't have to have an equal share. A spouse might get 90 percent while a charity might get only 10 percent.

Contingent Beneficiary—If all of the named beneficiaries are deceased, those listed as contingent beneficiary receive the death benefit. When would this occur? If the insured and the beneficiary die together, the contingent beneficiary becomes very important. For example, if Mike and Cheryl still go on an annual ski trip together, Cheryl might want to name her children as contingent beneficiaries in case she and Mike get into a fatal car accident on the way to the slopes.

Death Benefit (or Face Amount)—This is the amount of money paid by the life insurance company at the death of the insured to the beneficiary.

Premium—The premium is the cost of owning life insurance. When you send a check to the life insurance company after getting a bill, you are paying the premium. Why is it called a premium? It's a marketing trick. Premium sounds good and positive—a lot better than bill or expense.

Rider (or Endorsement)—Legally speaking, a rider is an amendment to a life insurance policy that becomes part of the insurance contract.

In other words, a rider is an option or feature for which you are willing to pay extra. When you're buying a car and the salesperson is discussing car undercoating, premium sound systems, and satellite navigation, he is trying to sell you riders. Some riders are worth their cost; others are not.

What Riders Should You Get?

Most riders are expensive add-ons that you should avoid. However, there is one that I normally consider. It's called "waiver of premium." If you have this rider and become disabled, you don't have to pay your life insurance premium for as long as you are disabled. This rider can save you a few hundred or thousand dollars a year at a time when you need it. Is it right for you? The answer lies in the cost of the rider. If it's less than 5 percent of your annual life insurance premium, it probably makes sense to add it to your policy. If it's more expensive than that, a better move for you is simply to increase the benefit amount on your disability policy by the amount of your life insurance premium.

In force—When you hear that a life insurance policy is "in force," it simply means that the policy is active and you are insured.

Life insurance broker/agent—A life insurance agent is a salesperson who sells life insurance for one company. When you go into a Toyota dealership, the salesperson will try to sell you a Toyota. Don't expect her to recommend a Honda. On the other hand, a life insurance broker represents multiple insurance companies and can sell you policies from more than one company.

Tax Loophole?

Life insurance proceeds are not taxed! Well, that's half true. They are not subject to federal or state income tax but they are included in your estate and will be subject to an estate tax if your assets exceed the exemption amount. Don't worry, there are some pretty slick ways to avoid having insurance proceeds subjected to estate tax. Visit www.SixDayFinancialMakeover.com to learn how.

Types of life insurance.

There are two basic types of life insurance: (1) term and (2) permanent. It's very important to know the differences between these two types of life insurance.

(1) TERM LIFE INSURANCE

Term life insurance is easy to understand. It provides protection for a set amount of time—usually between one and 30 years (10, 20, and 30 years are common). At the end of the term, the agreement ends and your insurance ends. If you still want or need life insurance, you have to enter into a new agreement by purchasing a new insurance policy or pay a higher premium each year for the one you had.

If you have a term life insurance policy, you don't really own it. Instead, you're renting it. Just like you would rent an apartment or lease a car. During the time of the lease, it is yours to use, but once the lease expires, it's no longer yours. If you want to keep living in the apartment, you have to enter into a new contract.

If the insured dies during the "lease" period, the insurance company is obligated to pay. On the other hand, if the insured survives the term of the policy, the insurance company isn't obligated to pay anything.

(2) PERMANENT INSURANCE

If term insurance is like renting an apartment, permanent life insurance is like buying a home. Instead of being protected for a limited number of years, permanent insurance provides protection for as long as you live—that's why they call it "permanent."

There are several different types of permanent life insurance, including whole life, universal life, and variable. Then there's variable universal life. Of course, with permanent insurance, you have cash value, guaranteed and projected interest rates, in-force illustrations, maybe even investment options. Long story short, permanent insurance can get pretty complicated. It can also get pretty expensive.

I don't like rules of thumb, but for most people most of the time, term insurance is what you want, and permanent is what you want to avoid. Permanent life insurance *does* have a purpose, but it is a very narrow purpose that I will discuss later in the chapter.

How much does life insurance cost?

Life insurance can be affordable or downright expensive. It all depends on the following five factors:

1. **Policy.** Different life insurance policies will cost different amounts. Just as a Cadillac is going to cost you more than a Honda, you can get relatively cheap life insurance or you can get more expensive policies. The type of life insurance—term versus permanent, the amount of death benefit, how long you want coverage, and the type of riders you select—are all factors that affect the cost.

2. **Age.** A lot of things come with age—maturity, confidence, wisdom, and character. You can also add "higher life insurance costs" to that list. The older you are, the more expensive life insurance will cost. This should make sense. Life insurance companies live and die (pun intended!) by averages and statistics, mainly life expectancy numbers. The older you are, the greater the chance the life insurance company will have to cut a check to your beneficiaries. Someone who's thirty has a longer life expectancy than someone who is seventy. If the insurance company thinks they will have to pay a death benefit sooner rather than later, they'll want to charge you more to cover the risk.

3. **Health.** It pays to be in good health. Life insurance companies will go to great lengths to determine your health. Insurance companies require you to complete a long medical application that includes questions about past surgeries, the health of your parents or their cause and age of death, medications you're currently taking or have taken in the past, and a list of all doctors you've seen in the past ten years and the purpose for each visit. They won't just take your word for it, either. They'll go through all of your medical records to verify your application and to make sure you didn't "forget" anything important. In addition to a comprehensive application, they will also perform a medical evaluation. The medical evaluation normally doesn't take more than thirty minutes, during which time they will take your blood pressure, height, weight, blood sample, and urine sample. If you're in good health, the life insurance company won't charge you as much since a healthy person has less of a chance of dying sooner.

4. **Smoker/Nonsmoker.** Life insurance companies read the warning labels on cigarette packages. They know all of the problems smoking can cause, and aren't thrilled about insuring a smoker unless they charge the smoker a lot more in premiums. Bottom line, if you smoke, expect to pay more for life insurance.

5. **Insurance Company.** Remember, a life insurance policy is a contract. You pay premiums today and the life insurance company pays a death benefit at some point in the future. The assumption is that the life insurance company will (1) be around when it is time to pay the death benefit and (2) have enough money to pay the death benefit. You're betting that the life insurance company will be able to honor their end of the agreement in the future. Better, more financially stable life insurance companies can charge a little more.

Standard, Preferred, Super-Preferred: What It All Means and Why It Matters

Life insurance companies spend a great deal of time and effort analyzing your medical history, the answers you've supplied on your application, and the results of your medical exam to evaluate the risk they are taking by providing you with life insurance. The greater the perceived risk, the more they are going to charge you. Most companies use three risk classifications: Standard, Preferred, and Super-Preferred.

A Standard rating means the life insurance company has determined that you are an average risk. As a result, it will not offer you any special discounts. For example, if you are a smoker—even a smoker in perfect health—you will typically be given a Standard rating (or even Substandard). Preferred and Super-Preferred ratings mean the life insurance company has determined you are less of a risk for them and will give you a discount.

If your insurance agent tells you that you've been "rated up," don't take it as a compliment. It means the insurance company has increased your risk classification—maybe from Preferred to Standard, or Super-Preferred to Preferred. Hearing that you've been "rated up" is deceptive, but I guess the insurance companies figured it sounded a lot better than, "The insurance company thinks you're in worse health than your peers and will only insure you if you pay more."

Do I or my spouse need life insurance?

The answer to this question has several important consequences that can affect your financial health while you are living and the financial health of those you love after you've passed away. Don't waste your time wondering if you need term or permanent, coverage for ten years or twenty, or $500,000 or $1 million. The first thing you should do is evaluate whether you need *any* life insurance.

Unlike auto insurance, where consumers look through their phone book and proactively buy it, life insurance tends to be sold by salespeople. Don't buy life insurance just because you've heard it is the right thing to do or because an aggressive salesperson tells you that you're neglecting your family if you don't have a policy.

Sometimes life insurance is not necessary. For example, if you are financially independent, retired, or have no family or dependents to support, you may not need life insurance. Owning a policy you don't need or having too much life insurance can mean paying hundreds or thousands of dollars a year in needless insurance premiums. Every dollar that you spend on life insurance is one less dollar you can use to improve the quality of your life and your loved ones' while you are alive. The money keeping your policies in force could be used to buy groceries, fund a vacation, go to a baseball game with your kids, give to a charity, or save for retirement.

But what would happen if you passed away tomorrow? If you die without life insurance and you don't have enough money in the bank or in your investment accounts, your family may experience financial hardship at a time when they are trying to deal with the emotional hardship of losing you. Would your family be able to recover financially? Would your spouse have to sell the house? Go back to work? Work two jobs? Take the kids out of piano lessons? If you have life insurance when you pass away, your loved ones can use the proceeds to help them fulfill their goals.

THE 6½-STEP LIFE INSURANCE MAKEOVER

Everything starts with a purpose and selecting life insurance is no different. If the life insurance doesn't solve a problem then you don't need it, period. Don't waste your hard-earned money buying life insurance you may not need or buying too much life insurance.

Once you've identified the purpose of life insurance, you can use this 6½-step process to guide you through obtaining an appropriate policy.

1. Determine your need for life insurance.

2. Choose which type of life insurance coverage is best suited for that purpose.

3. Calculate how long you need to have the life insurance.

4. Figure out how much life insurance you need for that purpose.

5. Get quotes from several companies.

6. Choose a life insurance company and contact them to purchase it.

6½. Buy the policy!

Keep in mind—it's entirely possible that you may need more than one life insurance policy. For example, you might have a ten-year term policy with a death benefit of $250,000 and a thirty-year term policy with a death benefit of $1.5 million. That's okay. Just like you have several pairs of shoes for different occasions, you also might have different policies that serve different purposes. You wouldn't wear gym shoes with a tux and you wouldn't run in loafers. Your life insurance policies should also serve a particular purpose.

Regardless of what you read or what fancy charts and graphs your friendly life insurance broker presents, there are four reasons to own life insurance:

- Purpose #1—Pay for Large, One-Time Expenses

- Purpose #2—Replace Earned Income

- Purpose #3—Provide a Small Cushion

- Purpose #4—Pay Estate Taxes

Whoops . . . Did I Forget to Do My Homework?

You may find it surprising that I didn't mention life insurance as a savings and investment vehicle. Surely I must not have done my homework. There are few life insurance brokers who don't praise the many benefits of using life insurance as a tax-deferred savings and investment vehicle. It's true that for the right person under the best circumstances, it may be an alternative way to save and invest; but for 99 percent of the population, it's not a good idea. There are plenty of other (less expensive) places to invest your money—even tax-deferred. So unless you're one of the 1 percent[1], don't get caught up in this sales pitch.

PURPOSE #1—PAY FOR LARGE, ONE-TIME EXPENSES

The role of life insurance in this situation is to use the death benefit to pay for large, one-time expenses. Here, the family has identified one or more big expenses—such as college or a mortgage—that they want to make sure they can cover if there is a premature death.

You should consider using life insurance to pay one-time expenses if:

- You want to pay for specific large expenses but you don't yet have sufficient assets to cover them.

- You have enough to pay for these large expenses, but doing so would jeopardize your family's financial stability.

- You are married and your spouse makes enough to support the family but not enough to cover the large expenses.

Step 1—Determine need.

Do you have any large expenses that your family wouldn't be able to cover if you or you spouse died tomorrow? If not, skip to Purpose #2 (Replace Earned Income) below. If so, list them here:

EXPENSES:

_____

_____

_____

_____

---

1. So how do you know if you are part of the 1 percent? If in doubt, work with a fee-only financial advisor who can evaluate your situation and provide you with unbiased insurance advice.

Step 2—Determine the best type of insurance.

There are really only two primary flavors of life insurance, term and permanent. Term is for a limited period of time and permanent is for life. Look at your list above. Nearly all one-time expenses are for a limited duration. For example, if you want to pay for your children's college education, once they go to college this isn't a pending expense anymore. Because one-time expenses have a limited life, term insurance is the way to pay for them.

Step 3—How long do you need to be covered?

Since you know these large, one-time expenses won't be debts you owe forever, you need to figure out how long they will be around. For example, if your son is twelve, you will need to start to pay for his college tuition in six years. Once your son is twenty-two, you won't have this potential expense and as a result, you won't need life insurance to pay for it.

For each of the future one-time expenses you listed above, determine their life span.

EXPENSES   **LIFE SPAN OF EXPENSE**

_____   _____ years

_____   _____ years

_____   _____ years

_____   _____ years

Step 4—How much insurance do you need to cover these expenses?

For each of the expenses you listed above, calculate how much each will cost based on when you will need to pay the expense. For example, let's say your son is ten and you want to pay for his four-year college education. Instead of using today's cost for one year at college and multiplying it by four, you need to adjust the expense out ten years. Here's why. One year of tuition and room/board at Harvard today costs more than $40,000. Assuming college tuition keeps rising like it has, it could cost more than $80,000 per year in just ten years!

How do you know how much to increase the expense each year for inflation? For most one-time expenses you can use 5 percent, but for things like education that have increased much more every year, you should use at least 7 percent. For expenses that actually decrease with time, like a mortgage, use today's cost.[2]

List the expenses and the future values here:

EXPENSES	LIFE SPAN OF EXPENSE	FUTURE COST
_____	_____ years	$_____
_____	_____ years	$_____
_____	_____ years	$_____
_____	_____ years	$_____

Now that you've listed the one-time expenses, their life span, and their future cost, you know how much insurance you need and how long you need it. For example, let's look at the one-time expenses Jose wants to pay if he passes away, their life spans, and their future cost.

EXPENSES	LIFE SPAN OF EXPENSE	FUTURE COST
College education (Rosa)	10 years	$125,000
College education (Vincent)	20 years	$225,000
Pay off mortgage	20 years	$275,000[2]

Jose needs a 10-year term policy for $125,000 and a 20-year term policy for $500,000 (Vincent's college education of $225,000 plus paying off the mortgage of $275,000).

PURPOSE #2—REPLACE EARNED INCOME

This is the biggie. Rather than using life insurance to pay one or two big expenses like the kids' college tuition, the role of life insurance in this situation is to provide ongoing income to support the survivor's normal and daily expenses. This was the original purpose of life insurance and is the most important reason to own it. The answer to the question, "If I die tomorrow, how will my family survive without my income?" is "life insurance."

Life insurance is the perfect tool for providing income to loved ones after a death. Beneficiaries get a check from the insurance company and don't

---

2. Remember, expenses that decrease with time are listed at their current cost since you'd want to have enough coverage if you died tomorrow.

have to pay any tax. They can then invest the proceeds and live off of the income. In this case, the income that was once being earned has now been replaced with the income generated by the investments.

Here's a quick example of how it might look. Let's say the Chang family needs $75,000 a year to live. If Jane is the sole breadwinner, her family would be in financial trouble if she passed away and wasn't able to provide her family with an income. With a little planning, Jane could protect her family from financial disaster. If she had $1.5 million in life insurance, her family could invest it and by earning a 5 percent return, produce $75,000 a year in income to pay the bills. Voilà! Disaster averted.

You should consider using life insurance to replace income if:

- There is only one breadwinner and family members wouldn't be able to support themselves if the breadwinner passed away.

- You will incur child care expenses if a nonworking spouse passes away.

- There are not enough investments to generate the income your family needs to live.

Step 1—Determine need.

How do you know if you need life insurance to replace your income or your spouse's income? Way back in Chapter 1, you calculated your Independence Factor. If you recall, this number tells you how many days per month you could pay your bills before running out of money. If you didn't complete the quiz yet, you can take it here.

Step #1 - Approximate how much you spend per month. Include everything—entertainment, mortgage, rent, taxes, insurance, food, etc.   **Monthly Expenses** (A) $_____

TOTAL MONTHLY EXPENSES (A) $_____

Step #2 - Add all of your sources of passive income per month, excluding investment income   **Rental Income** (B) $_____

Royalties/Licenses (C) $_____

Social Security/Pension Partnership Income (D) $_____

MONTHLY NON-INVESTMENT PASSIVE INCOME (E) $_____

Step #3 - Total all of your investment accounts
(e.g., 401(k), IRA, Savings) and multiply
by 0.33% (i.e., 0.0033):   **Monthly**
$_____ × 0.33% = Enter total →   **Investment Income** (F) $_____

MONTHLY INVESTMENT PASSIVE INCOME (F) $_____

TOTAL MONTHLY PASSIVE INCOME (E+F) (G) $_____

Step #4 - Divide your Total Monthly
Passive Income by your Total Monthly
Expenses (G ÷ A)   **Passive Income Ratio** (H) _____

Step #5 - Multiply your Passive Income
Ratio by 31 (H × 31)   **Independence Factor** (I) _____

If you scored more than 31, that means you earn enough passive income to support your family if you passed away. If your score is less than 31, you need life insurance to replace your income and make up the difference.

Step 2 —Determine best type of insurance.

Again, there are really only two primary flavors of life insurance, term and permanent. Term is for a limited period of time and permanent is for life. So what type of insurance is better to replace income, term or permanent? Term is the way to go. Here's why. The closer you are to retiring the less of a need for life insurance to replace income. Let's look at two examples:

EXAMPLE #1—PRE-RETIRED

If you're forty years old and you pass away tomorrow, your family will need to replace your income. The life insurance death benefit your family receives tomorrow could be invested and the income used to pay living expenses.

EXAMPLE #2—RETIRED OR NEAR RETIREMENT

If you're retired or near retirement age, there isn't any earned income to replace since you are no longer working (you're retired!). Theoretically, if you're retired and paying the bills without working, your spouse or family could continue to live their lifestyle without needing any additional income. Although earned income stops when you retire, other sources of income such as passive income from your investments and Social Security become the dominant source of income.

Step 3—How long do you need to be covered?

Since we are replacing earned income with life insurance, you need the insurance for as long as you are receiving earned income—that is, up until you retire.

If this still isn't clear, think about disability insurance. Disability insurance provides income if you become disabled and can no longer work. Do you need disability income when you are retired? No. Once you are retired, you are no longer working. The same holds true with needing life insurance to replace earned income. If you aren't working and receiving earned income (i.e., you're retired), you don't need life insurance.

Step 4—How much insurance do you need to replace earned income?

So far we've established that you need term insurance up to your retirement age to replace earned income. The question now is, "How much?" Take a look at the Independence Factor calculation from Chapter 1 or above. Subtract your monthly expenses (column A) from your monthly passive income (column F) and multiply it by 12 to look at what your income shortfall is for the year. Divide this number by 4 percent (0.04). This is the minimum amount of life insurance you need to replace your earned income.

	Total Annual Expenses	Annual Passive Income	Net Annual Expenses	Insurance Needed
Example #1	$ 63,000	$ 1,500	$ 61,500	$1,230,500
Example #2	$155,000	$26,500	$128,500	$2,570,000
Example #3	$ 75,000	$55,000	$ 20,000	$ 400,000

Now you try it!

A	B	C	D
TOTAL ANNUAL EXPENSES	**ANNUAL PASSIVE INCOME**	**NET ANNUAL EXPENSES**	**INSURANCE NEEDED**
Multiply your monthly expenses by 12	Total your annual passive income	B – A	0.04 ÷ C
$_____	$_____	$_____	$_____

Column D represents how much insurance you need to replace your earned income. If you currently have some savings or existing life insurance, you would just reduce column D by what you already have saved or by what is in your current policies. For example, if your calculation shows you need $1 million in life insurance, but you already have $250,000 in savings and investments and you already have a $250,000 life insurance policy, you would only need an additional $500,000 of life insurance.

PURPOSE #3—PROVIDE A SMALL CUSHION

Don't underestimate the value in using life insurance to provide a cushion, even a brief cushion after the death of a loved one. Most of us have no idea how we will respond when a spouse or significant other dies—especially when it is unexpected. Even if you are a high-powered executive making hundreds of thousands a year, it still can make sense to have life insurance on your spouse. You might need to take a few months off, and even when you go back to work it could take several more months or even years to get back to the same level you were at before your loss.

Maybe you could bounce back but your children might have more trouble. After losing a parent, they might need you home a lot more. Maybe you need to get away as a family for a while? Or maybe it would be helpful to bring in a grief therapist to work with the family? After the death of a loved one, the last thing you want or should be worried about is money. A small chunk of life insurance is sometimes exactly what you need to get through it.

There are no hard and fast rules or formulas to determine how much of a cushion you might need. I generally recommend one to two years' salary.

PURPOSE #4—PAY ESTATE TAXES

Maybe by completing the *Six-Day Financial Makeover* and saving and investing wisely you've built a nice nest egg. The IRS is kind enough to exempt a base amount ($2,000,000 per person in years 2006–2008) from tax, but your estate may be large enough that it will owe an estate tax on the value over this amount (the estate tax is nearly 50 percent!). Before your loved ones get a single dime from your estate, they will have to pay this estate tax bill. If your entire estate consists of one big savings account, it is easy for your loved ones to write a check to pay the tax. Most of the time, though, paying the bill is not as easy as writing a check. Typically assets must be sold to generate the cash needed to pay the tax. If the estate consists of liquid assets like cash, stocks, and bonds, it is pretty easy and inexpensive to convert these to cash.

If an estate has a bunch of illiquid assets (stuff that can't be sold quickly or easily), how do the beneficiaries pay the tax bill when all they have are two houses and an apartment building? Can they write to the IRS and tell them that there just isn't enough cash to pay? That letter would get a chuckle from someone at the IRS. The estate tax return must be filed within nine months of the date of death (a six-month extension may be available, and an installment plan may be allowed in certain circumstances). If there's not enough cash, your family will need to start selling some of the real estate to convert it to cash. Real estate can take several months or years to sell, but the looming IRS clock continues to tick. You may be forced to sell the real estate at a bargain just to be able to pay the estate tax. In this case, wouldn't it be nice to have a lump of cash available that you could use to pay the tax? Where would this lump of cash come from? Life insurance, of course!

If your loved ones will owe an estate tax, where will they get the cash to pay the bill? Before you jump into a big life insurance policy, you should first consider a few advanced estate planning techniques that could reduce the taxes you owe (visit www.SixDayFinancialMakeover.com to learn how).

As the "greatest transfer of wealth in the history of America" occurs—this describes the trillions of dollars that will be passed to and from baby boomers in the coming years—more and more families will be subject to an estate tax. If you fall into this category, you might want to consider using life insurance to pay part or all of the projected estate tax.

Do you think you will have a large estate tax bill that you'd prefer to have paid with life insurance instead of out of the assets in your estate? If so, you should speak to an experienced estate attorney to make sure you are taking advantage of all of the estate tax minimization strategies available to you. If you're still going to have to pay an estate tax, have your attorney refer you to a fee-only financial advisor to help you determine the type and amount of life insurance to purchase. This is one area where permanent insurance is necessary.

After you've completed steps 1–4 for each life insurance purpose (one-time expense, replace income, cushion, estate tax), proceed to steps 5–6$\frac{1}{2}$.

Step 5—Get quotes from several companies.

There are many places you can get term life insurance quotes. If you're in good health and are under sixty years old, the Internet is a good place to start. If you have a medical history or are over sixty years old, work with a fee-only financial advisor or life insurance broker. They'll usually know which insurance company is best depending on your particular medical history.

If you work with an insurance broker, be sure to tell him exactly what you want. You're making his job easy. He's just there to get you a quote. Make sure that you are comparing apples to apples. All of the quotes you get should be for the exact same policy. Insurance brokers and financial advisors can make one policy look better than another by changing the characteristics of the contract.

This means that all of the following should be identical:

- Type (term or permanent)

- Length of term

- Amount of death benefit

- Underwriting category (standard, preferred, super-preferred)

Step 6—Choose an insurance company and contact them to purchase a policy.

With quotes in hand, you may be tempted to buy the cheapest policy you can find. While I'm all for saving a buck, you have to look at the quality and reputation of the insurance company. When it comes time for the insurance company to pay the death benefit, you want to make sure they're still in business.

How do you gauge the financial stability of each insurance company? You have two options. You could do a thorough analysis of their financial records, including how many millions of coverage they have outstanding, and their assets, and hire an actuary to predict the company's future cash flows. This would probably take you a few weeks for each insurance company, and you wouldn't necessarily have all of the information you need to make a decision. The other option is to review the company's insurance rating. There are several independent rating agencies that provide a letter grading system, including A.M. Best Company (www.ambest.com), Weiss (www.weissratings.com), Fitch (www.fitchratings.com), Moodys (www.moodys.com), and Standard & Poor's (www.standardandpoors.com). These companies do all of the work for you. They have teams of analysts studying each insurance company.

So what should you look for? Each insurance rating company has its own grading system. For example, A.M. Best uses the following:

A++, A+ (Superior)

A, A– (Excellent)

B++, B+ (Very Good)

B, B– (Fair)

C++, C+ (Marginal)

C, C– (Weak)

D (Poor)

E (Under Regulatory Supervision)

F (In Liquidation)

S (Rating Suspended)

You want to buy your policy from a highly rated insurance company. That means it should have a grade of A or better. Additionally, you should ask your insurance broker or financial advisor for the Comdex rating for each of the insurance companies. The Comdex rating summarizes all rating agencies' grades and assigns each company a single numerical score between 1 and 100. The higher the score the better the insurance company. Look for a Comdex rating over 90 when selecting an insurance company.

Do Insurance Companies Go Bankrupt?

Yes. In the early 1990s, Executive Life Insurance Company did the unthinkable. They went insolvent. Executive Life, once the largest life insurance company in California, had 245,000 clients holding $40.5 billion of life insurance and annuities. Executive Life invested heavily in junk bonds to try to meet the high interest rates it promised policyholders, but after the junk bond market crashed, Executive Life declared insolvency in 1991 and was seized by the California Department of Insurance.

Why is this significant? According to a *Los Angeles Times* article on Executive Life, "many of its policyholders, some of them elderly and disabled, are struggling to get by on monthly annuity payments that are 30 percent to 50 percent less than what they had been promised."

Step 6½—Buy the policy!

It seems ridiculous to include this step. After all, you've gone through a lot of work to get to this point. Of course you are going to purchase the policy! This book is about improving your financial life by taking action! All of the research and calculations you've done to this point are worthless unless you pull the trigger and actually purchase a policy. Yet, you would be amazed at how many people don't follow through and buy a policy. Don't hesitate. If you need the insurance, pick up the phone and buy it.

Don't Let This Happen to You

Vince was a tough guy who grew up on the streets of Philly. With four older brothers and an overbearing father, Vince had to fight to get everything. Nothing came easy to him until he discovered he had a knack for science and biology. He never studied or did much homework in high school, but he always aced his science classes.

With some encouragement from his advanced chemistry teacher, he decided to apply for a college scholarship. Lo and behold, he got a partial scholarship to the University of Pennsylvania! Although he was working nearly full-time to support himself, his grades didn't suffer. He graduated with honors from their premed program. Vince went on to become an emergency room trauma physician. He met Karen, a nurse at the hospital, and fell in love. After their first child, they decided it would be best if she stayed home. It was a hard decision for Karen—an independent woman—but Vince convinced her it would all work out.

Vince met with his financial advisor alone. It was nearly impossible to get a babysitter during the day, but he also wanted to meet without Karen because he didn't want to have to argue with her about life insurance. You see, their financial advisor had been recommending they have more life insurance on Vince for several years. Vince argued that he worked for everything he had and that his children would have to as well. He didn't want to raise "trust fund" kids. Reluctantly, he finally bought a $250,000 term policy.

As far as Karen knew, Vince was taking care of everything. That was the deal. She quit working and he provided for the family. Unfortunately, that wasn't the deal she got. At 3:28 A.M. one morning on his way home from work, Vince was struck by a drunk driver and killed instantly. The grieving process was almost unbearable for the family and was made worse once Karen discovered the financial turmoil she faced.

The $250,000 life insurance policy was painfully inadequate. After selling their home, moving in with her parents, and telling her kids they had to drop out of their music and sports activities, Karen was devastated. Karen's mom asked, "Why would he have left you so unprepared? I thought you had a deal. How could he have done this to you?"

Congratulations! You've read a very important chapter in your Six-Day Financial Makeover. As you know by now, reading is good but doing is better. Make sure you take the next step by going through the Action Steps below!

Action Steps

Poor insurance. It's boring, confusing, and pretty much universally hated. Be that as it may, it is also a critical part of your financial makeover. This is probably one of the most likely chapters to be skipped, but if you read it, go the extra inch and implement the advice. If you don't, you'll be no better off and your financial transformation will have a big hole in it.

Go through the Action Steps below and put a check mark in one of the following boxes for each one.

Automobile Insurance

1. ☐ COMPLETED   ☐ NEED TO COMPLETE   ☐ DOES NOT APPLY

   Pull out a copy of your automobile insurance policy.

2. ☐ COMPLETED   ☐ NEED TO COMPLETE   ☐ DOES NOT APPLY

   Fill in these boxes or use the online worksheet at www.SixDayFinancial Makeover.com:

	Amount you have now	Amount you should have	Amount you need
Bodily injury per person	$_____	$100,000	$_____
Bodily injury per accident	$_____	$300,000	$_____
Property damage	$_____	$100,000 (or at least $50,000)	$_____
Medical payments	$_____	$5,000	$_____
Uninsured/ Underinsured	$_____	$100,000	$_____

3. ☐ COMPLETED   ☐ NEED TO COMPLETE   ☐ DOES NOT APPLY

   If you need more insurance than you currently have, call your auto insurance company right now and increase your limits.

4. ☐ COMPLETED   ☐ NEED TO COMPLETE   ☐ DOES NOT APPLY

   Do you need collision or comprehensive insurance? Can you afford to replace your car tomorrow? If not, you need collision and comprehensive insurance for the value of your vehicle. Call your insurance company now and get this coverage.

Homeowner's Insurance

1. ☐ COMPLETED   ☐ NEED TO COMPLETE   ☐ DOES NOT APPLY

Pull out a copy of your homeowner's insurance policy.

2. ☐ COMPLETED   ☐ NEED TO COMPLETE   ☐ DOES NOT APPLY

Home property coverage
    If you had to replace your home, how much would it cost: $_____
    How much is your home property coverage now: $_____
    If you need more protection on your home, call your insurance
       agent right away and increase your coverage to the full
       replacement cost of your home.

3. ☐ COMPLETED   ☐ NEED TO COMPLETE   ☐ DOES NOT APPLY

Home content coverage
    If you had to replace the contents in your home, how much
       would it cost: $_____
    How much content coverage do you have now: $_____
    If you need more protection on the contents of your home, call
       your insurance agent right away and increase your coverage to
       the full replacement cost of your contents.

4. ☐ COMPLETED   ☐ NEED TO COMPLETE   ☐ DOES NOT APPLY

Do you have jewelry, furs, antiques, artwork, or a stamp collection? If so, call your insurance agent to make sure these items are covered under your homeowner's policy.

5. ☐ COMPLETED   ☐ NEED TO COMPLETE   ☐ DOES NOT APPLY

Do you live in a high-risk fire zone, flood zone, or earthquake area? If so, your existing homeowner's policy may not cover you against these perils. Call your insurance agent and make sure you are financially protected against these devastating disasters.

6. ☐ COMPLETED   ☐ NEED TO COMPLETE   ☐ DOES NOT APPLY

Make sure your liability protection is at least $300,000. Ask your insurance agent to increase your liability limit on your homeowner's policy so there is no gap between where it ends and where your umbrella policy liability begins.

7. ☐ COMPLETED   ☐ NEED TO COMPLETE   ☐ DOES NOT APPLY

Take a video inventory of your home and the contents and store it in a safe-deposit box (for more information on safe-deposit boxes read Chapter 11). If your property is destroyed, this video will help you prove you owned the contents for insurance purposes.

Health Insurance

1. ☐ COMPLETED   ☐ NEED TO COMPLETE   ☐ DOES NOT APPLY

If you have health insurance, make sure it is a comprehensive policy that will cover you against all types of sickness or injuries and that it provides at least $1 million in lifetime benefits.

2. ☐ COMPLETED   ☐ NEED TO COMPLETE   ☐ DOES NOT APPLY

If you do not have health insurance, do not do anything else until you buy a policy. You absolutely must have at least a catastrophic health insurance plan.

Disability Insurance

1. ☐ COMPLETED   ☐ NEED TO COMPLETE   ☐ DOES NOT APPLY

Determine if you have a need for disability insurance. Complete the Disability Insurance Calculation on page 176. If you don't need disability insurance, skip ahead to the next section. If you need disability insurance, continue to Step 2.

2. ☐ COMPLETED   ☐ NEED TO COMPLETE   ☐ DOES NOT APPLY

Call your friendly insurance agent and get disability insurance quotes. I suggest you get quotes on the best policy you can find (i.e., the Rolls Royce version) and then, to reduce costs, make changes.
Best Policy:
Waiting Period: 30 days
Disability Definition: Own occupation
Years of Benefits: To age 65
Monthly Benefit: As much as possible based on your total income
  (salary, bonuses, commissions, etc.)

Inflation Protection: At least 5% per year
Type: Non-cancelable

Chances are this policy will be very expensive. If you need to cut costs, and you'll probably want to, you can change each of these factors to make the policy more affordable. Instead of haphazardly changing these factors, change them in this order:

Type: Guaranteed-renewable instead of non-cancelable
Waiting Period: 90 days instead of 30 days
Monthly Benefit: Based on what you calculated from the Disability Insurance Calculation rather than the maximum you can get
Disability Definition: Modified own occupation instead of own occupation
Inflation Protection: None instead of 5% per year
Years of Benefits: Anything less than to age 65

For example, if you need to reduce your annual premium by $1,500, change the Rolls Royce version by getting a quote on the identical policy except make it guaranteed-renewable instead of non-cancelable. If it drops the premium by $1,500 or more, you can stop there. If you still need to reduce the premium, get a quote on the Rolls Royce version with guaranteed-renewable and change the waiting period from 30 days to 90 days. Continue going down the list until you get a policy you can afford.

Life Insurance

1. ☐ COMPLETED   ☐ NEED TO COMPLETE   ☐ DOES NOT APPLY

Go through the 6½-Step Life Insurance Needs Formula to determine if you need life insurance, the amount, the type, and the length.

Update Your Online Financial Makeover Account

1. ☐ COMPLETED   ☐ NEED TO COMPLETE   ☐ DOES NOT APPLY

Before you do anything else, update your Six-Day Financial Makeover account at www.SixDayFinancialMakeover.com.

CHAPTER 8

Survive . . . Old Age (Long-Term-Care Solutions)

Designing the perfect vision for your life and investing to accomplish your goals are not only important to a financial transformation, they're fun to read and think about. Sometimes we need to think about and plan for the worst. This chapter is one of those times. Long-term-care planning can be a sobering topic, which makes it very tempting to skip over.

The average cost of nursing home care is more than $66,000 per year. Your chances of needing long-term care far outweigh your chances of needing your auto insurance policy, yet most of us have not planned for long-term care. How do you know if you can skip this chapter or if you need to think about long-term-care planning?

Do yourself and your loved ones a favor, read this chapter and implement the advice if (1) you or your spouse is over forty-five years old, (2) if you have aging parents who can't afford care, or (3) if you are caring for someone, regardless of age, who requires prolonged support.

Should I read this chapter?

	TRUE	FALSE
1. Medicare and Medicaid will pay for my long-term care.	☐	☐
2. I already own a long-term-care insurance policy.	☐	☐
3. I don't care about planning for long-term care because I will never live in a nursing home.	☐	☐

TRUE   FALSE

4. I don't need to know about planning for
   long-term care because I'm still too young.   ☐   ☐

5. I would like to learn more about long-term-
   care solutions for my parents and/or myself.   ☐   ☐

If you answered any of these questions TRUE, you should read this chapter.

Chapter Toolbar

Cost to Implement Advice	Likelihood of Needing Strategies in Chapter	Need Professional Advice?	Website Tools
$1,500–$3,000 Per Year	1 2 3 4 5 6 7 8 **9** 10 Not Likely Very Likely	↑ ↑ ↑ ↑ ↑ No Definitely	Yes

---

"When I die, I want to go peacefully in my sleep like my grandfather did—not screaming like the passengers in his car."

What does this gruesome joke have to do with long-term-care (LTC) planning? Surprisingly, quite a bit. First, unlike the grandfather in the joke, most people do not die quickly. If everyone remained healthy and mobile until death, LTC planning would be unnecessary. However, most people require weeks, months, or even years of medical care and support before they pass away. If you are over the age of sixty-five, you have a greater than 70 percent chance of needing LTC.[1]

Second, men have shorter life expectancies than women and men typically require medical care and support first. Usually the woman is in better health and can be the in-home caretaker for her husband—in fact, a whopping 75 percent of caregivers are women.[2]

Third, like the screaming passengers in the car, watching and providing extended care to an ailing loved one can be a horrible experience and an

---

1. "Americans Fail to Act on Long Term Care Protection," American Society on Aging, May 2003. www.asaging.org/media/pressrelease.cfm?id=35 (accessed May 12, 2005).

2. Errold F. Moody, *No-Nonsense Finance* (New York: McGraw-Hill, 2004), p. 244.

unbearable burden. In addition to the physical problems caused by overexertion and sleep deprivation, caregivers frequently experience depression, anxiety, and other psychological problems. A friend of mine spent his twenties taking care of his father, who was afflicted with Alzheimer's. He doesn't regret the time spent caring for his father, but he lost a decade of his youth to the task. As we age, more and more of us will be called upon to take care of our parents.

Last, although the chapter started with a joke, LTC is a serious subject[3] with long-lasting implications for you, your spouse, your family, and your parents.

Is Long-Term-Care Planning Necessary?

Financial planning is often more of an art than a science. There are only a few hard and fast rules that apply to most everyone. LTC is different; for the majority of middle-class or affluent families, LTC planning is absolutely necessary.

- The average cost for a private room in a nursing home is more than $66,000 per year.[4]

- The average cost for a shared room in a nursing home is more than $57,000 per year and rising rapidly.

- The average nursing home stay is 2.4 years.

- The current cost of an average entire nursing home stay is $158,766.[5]

- 10 percent of nursing home residents will stay there five years or more.[6]

---

3. Not all companies think long-term care is serious. One long-term-care insurance company has an advertisement that states, "LTC is a lot like pizza." The ad continues by comparing LTC insurance and pizza, answering questions like, "Can I get it delivered?" and "Do you still have the 30 percent off deal?"

4. *Wall Street Journal*, "How Getting Sick, or Staying Well, Can Upset a Solid Retirement Plan. July 1, 2004.

5. MetLife Mature Market Survey, Aug. 5, 2003, in "Who Pays for Long-Term Care?" http://www.ltc.com/ltcbasics_whopays.html (accessed July 25, 2006).

6. "A Guide to Long-Term Care Insurance," Health Insurance Association of America, 2003, in "Who Will Need Long Term Care?" www.ltc.com/ltcbasics_whowill.html (accessed July 25, 2006).

- 43 percent of people receiving LTC are under age 65.

- 12.1 percent of people between the ages of 65–74 need LTC.

- 27.2 percent of people between the ages of 75–84 need LTC.

- Almost 70 percent of people over age 85 need LTC.

Don't expect the government to help. Contrary to popular belief, Medicare doesn't provide LTC benefits and only the most destitute receive LTC support from Medicaid. Even those receiving help from Medicaid, the provider of last resort, may be out of luck since Medicaid will soon have problems providing for the increasing aged population. The population over age sixty-five in the United States will nearly double in the next thirty years, placing significant financial pressure on our government. According to *The Coming Generational Storm*,[7] "The longer people live, the more likely they are to outlive their assets. This means rising calls on Medicaid." With the long-term viability of Medicare and now Medicaid in question, it is only prudent to plan your own LTC strategy.

We dutifully invest in auto and homeowner's insurance but neglect the insurance that we may need the most. We neglect to plan for LTC for the same reasons we don't like to talk about life insurance or Wills. The potential need for LTC, for our loved ones or us, is depressing. The other Financial Makeover topics you've read about and implemented have been much more positive topics—they imply the potential for a happy, financially secure future. Planning for LTC implies the possibility of disability and the inevitability of aging. Unfortunately, having no plan is still a plan. The statistics tell us that sooner or later we all need to think about LTC.

Your LTC plan should be to hope for the best, but to prepare for the worst. You can either proactively plan an LTC strategy, or you can avoid the issue and leave your spouse's, parent's, and children's LTC plan to chance.

If you think you are too young to plan for LTC, you are wrong. Regardless of *your* age, you're likely to have parents who need to think about their LTC plan. Too often parents' lack of planning can decimate their children's finances. Why? Most children want their parents to be happy and comfortable. When care is required, nearly everyone wants to stay at home as long as possible. Although home health care is usually less expensive than nursing home care, it is often still a huge burden. If more skilled care is

---

7. This is an excellent book on the aging trend and its potential financial impact on our economy and government. I highly recommend it.

needed, the annual costs can reach $50,000 to $75,000. If the parents can't afford this, their children must make a decision. They can send their parents to a Medicaid facility or pay for better care themselves. With a little advance planning, they won't have to make this difficult and costly decision.

If your parents or loved ones don't have an LTC plan, help them sort through their options, the cost of the care, and develop a strategy for paying for the care. Since you are ultimately responsible for your parents' and spouse's well-being, you should make it your responsibility to help them create an LTC plan.

Don't Let This Happen to You

Rick grew up in Brooklyn with his mother and father. Because he was an only child, his parents were quite attentive and, as a consequence, Rick was a little spoiled. His parents weren't wealthy, but they were able to save for Rick's undergraduate school and his law degree at Harvard. After passing the bar, Rick accepted a position in a Los Angeles–based entertainment law firm. He worked long hours and was determined to make a name for himself. His parents were sad to see him move so far away but supported their son's career and were proud of his accomplishments. Shortly after Rick moved to Los Angeles, his father passed away from a heart attack. Rick considered moving back, at least temporarily, to help his mother, but he was unable to take the time off. Rick never discussed money with his parents and thought his mother was well-off. A few years went by and his mother had a stroke. Her condition was severe enough that the doctor told Rick she would need full-time supervision and assistance for the rest of her life. Although numbers were never his strong suit, Rick started analyzing her bank and brokerage accounts to see what level of care she could afford. What Rick found shocked him. His mother had very little. She would be able to pay for only two years in a mediocre nursing home. He reluctantly agreed to send her to the nursing home, promising to find her a better living situation. Two years and thousands of dollars later, his mother was out of money. Rick faced two choices: send her to a Medicaid nursing home or pay for her care. After researching many Medicaid-approved homes, he decided the right thing to do was to pay for her care. Rick paid for her care at the better facility for four years. After four years he was so far in debt he couldn't justify it any longer. He was forced to transfer her to a Medicaid facility—something he had promised her he would never do.

What Are My Long-Term-Care Options?

There are many more LTC solutions available today than there were just a few years ago. In the past, you had only two options. Either you received support from a spouse at home or you were thrust into a full-time nursing home and received care from nurses and doctors. Not anymore!

Staying at home

The good news is that people can safely stay at home much longer than they used to if they have the proper care. One solution is to hire a home health aide caretaker. Home health aides provide a variety of services including cooking, cleaning, laundry, and providing assistance with eating, bathing, transportation, and exercise.

Moving in with your children

If your children are willing and able to care for you, this is certainly a viable option. However, moving in with children involves a lot of practical questions. Will someone be home or available twenty-four hours a day? Is there an extra bedroom? Is the bedroom on the first floor? Are there pet allergies? How close is the nearest hospital? Are there sidewalks for exercise?

Adult communities

These communities do not provide LTC solutions per se, but are perfect for couples looking for a "new lifestyle." Adult communities are developments typically built for older residents who want a social community.

Shared housing

Shared housing is ideal for single or widowed individuals who are in good to fair health and don't want to live alone. Residents can take advantage of shared costs and reap the social benefits of having roommates.

Adult day care centers

Adult day care centers provide a place for seniors to gather during normal working hours, transportation to and from the facility, food, care, and supervision. Just as important, they provide companionship and a positive social atmosphere.

Assisted living residences

Assisted living residences vary dramatically, from small bed-and-breakfast-style homes to high-rise apartment complexes and everything in between. These residences are designed for temporary living—the average stay is approximately two years.

Nursing homes

Nursing homes provide two types of care—skilled nursing care and custodial care. Skilled nursing is provided twenty-four hours a day by licensed medical staff under a doctor's supervision. Custodial services include help with eating, dressing, toileting, and bathing. Many nursing home residents only need custodial care.

How Are You Going to Pay for Long-Term Care?

LTC is not cheap and costs vary depending on the type of care needed. Adult day care is less expensive than assisted living, which is less expensive than nursing home care. On the low end, an adult day care center might cost $35,000 per year and on the other end of the spectrum, a nursing home may cost more than $100,000. Remember that LTC expenses are new expenses that are in addition to the existing cost of living. In other words, just because you have a long-term-care expense doesn't mean your other expenses vanish.

For example, an adult day care center may cost $35,000 a year and will provide three meals per day. While it's true that without the adult day care, you'd be paying for and providing these meals yourself, the actual savings of having the day care center provide the meals represent less than $4,000 a year. The remaining $31,000 is a new expense. Even if you move into an assisted living residence or nursing home full-time, you may very well have other ongoing expenses. The problem is magnified if one spouse requires LTC and the other spouse remains at home with a mortgage, homeowner association dues, utility bills, and so on. Do not make the mistake of thinking you will reduce your current expenses when considering the cost of LTC.

There are three ways to pay for LTC: out of pocket, with government dollars, or with an insurance policy. This chapter will discuss the benefits and problems inherent in each method to help you create the best LTC strategy for you and your family.

Pay for Long-Term Care Yourself

It is impossible to know if you will need LTC or for how long. LTC statistics can be misleading and I would not rely on averages in creating a plan. For every person who manages to avoid LTC, there is another one who will need it.

Paying for all of your LTC yourself is a dangerous plan. An LTC event can quickly decimate your financial resources. It doesn't take long paying $75,000 a year to burn through an entire retirement nest egg. A family's life savings will vanish twice as fast if both spouses require extended LTC. Approximately 90 percent of people entering a nursing home will deplete their assets within four months.[8]

If you are determined to pay for LTC yourself but do not have enough income, there are alternative strategies. If your house comprises most of your assets and you are sixty-two or older, you may qualify for a reverse mortgage. A reverse mortgage allows you to tap into the equity of your residence by receiving a monthly check for as long as you live in your home. The size of the check is determined by the value of your home, current interest rates, and ages of its resident-owners. This monthly check may be all it takes to pay for home health care services. This strategy works best when all other assets have been depleted.

> If your only asset is your residence and you expect to live at home for several more years, you can quickly determine how much your monthly check will be by using the reverse mortgage calculator at www.aarp.org/revmort. You will need to enter your date of birth, your spouse's date of birth, the value of your home, and your zip code.

Self-funding your LTC is only a good strategy if you manage to avoid LTC. Yet it is impossible to guarantee that you will not need care. I encourage you to first talk to a financial professional to help you sort out the options.

---

8. Moody, *No-Nonsense Finance*, p. 254.

Have the government pay for your long-term care

Most people believe that Medicare and Medicaid will pay for their LTC. Medicare covers the cost if you are not poor and Medicaid if you are. The rules for both Medicare and Medicaid are complex. I'll save you a lot of time by saying the government is *not* in the business of providing long-term care and that you shouldn't count on it for paying for your long-term care.

I don't have to worry about long-term-care planning because Medicaid will pay my bills! The good news is that Medicaid offers LTC coverage. Medicaid pays the entire nursing home bill for 70 percent of seniors. The bad news is that you must be poor to qualify and Medicaid nursing homes have a bad reputation. If you plan on being poor, don't mind living in less than ideal conditions, and are confident the government will be able to continue to pay these expenses, don't read any further because Medicaid is your LTC solution.

Long-Term-Care Insurance

LTC insurance is the best way to pay for LTC. Like any insurance policy, you hope you never need it. LTC insurance provides a solution to a real problem. You have a much greater chance of using your LTC policy than other policies you would never go without:

- The odds of incurring property damage or bodily injury at home and using your homeowner's insurance are 1 in 88, according to "Long-term Care Insurance: A Product for Today," *Journal of the American Society of CLU & ChFC.*

- The odds of using your auto insurance are 1 in 248, according to *The Road to Wealth* by Suze Orman.

- The chances of needing fire insurance are 1 in 1,200, according to *The Road to Wealth* by Suze Orman.

- The odds of needing your LTC insurance policy are 1 in 2, according to the article "Baby Boomers Need to Plan for Their Future," by the American Health Care Association.

How does a long-term-care policy work?

The first significant difference in a LTC insurance policy is that the "benefit" is expressed in dollars of coverage per day. Other insurance policies like auto or homeowner's pay a flat dollar amount. Your homeowner's policy may cover up to $350,000. In contrast, LTC insurance may pay $150 per *day.* There are also policies that accumulate unused LTC benefits. These will be discussed later in the chapter.

This distinction in daily coverage is important because if you have a three-month stay in a nursing home that costs $200 a day, when you have a policy that pays $150 a day, you will be required to pay $4,500 out of pocket (90 days × $50 = $4,500). Conversely, you could have a thirty-year stay in a nursing home that costs $150 a day and not be out of pocket at all. LTC costs vary dramatically from state to state and even from city to city. This is why it is imperative you know how much LTC costs in your area. A slight miscalculation can cost you thousands of dollars per year.

The second thing different with an LTC insurance policy (but similar to a disability policy) is how these policies determine when you are eligible for LTC. This problem isn't found in most other insurance policies. If you smash your car into a tree, your house burns down, or you break your arm, no insurance policy will claim you are not eligible for a claim. While it is normally an easy decision for other insurance policies, it is much more difficult to determine when someone actually needs LTC. For example, if someone cannot bathe himself, does he need some form of LTC? What if he just needs help cooking and cleaning? What if he needs help taking medications? What if he just needs supervision? Should the insurance company cover all of these claims?

Insurance companies defined six activities of daily living (ADL) to standardize the needs of LTC. ADLs are a fancy term for those things most of us do throughout the day without thinking about it. In the first hour of the morning, you probably zipped through all six ADLs:

1. Transferring—Getting out of bed

2. Continence—Controlling bowel and bladder functions

3. Toileting—Using the toilet

4. Bathing—Taking a shower

5. Dressing—Putting on clothes

6. Eating—Having a bowl of cereal and a cup of coffee. (Note that this ADL only includes the physical act of eating and does not include preparing the food.)

Certain states, including California, include a seventh ADL for some LTC policies:

7. Ambulation—Walking throughout your home and outside your residence

ADLs are important because they are how insurance companies determine if they will pay for your LTC. Most insurance policies will cover your LTC if you are unable to perform at least two ADLs or have an impairment of cognitive ability. You may find a policy that will provide benefits when you can't perform just one ADL. These policies will be discussed later in the chapter.

For example, if you cannot get into or out of bed by yourself and cannot bathe, your LTC policy would provide coverage since you can't perform two of the ADLs—transferring and bathing. However, if you just have trouble eating, your insurance policy would not cover your LTC bills since you can perform all but one of the ADLs.

The third difference between LTC insurance and other forms of insurance is that LTC policies are divided into two types, tax-qualified (TQ) and non-tax-qualified (NTQ). Which type you own can make a difference in when you are covered, how your benefits are taxed, and if your premium payments are tax-deductible.

TQ policies were conceived in August of 1996 as part of the Health Insurance Portability and Accountability Act (HIPAA). Prior to this act, there was just one kind of LTC policy. The HIPAA law provided rules for a TQ LTC policy.

- Uses a standard and consistent definition of the six ADLs;

- Defines an LTC need when a policyholder is unable to perform at least two ADLs or has a severe cognitive impairment;

- Requires a licensed health-care practitioner to certify that the policyholder will need help with at least two of the ADLs for at least ninety days; and

- Provides a thirty-day money-back guarantee (also called a "free-look" period).

If an LTC policy conforms to these and a few other restrictions, the policyholder gets certain "benefits." These benefits may or may not be worthwhile, but can include the deduction of LTC premiums from income tax, not considering LTC reimbursement as taxable income, and state tax credits or deductions.

What your LTC Policy Should Contain

Before you start researching LTC insurance policies, first determine if you are a good candidate. Individuals with a net worth less than $300,000 or greater than $3 million may not need to consider LTC insurance—if this is you, consult a fee-only financial advisor to see what approach is best for you.

There are a large number of options with LTC insurance. Each option requires analyzing your unique situation, but the following are general guidelines that will help determine what your policy should contain.

How long the coverage should last

In the insurance world, this is the "term" or period of coverage. LTC policies can last one year, two years, or for the rest of your life. The longer you want coverage, the more expensive the policy. If you can afford it, a policy that lasts for life (i.e., full coverage until you die) is obviously best. Medical advances are pushing the limits of longevity. In fact, the 85+ population is expected to see tremendous growth, from 4.3 million in 2000 to 18.2 million in 2050—a 323 percent increase.[9] The centenarians—those 100 or older—are expected to rise 1,000 percent over the same period.[10] You will want a policy that will support you for as long as possible.

If the cost of getting a policy that lasts for life is too expensive, you have to make a more difficult decision. Should you get a two-year policy? A four-year policy? Should you get policies with the same period of coverage for both spouses? Take these factors into consideration:

- **Age**—Is there a big difference in age between you and your spouse? It might make sense to purchase a longer-term policy for the older spouse and a shorter-term policy for the younger spouse. Chances

9. Laurence J. Kotlikoff and Scott Burns, *The Coming Generational Storm* (Cambridge, Mass.: MIT Press, 2005), p. 10.

10. Ibid.

are the older spouse will require LTC first. This will protect the assets of the younger spouse, who will need the use of them for a longer period of time. Also, with the money saved on the younger spouse's shorter-term policy, you might be able to purchase a life insurance policy on the older spouse. At the older spouse's death, the proceeds of the life insurance can be used either to fund a new LTC policy for the surviving spouse or be used to pay for care directly.

- **Sex**—Women live longer than men. As a result, women are typically their husband's first caregiver. LTC insurance is also sometimes called "woman's insurance" because women greatly outnumber men in nursing homes. Consequently, women should generally obtain LTC coverage for a longer period than men. A minimum term for women is four years, and a minimum term for men is two years.

- **Medical History**—Take a look at both spouses' individual and family medical history. You are looking for important signs that may help you determine who might need care longer. Does heart disease run in your family? Cancer? Alzheimer's? Some conditions, like a heart attack, tend to require less LTC while Alzheimer's can require ten years or more of care.

  One of my clients has a condition that increases his chance of having multiple strokes. A stroke victim can live for years but will require advanced nursing care. In this situation, it made sense to get him a longer-term policy.

- **Support Network**—Although not ideal, consider the care that can be provided by an informal support network of friends and family. If both spouses have the same support, this won't be a factor in determining who should get a policy with longer coverage. However, there are often differences between spouses' networks. One spouse may have children from a previous marriage or siblings who can provide support and the other spouse may not. One spouse may be active at a place of worship and the other may not. If you determine that one spouse is deficient in the support of friends or family, it may be appropriate for this spouse to have a longer-term policy.

  One of my younger clients inherited several million dollars. She is in great health and could afford to pay for LTC out of her own pocket. We looked at her support network and found that there was nobody who could take care of her. The comfort of knowing she had the policy, and more importantly the support, was well worth the LTC premiums.

- **Availability of a Pooled Account Policy**—Depending on your state, you may be able to get a pooled policy. A pooled policy is one in which you have a pool of LTC money available to you. For example, if you have a two-year policy paying at $150 per day, you would have a total of $109,000 (365 days×2 years×$150 per day) of LTC dollars for as long as you live even though your policy is for two years. If you needed coverage for two years and the cost per day was $100, at the end of two years you would still have $36,500 remaining to pay for additional care.

Conversely, if you had a non-pooled policy, you would only have coverage for two years (730 days) at $150 per day, regardless of the cost of coverage per day. In the example above, you had $36,500 left after two years, but if you had a non-pooled policy you would have to start paying for the care yourself on the 731st day. Keep in mind that even with a non-pooled policy, your coverage is based on days of care needed. If you have a two-year policy and receive care at home every other day from a home health aide, you can continue to receive the care for four years even though it is a two-year policy.

If you have an LTC policy that pays for life, a pooled account doesn't apply since your benefits will never run out. If you are getting anything but a policy that pays for life, it is advantageous to get a pooled account when available.

Daily benefit amount

LTC is expensive and in some cities it is more so than others. Determining how much daily benefit you need is slightly more difficult than it may seem. You can't just get a policy that covers the cost of care today. I recommend getting a policy that keeps up with the rising cost of LTC inflation (see below for a more detailed description of inflation protection options).

Unfortunately, most policies rise at a maximum annual rate of 5 percent even though LTC costs are rising at an average of 6 percent per year. For example, if care in your city costs $160 a day, in fifteen years it will cost $383 per day. If you purchase a daily benefit of $160 a day with a 5 percent compound inflation protection, your daily benefit will grow to $332 per day in fifteen years. Under this scenario, you would be out of pocket $51 per day or nearly $19,000 per year.

This is why it is important to get the inflation protection *and* to pad the daily benefit amount. How much you pad the amount will depend on how old you are. The younger you are the more you will need to add to the daily benefit. Use this guide below:

Age 50–60:   Add approximately 25 percent to current daily benefit amount

60–70:   Add approximately 15 percent to current daily benefit amount

Over 70:   Add approximately 5 percent to current daily benefit amount

For example, if you are fifty-five and live in an area where the average cost of LTC is $160 per day, you would buy a policy that provides a $200 daily benefit. If you are sixty-three and live in an area where the average cost of LTC is $130 per day, you would buy a policy that provides a $150 daily benefit. Semiprivate nursing home room rates are less expensive, so if you don't mind sharing a room, you might be able to save some money in premiums.

Elimination period

The elimination period, also called the waiting period, functions like a deductible on your auto policy. Instead of requiring you to pay a certain dollar amount before coverage kicks in, an LTC policy requires you to pay for a certain number of days of coverage. It is important that you understand that the elimination period is only satisfied when you pay for a certain number of days of care. In other words, if you know you will need LTC and try to save money by having friends and family take care of you, the elimination period won't start until you actually start *paying* for the care.

Elimination periods commonly found on LTC policies are 0, 30, 60, 90, or 180 days. The shorter the elimination period is, the more expensive the policy. A zero-day elimination period seldom makes sense. Depending on the cost of the policy and the LTC budget, 30- and 90-day elimination periods are best. Avoid 180-day elimination periods if possible. Based on the skyrocketing costs of care, the cost of paying for five months of care (30-day versus 180-day) in fifteen or twenty years when you need the coverage can be $50,000 or more. Usually the difference in the premium between a 90- or even a 30-day elimination period is not enough to make it a worthwhile chance to take.

Inflation protection

Choosing the right policy involves sorting through a lot of complicated advice. However, nearly all experts agree on the need for inflation protection, or "compounding." Compounding protects you from the rising costs of LTC. If nursing-home care costs $150 a day in your city, what will it cost in ten, fifteen, or twenty years when you need it? Will it still be $150 a day? Not likely. LTC costs have increased dramatically in recent years (approximately 6 percent per year[11]) and are expected to continue to outpace general inflation. The $150 per day nursing home cost will be $360 in fifteen years! If you have a policy that covers $150 a day but doesn't increase each year, you will be out of pocket $210 per day when you need the coverage. Over several years, such a deficit in your policy will cost you staggering amounts of money.

If you are young when buying the policy, inflation protection is even more important. It's also important to get a policy that doesn't place a cap on the daily benefit. For example, some policies will stop increasing your daily benefit after you reach a certain age or when the benefit doubles. Avoid these policies. Just because you turn eighty—or through compounding, your daily benefit is twice the original value—doesn't mean the cost for LTC suddenly stops increasing. Bottom line, you want a policy that will pay for your LTC today and in the future.

LTC policies have four common methods of inflation protection. It's important to understand the differences in these methods because the first type is definitely better than the others.

1. **Compounding Inflation Protection.** This method provides an annual increase in your daily benefit amount by a set percentage— typically 5 percent. This is computed automatically and without an increase in your premium. This is the preferable method but it can be an expensive rider—sometimes increasing the cost of the policy by 50 percent or more. The 5 percent inflation protection increase

---

11. Dykes, J. S., "The Outlook for Long-term Care Insurance," *Kiplinger's Retirement Report*, April 2004.

is not based on the original daily benefit but on the value of the benefit the year before. For example, if you buy a policy with a $150 daily benefit and have a 5 percent compound inflation protection rider, in year ten the daily benefit amount will have increased to $245. If you are age sixty-five or younger, opt for a policy with compounding inflation protection.

2. **Simple Inflation Protection.** This method functions in exactly the same way as compounding protection, except that the annual increase is a set dollar amount. Typically, the simple inflation protection amount is 5 percent. If you purchased a $150 daily benefit, the policy would increase by $7.50 per year automatically. In year 10, the daily benefit amount would be $225. If you are age seventy or older, a simple inflation protection rider may be appropriate for your policy.

3. **CPI Inflation Protection.** If you buy a policy with this method of inflation protection, your daily benefit will increase annually based on the rise in the Consumer Price Index (CPI). The problem with this method is that while the CPI generally rises less than 5 percent per year, nursing home costs are increasing at approximately 6 percent per year. You may find that your policy is not keeping pace with the rising costs of LTC. If you are age seventy or older, a simple inflation protection rider is preferred. If it is too expensive, an automatic inflation protection based on CPI may be okay. If you are younger than seventy, however, this will not be the right inflation protection choice for you.

4. **Option.** The last method allows you to increase your daily benefit at set intervals by paying an additional premium. The additional premium is based on your current age, and not when you originally purchased the LTC policy. This can lead to hefty increases in premium for small increases in the daily benefit. This rider is better than nothing, but it is inferior to the other inflation protection riders.

Guaranteed renewable versus non-cancelable

These two contrasting options aim to answer the questions, "Can the insurance company cancel my policy and will my LTC premiums increase?" A guaranteed renewable policy means that as long as you pay your premiums on time, the insurance company cannot cancel your policy—regardless of your health. It also means that while the insurance company cannot selectively raise just your premiums, it *can* (and most likely will!) raise rates for all policyholders.

A non-cancelable policy is more difficult to get but offers much greater protection. If you have this type of policy, as long as you pay your premiums on time, the insurance company cannot cancel your policy or raise your premiums. There are few companies that offer non-cancelable policies, but their policies may be cost prohibitive or require a large single premium payment.

Requirements for coverage to begin

As discussed earlier, most policies require the loss of ADLs in order for benefits to begin. If you have a tax-qualified (TQ) policy, you must lose two ADLs for coverage to start, but there are non-tax-qualified (NTQ) policies that only require the loss of just one ADL. The additional cost of these policies must be weighed against the benefit of receiving coverage earlier. If you are predisposed to a condition—like arthritis—that may prevent you from performing one of the ADLs (like dressing), a NTQ policy that starts coverage with one ADL may be more appropriate for you.

Levels of care

LTC policies come in different forms. The three basic policies are nursing home care, home health care, and comprehensive LTC. The first two policies cover only nursing home costs and home-health costs, respectively. The comprehensive policy covers home health care, assisted living, and nursing home care.

Because it is impossible to determine what kind of care you will need, I recommend a comprehensive LTC policy. There was a time when the majority of policies sold were only for home care and not nursing home care. Those buying these policies were obviously optimistic, but also short-sighted. The overriding theme of LTC planning is to expect the best, but plan for the worst. You wouldn't buy a health insurance policy that just covers urgent care clinics and not emergency rooms, so don't make this same mistake when buying an LTC policy.

Typically you can get a nursing home policy and add a home health care rider to the policy. Although it can add 50 percent or more to the premium, it is usually worth the added cost. Determine if the home health care benefit is limited. Some policies are designed to pay only 25 percent, 50 percent, or 75 percent of your daily benefit if used for home health care costs. There is nothing wrong with this stipulation, you just need to be aware of the costs for home health care in your area and get a policy that will cover you.

There is one caveat with home health care. If you live alone and do not have a local support network, the home health care rider may not be worth it for you. Home health care tends to work best when a spouse or family member can coordinate it and provide some level of care.

Premium waiver

An LTC insurance policy with a "premium waiver" rider allows you to stop paying premiums as soon as you start collecting LTC benefits from the policy. Do not buy a policy without this protection. Be alert, insurance companies are tricky with their policy wording. Some premium waiver riders do not begin until you require nursing home care. In this situation, if you are receiving home health care you will still have to pay your LTC insurance premiums. You don't want to have to keep paying in that situation. Get a policy that allows you to stop paying premiums regardless of the type of LTC you are receiving.

Researching the Financial Soundness of the Insurance Company

The best LTC policy is virtually worthless if the insurance company cannot pay your claim when you need it. While analyzing individual LTC policies is a must, don't forget to also analyze the insurance companies themselves. Too often LTC policies are purchased based on cost alone. Beneficiaries of such policies end up with inferior coverage because they compared policies with significant differences to one another, or insurance through an inferior company because they failed to notice that one of the insurance companies is less secure financially.

Nothing can guarantee that your insurance company will be solvent and able to pay your claim in ten, twenty, or more years, but you can do the following three things to improve the chances:

1. **Research Credit Ratings.** Only go with a large, top-rated LTC insurance company. There are several independent services that provide financial size and credit ratings for insurance companies:

Weiss—www.weissratings.com or (800) 289-9222

A.M. Best—www.ambest.com or (908) 439-2200

Standard & Poor's—www.standardandpoors.com or
(212) 208-1527

According to a special report issued in 1994 by the United States General Accounting Office, not all credit reporting agencies are equal. It found that on average, Weiss's ratings reflected financial vulnerability much sooner than the other credit rating companies.

I highly recommend that you purchase a credit report from Weiss for $14.95 (per company report) on all of the companies you are seriously considering. You can also visit Weiss's website and view (for free!) their top-rated and lowest-rated LTC insurance companies. This quick glance shouldn't replace their credit report, but can be a good place to start. You should also visit A.M. Best's website. They offer free online credit and financial size ratings. If you are working with a financial advisor, insist that she provide a current Weiss and A.M. Best report on each company she recommends.

The policy you purchase should be from an insurance company with an excellent rating ("A" for Weiss and "A+"/"A++" for A.M. Best) from all rating agencies.

Just what does an "A" rating mean? Weiss reports that an A rated company ". . . has the resources necessary to deal with severe economic conditions" According to A.M. Best, an A or A+/A++ rated company is one that "has an *excellent/superior* ability to meet their ongoing obligation to policyholders."

2. **History of Rate Increases.** Nobody wants to see their LTC premium increase, but unless you have a non-cancelable policy, the insurance company can (and probably will) raise your premiums. Always request a written history of premium increases on existing LTC policyholders from each company you consider. Avoid those companies that have a track record of frequent and/or large rate increases.

3. **Consumer Complaints.** Check with the insurance department in your state. They can provide information on formal complaints from unhappy policyholders. A single complaint doesn't mean you shouldn't consider the company. Look for patterns that may indicate an ongoing problem.

Determining How Much You Should Spend on a Long-Term-Care Policy

If you have decided you want an LTC policy, you next need to decide how much you should spend on it. There is no maximum or minimum dollar amount that will be appropriate for everyone. However, for most people your annual retirement income will determine how much LTC insurance you can afford.

Generally, your LTC premiums should not exceed 5 to 7 percent of your annual retirement income. For example, if your total annual income was $65,000, you would not want to spend more than $3,250 or $4,550 per year on LTC insurance for you and your spouse. Even though you might—and should—purchase your LTC policy while you are still working, you should calculate what percentage of the premiums will be based on your retirement income. A policy you can easily afford during your working years may become burdensome during retirement. Get a policy that you can live with today and tomorrow.

When You Should Buy a Long-Term-Care Insurance Policy

The best time to buy is when you are young and healthy. Everyone wants to buy a policy the day before they need it, but it is impossible to predict precisely when you will need care. Unfortunately, the longer you postpone the decision, the greater your chances of suffering an illness or developing a condition that will disqualify you from coverage or cause the premiums to be too expensive. Use the guide below:

Under Age 45:   Might be premature, as the likelihood of needing LTC is small. If you have a limited support network, the peace of mind in having a policy may be worth it. Rates will be low. Consider a "limited pay" option, which requires premiums to be paid for a set number of years, after which the policy is paid up and no further premiums are due. This can be a good strategy because it allows you to pay for LTC during your income-producing years rather than during retirement when you will be on a limited budget. Also, most limited pay policies are non-cancelable. This means that the insurance company cannot ever increase your premiums or cancel your coverage.

Age 45–55:   Good time to start looking. The rates are still attractive. Consider the limited pay option discussed above or a traditional payment policy.

Age 55–60:   If you haven't looked yet, now is a very good time. Don't put it off any longer; you are young enough where rates are still attractive.

Age 60–65:   If you fall within this range, time is still on your side. Rates will not necessarily be "attractive," but they should still be reasonable.

Age 65–70:   Statistically, you have another fifteen years until you will need LTC, but premiums are going up dramatically. Lock in a policy now before it is too late.

Over Age 70:   If you are seventy or older, you can still get an LTC policy. Premiums will be a lot higher, but it may still make sense. The underwriting process, the process by which insurance companies determine if they want to provide you with insurance, is more difficult. Most companies will require an in-person interview. Even if you think the cost will be too much, get several quotes anyway. You might be surprised.

Where You Can Get Independent and Unbiased Help

The Administration on Aging (AoA) is a federally sponsored organization addressing the needs of older Americans. The AoA supports the Long Term Care Ombudsman program, which is a network of advocates for residents of nursing homes, board and care homes, and assisted living facilities. The Ombudsman network consists of nearly 8,500 volunteers and more than 1,000 paid staff. Each state is mandated to have an Ombudsman Program to help people find the best care possible.

They can be an invaluable resource for current long-term-care residents, too. Information on the Ombudsman program can be found online at www.LTCombudsman.org. Here is a sampling of how it can help you:

- Resolve complaints made by or for residents of LTC facilities.

- Provide information to the public on nursing homes and other LTC facilities and services, residents' rights, and legislative and policy issues.

- Advocate for residents' rights and quality care in nursing homes, personal care, residential care, and other LTC facilities.

It is a watchdog organization looking out for the interests of LTC residents and is charged with addressing the following concerns:

- Violation of a resident's rights or dignity.

- Physical, verbal, or mental abuse, deprivation of services necessary to maintain residents' physical and mental health, or unreasonable confinement.

- Poor quality of care, including inadequate personal hygiene and slow response to requests for assistance.

- Improper transfer or discharge of a patient.

- Any resident concern about quality of care or quality of life.

Action Steps

There are few things in life that can cost as much as a prolonged long-term need for you or a loved one. High costs for care can decimate even the strongest finances. Now that you have a good understanding of the types of long-term care, what the government covers, and long-term-care insurance, it's time to complete this piece of your financial makeover by focusing on this chapter's Action Steps.

Go through the Action Steps below and put a check mark in one of the following boxes for each one.

Determine Who Needs Long-Term-Care Planning

1. ☐ COMPLETED   ☐ NEED TO COMPLETE   ☐ DOES NOT APPLY

If you are forty-five or older, you almost certainly need an LTC plan. After reviewing LTC options, decide on an LTC plan.

2. □ COMPLETED   □ NEED TO COMPLETE   □ DOES NOT APPLY

If you are under forty-five but have aging parents or dependents who are likely to need LTC, have a discussion with them about LTC. If they don't have an LTC plan, it may fall on your shoulders. Walk them through the various LTC options and find a funding source that best meets their needs. Typically this will be LTC insurance. If they can't afford the policies, it may make sense for you and your siblings to pool your resources and pay LTC insurance premiums for them.

Long-Term-Care Options

1. □ COMPLETED   □ NEED TO COMPLETE   □ DOES NOT APPLY

If you are interested in home health care or in moving in with your children, evaluate whether you have a support network that is both willing *and* able to provide for your care. Examine this plan thoroughly. What looks good on paper may not make sense in reality. It is important to discuss your wishes openly. Ask the hard questions and encourage honest feedback.

Paying for Long-Term-Care

1. □ COMPLETED   □ NEED TO COMPLETE   □ DOES NOT APPLY

Do you have the resources to pay for your own LTC? Determine your ability to self-fund your own care by calculating your net worth (see Chapter 4 or go online to www.SixDayFinancialMakeover.com). For most people with assets between $300,000 and $3,000,000, it doesn't make sense to self-fund. If your net worth falls between these amounts, consider LTC insurance.

2. □ COMPLETED   □ NEED TO COMPLETE   □ DOES NOT APPLY

If you have a net worth less than $300,000, you may be able to rely on Medicaid to pay for your LTC. You should still research LTC insurance to determine if it fits into your budget.

LTC Insurance

1. ☐ COMPLETED   ☐ NEED TO COMPLETE   ☐ DOES NOT APPLY

    The best approach is to get several quotes on identical or similar LTC policies without worrying about the cost of the insurance. This way you can determine the maximum premium you will have to pay for a Cadillac-style policy. Once you have that figure, you can trim back some of the options to get a policy that fits within your budget.

2. ☐ COMPLETED   ☐ NEED TO COMPLETE   ☐ DOES NOT APPLY

    Obtain baseline quotes by providing the following:
    Period of Coverage: Life
    Daily Benefit: Research the average private nursing home rate for
        your area and add 25 percent if you are 50–60, 15 percent if you
        are 60–70, or 5 percent if you are over 70. This is the daily
        benefit you should use to get a quote.
    Elimination Period: 30 days
    Inflation Protection: 5 percent compound inflation protection
    Type: Guaranteed renewable (since there are so few non-cancelable
        policies available)
    Level of Care: Comprehensive
    Premium Waiver: Full waiver of the premium regardless of level of
        care
    Credit Rating: Only get quotes from companies rated "A" or better
        by Weiss and A.M. Best.

3. ☐ COMPLETED   ☐ NEED TO COMPLETE   ☐ DOES NOT APPLY

    Determine if you can afford the premium. If you can, request a written report on each company's history of premium increases and check with your state's insurance department. If the company hasn't had a history of large and/or frequent premium increases and there isn't a pattern of similar complaints, buy the policy. If you can't, go to Step 4. If none of the insurance companies will provide you with coverage, go to Step 7.

4. ☐ COMPLETED   ☐ NEED TO COMPLETE   ☐ DOES NOT APPLY

    If, based on your budget, you need to create a policy that is less expensive than the Cadillac-style policies found in Step 2, here is what you can do to reduce the premium on those policies:

Period of Coverage: For the first round of changes, get policies that pay for life. If you still cannot afford a policy, you can adjust this later.

Daily Benefit: Try to keep the daily benefit the same.

Elimination Period: Increase this from 30 days to 90 days.

Inflation Protection: If you are under age 60, keep the 5 percent compound inflation protection. If you are age 60 to 70, change this to 5 percent Simple Inflation. If you are more than 70 years old, change this to CPI Inflation Protection or eliminate altogether but increase the daily amount by 50 percent.

Type: Keep the guaranteed renewable option.

Level of Care: Keep comprehensive for now.

Premium Waiver: Keep the full waiver of premium regardless of level of care

Credit Rating: Continue to only get quotes from companies rated "A" or better by Weiss and A.M. Best.

5. ☐ Completed   ☐ Need to Complete   ☐ Does Not Apply

Can you afford a policy from Step 4 using the revised options? If so, request a written report on each company's history of premium increases and check with your state's insurance department. If the company hasn't had a history of large and/or frequent premium increases and there isn't a pattern of similar complaints, buy the policy. If you cannot, go to Step 6.

6. ☐ Completed   ☐ Need to Complete   ☐ Does Not Apply

Seek the help of an independent financial planner who will not earn a commission based on the policy you purchase. Whatever you do, do not change the following options:

Elimination Period: It seldom makes sense to increase above 90 days.

Level of Care: Keep comprehensive for now.

Premium Waiver: Keep the full waiver of premium regardless of level of care.

Credit Rating: Continue to get quotes only from companies rated "A" or better by Weiss and A.M. Best.

Determining How Much You Should Pay for Long-Term-Care Insurance

1. ☐ COMPLETED   ☐ NEED TO COMPLETE   ☐ DOES NOT APPLY

Generally, your LTC premiums should not exceed 5 to 7 percent of your annual retirement income. Calculate your expected retirement income—don't forget to add Social Security—to determine the maximum amount you should budget. If your retirement income won't support the kind of LTC policy you want and you are still working, consider a limited-pay option. This allows you to pay LTC premiums for a set period of time—usually five or ten years, after which you don't have to pay premiums ever again. This type of policy works best if you still have five or ten years until retirement.

Getting Outside Help

1. ☐ COMPLETED   ☐ NEED TO COMPLETE   ☐ DOES NOT APPLY

If you need professional help in determining which LTC plan is best for you, contact an Ombudsman by going to www.LTCombudsman.org.

Update Your Online Financial Makeover Account

1. ☐ COMPLETED   ☐ NEED TO COMPLETE   ☐ DOES NOT APPLY

Before you do anything else, update your Six-Day Financial Makeover account at www.SixDayFinancialMakeover.com.

SURVIVE . . . WHEN DISASTER STRIKES

CHAPTER 9

Survive . . . The Death of a Loved One (Estate-Planning Solutions)

Most of us don't like to think about death, but as uncomfortable as it may be to think about, if you put off proper planning, you risk subjecting your loved ones to a financial disaster—just as they're trying to deal with the emotional impact of a loved one's passing.

You've worked hard to design your life, to save and invest your money, and to survive all kinds of disasters, but do you know where your money will go when you pass away? Do you know who will take care of your children? Do you know who will make life-or-death medical decisions for you if you are unable to? Your financial makeover won't be complete without addressing these sensitive but critical issues.

Even if you consider your life "simple," you still need an estate plan. This chapter will guide you through the minimum you need to do to protect your family's assets.

Should I read this chapter?

	TRUE	FALSE
1. I don't have enough assets for an estate plan.	☐	☐
2. I don't need an estate plan because I'm just leaving everything to my kids.	☐	☐
3. My loved ones will probably owe taxes on my estate.	☐	☐
4. I have children from a previous marriage.	☐	☐

                                                     TRUE   FALSE

5. I'd like to learn more about how I can provide
    for my loved ones (and me!) with an estate plan.   ☐   ☐

If you answered any of these questions TRUE, you should read this chapter.

Chapter Toolbar

Cost to Implement Advice	Likelihood of Needing Strategies in Chapter	Need Professional Advice?	Website Tools
$250–$5,000	1 2 3 4 5 6 7 8 9 10 Not Likely Very Likely	↑ ↑ ↑ ↑ ↑ No Definitely	No

---

Estate planning conjures up images of death, aristocrats, mansions, and bitter family disputes. Most people are under the impression that estate planning is not for them because they think it's only for the rich. Yet neglecting to plan for your estate is a mistake—don't let the stereotype scare you.

Estate planning is the process of transferring your assets to others after you pass away. The assets involved in estate planning include cash in bank accounts, stocks and bonds in investment accounts, real estate, and other items such as your car, artwork, jewelry, and your baseball card collection. Estate planning doesn't just focus on financial assets; it also focuses on the transfer of care for children. As you will see throughout this chapter, successful estate planning offers so much more than simply transferring your assets at death. Your commitment to your family and your loved ones should last as long as they live, not only as long as you live.

Estate planning answers the following questions:

- Who do I want to take care of my children?

- At what age should my children have control over their inheritance?

- Who should get my great-grandmother's antique wedding ring?

- Who should make decisions for me if I'm unable to do so?

- Who should have access to my checking account if I leave the country?

- Which charity should receive my investment account?

- Do I want to have a traditional funeral?

- Do I want to be kept on life-support indefinitely?

What's the Purpose of Estate Planning?

Estate planning has three important purposes:

1. **It provides for your loved ones.** This is the most important reason for estate planning. If you have a spouse and/or children, estate planning gives you the chance to provide for them after you pass away. I work hard to provide for my family—financially, emotionally, and spiritually. Estate planning will help me continue to provide for my family after I pass away. It's not just about financial support. It is about making sure your loved ones are looked after and about helping them accomplish their dreams. Even if you don't have a spouse or children, would you like to help a niece, nephew, brother, sister, mother, father, or friend?

    Estate planning puts you in the driver's seat. You've worked hard for the money and things that you have. Planning gives you control over the benefits of your hard work. There are simple and quick things you can do today that will protect your family when you or a loved one passes away. This chapter will guide you through the minimum in estate planning that you will need to provide for your loved ones' future.

2. **It helps you achieve your goals.** If you have charitable goals, there is no reason that your death should put a stop to your achievement. For example, one of my IMPACT-Goals in life is to help as many people as possible reach their own goals. Another goal is to support the mission of my church. I'm also passionate about animal welfare. While all of these are goals I try to achieve today, my devotion to these causes doesn't have to stop when I pass away. With some planning, these goals can continue to be pursued and achieved.

3. **It helps you give as much as possible to your family or church/charity.** Depending on the size of your estate, your death may bring an unwelcome relative wanting his fair share of your estate—Uncle Sam. This is one of the first things most people think of when they think of estate planning—reducing their estate tax. I believe that taxes are the price of life in a civilized society, but I also strongly believe that I shouldn't pay any more tax than is legally necessary.

Billions of dollars are paid in estate tax every year that could have been easily avoided. We go to great lengths to reduce our taxes. We contribute to 401(k)s and IRAs, donate to charities, and keep detailed records. I used to live on the Washington-Oregon border. Because Oregon doesn't have a state sales tax, I knew people who would drive thirty minutes to Oregon to save less than five dollars in sales tax.

We'll drive across town to save a buck or two, but our lack of careful estate planning may cost our loved ones anywhere from thousands of dollars on up in easily avoidable estate taxes. With just a little bit of planning, the vast majority of the population shouldn't have to pay any estate tax. If you're fortunate enough to have enough wealth where estate tax is unavoidable, there are more advanced strategies that can dramatically reduce Uncle Sam's cut. Again, why pay more tax than is legally necessary?

Congratulations! You Already Have an Estate Plan

Maybe you didn't know it, but right now you already have an estate plan! Even if you've never written a Will or considered estate planning, you have a plan. Each state has developed an estate plan of last resort—called an "intestacy"—for residents who haven't created their own plan.

The intestacy laws say that if you die and don't have a Will, the state in which you live has a set system in place for distributing your assets. Many people believe that if you die without a Will the government will take your assets. Fortunately, this is not true! At the very least, your assets will stay within the family, but you'd better check the laws in your state—you might not like their plan for your hard-earned assets!

What's Wrong with My Default Estate Plan?

You do not want to be without an estate plan. Regardless of your state, their default plan is most likely not right for you. State laws vary, but in general they distribute your assets like this:

- **Single without children.** Most states give your assets to your parents. If your parents aren't alive, your assets go to your siblings equally.
  If you'd prefer your assets go to someone else, you need an estate plan.

- **Single with children.** There are two types of "assets" in this situation. There are your real assets (e.g., bank accounts, investments, real estate, etc.) and there are your children. All of your real assets go directly to your children equally. The more important question is always "What happens to my children?" The answer to this question depends. If there is a living parent in the same household, he/she automatically becomes the guardian (assuming the child/children are under age eighteen). If this is not the case, it gets a little bit more complicated. If there is a living parent but he/she does not live in the same household, the court will most likely name him/her as the guardian, but not automatically. If there isn't a living parent, a friend or relative will have to petition the court for appointment as guardian. If no one comes forward or the judge does not approve anyone, the children will be forced into foster care.
  You might want your assets to go to your children, but do you want them to have complete control over them when they turn eighteen?[1] On their eighteenth birthday, they can cash out and do whatever they want with the money. Most eighteen-year-olds are not mature enough to handle the responsibility of managing wealth. The very assets you worked so hard to accumulate and to pass on to better their lives can be squandered very easily.
  Larger sums can de-motivate a child. A friend in high school couldn't turn eighteen fast enough. His parents were both deceased and he was living with his grandparents. He skated by, getting

---

1. The legal age of adulthood in some states is twenty-one, but I would argue that this is still too young for most kids to have absolute control over an inheritance.

mediocre grades, and showing no interest in college or work. He rarely talked about it, but it would slip from time to time that he was going to have access to "a lot of money" soon. He was a smart guy. With a little motivation, he could have written his own check; instead he was just waiting for his birthday so he could cash the one that had been written for him.

The other issue to consider is the guardianship of your children. Wouldn't you like to choose who has the responsibility of raising your children? Without an estate plan, you have little control over that decision.

- **Married without children.** This might shock you but, depending on your state of residence, only a third to a half of your assets will go to your spouse. The rest goes to your parents, if they are alive, or to your siblings.

   If you're comfortable leaving only a third to a half of your assets to your spouse, the state's cookie-cutter estate plan may be right for you. Likewise, if you're comfortable receiving only a third to a half of your spouse's assets, the state's plan might work for you. Most couples who learn that they could be "cheated" out of what they consider rightfully theirs are anything but comfortable with this formula. If you don't agree with the state's plan for your or your spouse's assets, you need to create your own estate plan.

- **Married with children.** You might think that the surviving spouse gets all of the assets, but you're wrong. Most states direct a third to a half of the assets to the surviving spouse and the remainder to the children. If both parents die, a friend or a relative will have to petition the court for appointment as guardian. If no one comes forward or the judge does not approve anyone, the children will be forced into foster care.

   The married couple with underage children has some of the same problems facing the single person with children. In both cases, children get assets at age eighteen, which can de-motivate a child. If both parents pass away, both married and single parents face potential problems with guardianship. Again, if you like your state's plan for your financial assets and your children, you don't have to do a thing. On the other hand, if you'd prefer your spouse receive all of your assets, that your children have the guardian you choose rather than the one a judge appoints, or that your children are older when they receive an inheritance, you'd better develop your own estate plan.

Don't Let This Happen to You

Amber and Scott were inseparable as kids. They met in second grade and immediately became best friends. Amber spent as much time as possible with Scott and away from her alcoholic and verbally abusive father. Amber and Scott dated throughout high school and got married in college. Amber intentionally had very little contact with her father over the years and even less after she married. Aside from Scott, she had a hard time trusting men and always felt anxious and "on edge" around them. Although their life was far from glamorous, Amber and Scott were happy and had enough money to live the life they wanted. Eleven days before their twenty-fifth wedding anniversary, Amber died suddenly from an aneurysm. Without a Will or an estate plan, Amber's assets went through her state's cookie-cutter intestate plan and her father received half of her estate. Scott pleaded with the judge, explaining that Amber would have been devastated to know that her father received a single penny of her estate, but his pleas fell on deaf ears. Without a Will or an estate plan, there was nothing Scott could do.

On top of these disastrous problems, if you die without an estate plan of your own, you can't eliminate or even minimize estate taxes. The estate tax laws are pretty clear. They basically say, "If you put in the time to create an estate plan, you can reduce or eliminate the tax, but if you use the state's cookie-cutter plan, we won't give you any breaks." Consider it a speeding ticket where you have two choices. You can do nothing and pay the entire fee or you can write a simple letter and get the ticket reduced or even waived. By crafting your own estate plan, you can rest assured that your wishes and your goals are addressed during life and at death—and that you aren't paying any more in estate tax than is legally required.

The Top Ten Excuses People Use to Avoid Creating an Estate Plan

1. **I don't have enough assets to require an estate plan.** When I talk to some people about estate planning, they look at me like I'm crazy.

They say, "My last name is Jones, not Rockefeller. I've got a simple life with modest assets. I don't need estate planning."

A good estate plan is critical to protect even modest assets. You really don't need much to benefit from a good plan. Remember, the transfer of your assets is just one piece of estate planning. If you have children—even if you don't have a dime to your name—you need a plan.

2. **I don't want to think about dying.** Thinking about our estate plan forces us to acknowledge our mortality. We must consider who will receive our assets, who should raise our children, if we want to be cremated, who should make the decisions if we become incapacitated, if we want to be on life support, and other gloomy issues.

   I don't like thinking about death, either, but the thought of my child being placed in the wrong hands, of my wife watching me suffer on life support, or of having the wrong person make life-or-death decisions for me motivated me to get off the couch and create an estate plan. Let's face it, thinking about dying a little or a lot will not influence how long you live. Providing for your loved ones isn't always easy. Burying your head in the sand and hoping it "works out for the best" will make it harder for you and for your family. You don't need to dwell on your estate plan—just make sure you do it.

3. **I'm single and don't have children so I don't need an estate plan.** Young, single, or childless individuals frequently use this excuse. "If I don't have anything and I'm not responsible for anyone, what's the point of an estate plan?" Under the traditional view of estate planning, this might be the case, but not anymore.

   Even if you don't have assets or care where they go, a proper estate plan can help you while you are alive. Later in the chapter, you will learn about several types of estate planning documents that can literally save your life.

4. **I'm too young for an estate plan.** You probably feel good and are in excellent health. It may be decades before your estate plan will be needed. Why worry, plan, and pay for something that you won't need for ten, twenty, forty-plus years?

   Think of your estate plan as an insurance policy. Chances are you will pay for homeowner's insurance, year after year, and never use it.

But would you consider canceling the insurance policy protecting your largest asset? The only difference is that your estate plan will eventually be used. It's not a question of if, but of when. Why gamble with your family's security when you can quickly and easily create an "insurance" policy that will provide for them?

5. **Once I'm gone, I don't care what happens.** I call this the hotel-room syndrome. Do you ever notice that when you stay in a hotel, you make a bigger mess? I've seen hotel rooms that look like a tornado has hit them after only one night! Towels end up on the floor. The newspaper is strewn about. The blankets and pillows end up in a corner. Food is left out. The rationale is, "I'm leaving tomorrow and somebody else can deal with this mess." Would you behave differently if your children, parents, or spouse were maids at the hotel and had to clean your room?

   The last thing most people want is to make their death even harder on their loved ones. At a time of intense sadness and confusion, don't you want to make the administrative stuff as easy as possible on your family? Don't leave a big mess for someone else to straighten out—create a simple estate plan to help your loved ones.

6. **I don't know what I want to put in my estate plan.** An estate plan will force you to answer many questions. Who gets your assets? How much do they get? Who should take care of your children? The fewer of these difficult questions you can answer, the less valuable your estate plan will be.

   You will not be expected to have all of the answers when you begin creating a plan. These are important issues that will take time to consider. If you wait until you have all of the answers, you will never start your estate plan. In fact, most people discover that questions come up during the planning process that they never would have considered. If you are worried you might not have all of the answers, get started anyway. Even if you can't answer a single question, at least it gets you thinking and moving in the right direction.

7. **My life is in flux, so I'll just wait until things have settled before I start my estate plan.** Maybe you have a new baby on the way or are getting married. Maybe you're selling a business, buying a house, or getting a divorce. It can be tempting to wait to start your estate

plan until your life settles down. Why go through the hassle of completing a plan if you know you will need to change it a year from now?

If your life is anything like mine, chances are there will always be something on the horizon that will change things. Change is the only constant. If you wait for everything to be in place, you might be waiting a long time. I always suggest starting now—regardless of what lies ahead. Once you get your estate plan in place, it will be easy to modify it; rarely would you have to start over. Live like you will never die but plan as if you will die tomorrow.

8. **Creating an estate plan is too costly.** Like so many things in life, you can choose instant gratification or you can invest in something that will return riches later. An estate plan that covers the basics can cost between $500 and $1,500—depending on the complexity of your situation.

While I'm sure there are other things you'd rather do with $500, I can't think of any way to use that money that will have more important results than creating a customized estate plan. I don't think there is anything that will pay off in dollars, convenience, and peace of mind more than an estate plan.

9. **I don't have the time for estate planning.** We have a lot of priorities tugging at our time. Not too many people jump out of bed excited about planning their estate. Unfortunately, we often neglect important—but not necessarily urgent—activities in the rush of our daily lives.

Estate planning is rarely an urgent activity, but always an important one. If you spend all of your time putting out fires, you will never get around to those things that are simply smoldering until it is too late. The good news is that in the time it takes to watch a movie, you could have the professional help you need to create a customized estate plan. That's it! Your estate plan can be in place in just a couple of meetings. We all have the same number of hours in a week. Invest a couple of these hours into creating your plan—it is time well spent.

10. **I don't want my kids to be spoiled.** This is a real concern for many parents. "I worked hard for my money," they say, "and I want my

children to work hard, too." Warren Buffett summed it up nicely when he said, "I want to leave my children enough so they can do anything, but not so much that they can do nothing." This is a common concern among families with wealth. Like my friend from high school I previously mentioned, money—in amounts both small and large—can de-motivate.

If you're putting off your estate plan because you don't want your kids to get too much too soon, the only solution to your problem is to create your own plan. As explained above, if you use the default state plan, your kids could receive 100 percent of their inheritance as soon as they turn eighteen! If you'd prefer for your children to be older when they get their inheritance, to donate part of your estate to church or charity, or to fund your grandchildren's education, you must design your own plan.

Are you convinced that you need an estate plan? If you're hesitating, what's holding you back? Is it the time, the cost, or something else? Does it feel overwhelming? Try breaking your estate planning goals into smaller tasks, such as researching estate planning attorneys, calling three attorneys, and scheduling an appointment. Estate planning doesn't need to be overwhelming if you break it into manageable tasks.

The Essentials

When I turned seventeen, I was finally able to drive by myself. In the years preceding this monumental event, my stepdad diligently and patiently tried to turn me into an auto mechanic. He had me under the car, under the hood, and just about everywhere else in the car. He even gave me a toolbox full of screwdrivers, wrenches, sockets, and a bunch of other things as a Christmas present.

Unfortunately, unlike him, I'm not mechanically gifted. It was a strain to learn even the most basic elements of auto repair. So, when the time came for me to drive off alone for the first time, my stepdad took me aside and re-explained the tools and other car repair accessories he had loaded in my trunk.

When he was done explaining, I looked at him and said, "All this stuff is nice, but what do I really need to have with me?" He began to explain again when—impatient at seventeen—I cut him off and asked him, "If you could only bring four things, what would they be?" He told me I absolutely had to have jumper cables, a gas can, a wrench set, and a screwdriver set. I took everything else out and have always kept those four things in my car.[2]

The following are the absolutely essential tools you need in your estate plan toolbox.

Will

WHAT IS IT?

After you pass away, the courts must determine the distribution of your assets. A Will is a legal document that expresses how your assets should be distributed at death. Remember, each state has a predetermined plan for your assets that it will use unless you provide other instructions. A Will does just that. A Will tells the state that you have a better plan for the distribution of your assets and that it needs to distribute your assets according to your plan.

The Will is also the document in which parents can name a guardian for their children. The importance of this aspect of a Will cannot be overemphasized. If you pass away and your children do not have a living parent, the state decides who is responsible for raising your children. Your children may be sent to a relative who you might not think is ideal for this job. If you don't have a Will naming a guardian, this could easily happen.

WHO NEEDS IT?

If you're reading this book, you need a Will. The need for a Will is universal. Any adult with any assets at all, a spouse, or children needs a Will.

How long would you prepare if you knew you were going to be on business in China and unavailable for six months? If you're a single parent, would you get a nanny or find a relative who could take care of your child? Would you make a list of the bills that need to be paid? Would you make sure there was enough money for your family to survive in your absence? At the very least, there would be twenty or thirty things you would do to prepare your family for your six-month extended absence. If you would take the time and energy to prepare so extensively for a trip, why not prepare and protect your family for the most extended absence of all? Even if you're single, childless, and have no living relatives, you still need a Will! A Will helps you ensure your impact on the world around you will continue after you're gone.

---

2. I have, in fact, used the gas can and jumper cables on several occasions!

If you already have a Will, congratulations! Remember, a Will isn't something you do and then forget about. As things in your life change, your Will may also need to change. There are several situations that should cause you to review and possibly update your Will:

- **Change in asset values.** If the value of the assets in your Will has increased significantly, you will want to review the Will and make any necessary changes.

- **Family changes.** Review and update your Will to reflect family marriages, separations, divorces, births, adoptions, or deaths.

- **Move to another state.** Since state laws can vary considerably, you should review and update your Will if you become a resident of a different state.

- **Regulatory changes.** In the last few years, federal tax laws have changed in ways that can impact an estate. Always review your Will after state or federal tax law changes to keep the language and provisions in step with current legislation.

- **Personal changes.** If the named executor of your Will—the person responsible for managing the process of distributing your assets—or the guardian you chose for your children can no longer serve in that role, you should find someone who can and update your Will accordingly.

Luckily, changing a Will is pretty straightforward. You often need only use a codicil—or amendment—to the existing Will. Only if your life changes dramatically would you want to revoke your existing Will and start from scratch.

HOW MUCH SHOULD IT COST?
Some states, such as California, have fill-in-the-blank Will forms. If you are single with modest assets and no children, this should be just fine for you. If your state doesn't offer this, you can get by with a packaged software program to help you create your Will. Otherwise, I suggest using an estate-planning attorney (more on estate planning attorneys later in the chapter). A Will should cost somewhere between $250 and $750.

Power of attorney

WHAT IS IT?

This sounds much more complicated than it is. A power of attorney (POA) is a legal document that allows one person to act on behalf of another. The person setting up the POA is called *the principal* and the person given the power to act is called *the attorney-in-fact*. The scope of the attorney-in-fact can be limited to a single act or can be broad. For example, I can create a POA that allows my neighbor to pay my cable TV bill (limited scope) or that gives my neighbor all my legal power (broad scope).

There are four types of POA and each has its own purpose.

1. General POA.

A General POA grants certain rights—as limited or as broad as you wish—to individuals that enable them to act on your behalf. The General POA is valid and enforceable until any one of the following four things occurs:

1. The attorney-in-fact dies.

2. The principal revokes the POA.

3. The principal dies.

4. The principal becomes disabled or incapacitated.

Brett is going on a six-month sabbatical and has decided to earn a little extra money by renting his house. He needs someone to supervise the renters, deposit rental checks, and have the ability to initiate an eviction if necessary. In this situation, he can draft a General POA that gives Dave, his friend and neighbor, the power to deposit checks into his bank account and initiate an eviction. This legal document would allow Dave, his attorney-in-fact, to perform these actions for Brett. Once Brett returns from his sabbatical, he can easily revoke the General POA.

2. Durable POA.

At this point you may be wondering why a POA is so important. Perhaps you are saying, "I don't rent my house and I'm not going on a sabbatical." While you may not be in a situation where you need a General POA, you will probably need a Durable POA. The word "durable" means long-lasting and able to withstand wear. Unlike a General POA, which voids when the principal becomes disabled or incapacitated, a Durable POA does not terminate when the principal becomes disabled or incapacitated; it survives the disability.

Frank just turned seventy-six. His wife, Edith, always handled the household accounts—Frank has never had a head for figures. Although he's otherwise physically and mentally as fit as a fiddle, since she passed away five years ago he's had difficulty keeping track of bills and managing the money in his retirement plans. Frank creates a Durable POA that grants his daughter Lori the power to write checks from his bank account, deposit funds into his checking account, and buy or sell investments in his retirement plans.

3. Springing POA.

When you create a General or Durable POA, it becomes enforceable immediately. In other words, if you sign a General or Durable POA today that gives your best friend the ability to write checks from your bank account, your friend can immediately begin writing checks from your account. If your goal is to give your friend the ability to pay your bills if you become incapacitated, do you really want to grant him this power before you become incapacitated?

In this situation, you need a Springing Durable POA. A Springing POA "springs" into existence only after a specified event occurs. You choose the triggering event; it can be almost anything but most people choose disability or incapacitation as their trigger.

Ross trusts his friend Luis but decides that the only time he wants Luis to write checks from his account is if he is physically unable to do so. To do this, Ross creates a Springing POA that does not go into effect until he becomes incapacitated. As long as Ross is in good health, his friend can't write checks from his account. If Ross becomes incapacitated, the POA springs into effect—and gives Luis the power to write checks from his account.

4. Health Care POA

The Health Care POA is different from the other POAs in that the other POAs tend to focus on the management of property and the Health Care

POA grants the attorney-in-fact the ability to make health care decisions on behalf of the principal if he is legally incompetent.

Like the other POAs, the Health Care POA specifically addresses the decisions the attorney-in-fact can make for the principal—usually the decisions are related to medical treatment, medication, hospital discharge, blood transfusions, etc. State laws vary considerably in how much decision-making power you can grant in the POA.

Don't confuse a Living Will with a Health Care POA. A Living Will is a document that focuses exclusively on the extent that the attorney-in-fact can terminate treatment and/or life support. Regardless of your view on how much and what type of life-sustaining support you want, your wishes on this subject should be recorded. You still need to have a Health Care POA in place to name an attorney-in-fact who can make other medically related decisions on your behalf.

Bill creates a Health Care POA that grants his spouse or—if she is unable to do so—his sister the power to make all medically related decisions on his behalf. In the Health Care POA, he also has specified his wishes regarding life support.

WHO NEEDS IT?

A General POA is typically used to grant someone a specific power—such as cashing checks or buying and selling investments—or a broader power for a limited period of time.

The General POA can be extremely helpful if you are out of town or busy, but it is not an essential document. A Durable POA, however, is absolutely essential. The world doesn't stop when you become incapacitated: you still have a mortgage, credit card bills, and property taxes. If you're not able to pay these bills, who will? After reading Chapter 7, hopefully you have a disability policy that provides you with an income. Even with ample money available, someone must have the ability to write checks against your account.

If you're single, you will definitely need someone to manage your affairs if you become disabled and incapacitated. A Durable POA will give that person the ability to help you in a time when you can't help yourself. Marriage doesn't let you off the hook; depending on your state of residence, there are some transactions that require signatures from both spouses. Don't leave your spouse powerless at a time when she needs as many resources as possible.

Older individuals and those prone to incapacity (e.g., history of strokes or Alzheimer's in the family) must also have a Durable POA.

The only question is whether to have a Durable POA or a Springing POA. Remember, a Durable POA gives the attorney-in-fact the power to act on your behalf immediately, whereas the Springing POA is only effective if you become incapacitated. A few states still do not recognize a Springing POA, so in those states the only solution is a Durable POA. If your state allows a Springing POA, it can make more sense to choose it over a Durable POA.

A Health Care POA should also be part of your estate toolbox. It requires you to answer some tough questions and to get clear on sensitive subjects. If you don't answer these questions now, you might force loved ones to answer them for you. They will not be sure they are making the decision you would have chosen and their doubts may haunt them for the rest of their lives.

In short, everyone should have a POA. Whether you're married, single, with children or without, young, or old, you need a legal document that gives someone you trust the power to take care of you and your affairs. Incapacity is difficult enough for your loved ones—make it easy for them to help you.

With any type of POA, make sure you absolutely trust the individual you name your attorney-in-fact since he or she will be acting on your behalf. Depending on the powers you list in the POA, this person may have access to your bank and investment accounts and may be able to make life-and-death decisions for you.

Giving one person the legal authority to act on your behalf on all matters is not always prudent. We diversify investments to mitigate and spread risk and sometimes it is also smart to diversify among several attorneys-in-fact to mitigate risk. For example, if you create a POA in the event that you become incapacitated, you might grant a friend with a strong finance background the ability to deposit checks and to make buy or sell decisions within your investment accounts. You could then grant your brother the power to write checks from your bank account and to transfer funds from your investment accounts to your bank account. In doing so, you maximize the financial education and experience of your friend but avoid giving her carte blanche.

Married couples often, and understandably so, name each other as their attorney-in-fact. While this is normally the smart decision, it's not good enough on its own. If both you and your spouse become incapacitated in an auto accident, your POA will not be enforceable. It is critically important to name successor attorneys-in-fact if the primary attorney-in-fact (e.g., your spouse) is unable to perform the task.

One of the drawbacks with a Springing POA is first defining the springing trigger and then determining if it has occurred. The named trigger is typically disability and incapacity but these two terms alone are not precise enough for a POA. Have an estate attorney with experience drafting POAs help you write the language to avoid any ambiguity in the definition of your activating trigger.

As with any estate planning document, make sure you review it regularly—at least annually and immediately following a major life change or transition. Select one day a year to review all of your estate documents and put it on your calendar—then keep the appointment.

HOW MUCH SHOULD IT COST?

Use an estate planning attorney to draft a POA. This is especially true if you are creating a Durable or Springing POA. The language must be worded precisely; otherwise, the document may not have the necessary legal authority when you need it. Depending on the type of POA you require, drafting it should cost somewhere between $250 and $750.

What About More Advanced Estate Planning Strategies?

Nearly everyone needs the essential estate documents described above, but there are also more advanced strategies that can save hundreds of thousands of dollars in estate taxes including living trusts, bypass trusts, family limited partnerships, irrevocable life insurance trusts, and others. If you are interested in learning about these specialized estate solutions, go to www.SixDayFinancialMakeover.com.

Optional Estate-Planning Documents

Optional estate-planning documents are generally not legally binding documents. Their purpose has little or nothing to do with the transfer of assets and does not affect estate tax. Optional estate documents focus on values, lessons, and legacy issues. Not everyone wants to think about these issues since they can be much more emotional than the financial issues discussed in this chapter.

1. **Organ donor.** You are probably familiar with the organ donor program in which you place a "donor" sticker on your driver's license. These are well-intentioned programs but there are inconsistencies among various jurisdictions and potential problems in revoking gifts made this way. To avoid these problems, every state has enacted the Uniform Anatomical Gifts Act (UAGA). If you have strong feelings about being a donor or not being a donor, you should write your wishes in a separate document or you can even include it as part of your Will. Either way, don't force your loved ones to make this decision for you.

2. **"What I want you to know."** This is simply a letter that you write to your loved ones about what they've meant to you, what you learned from them, what you want them to learn from your experiences, or anything else you want them to know. This can be a great way to impart your values to your loved ones. What can be difficult to express out loud can be surprisingly easy on paper. You can have one letter for everyone or you can write separate letters. How you format it is entirely up to you. Be sure to mention this letter or letters in your Will so they can be given to the appropriate people.

3. **Autobiography.** Some people find great joy in writing an autobiography. Your autobiography can be a handful of pages or it can be a fifty-page document. It can be an incredible experience to learn about a loved one's trials, tribulations, successes, and fears. If the idea of writing your life story doesn't excite you or you want something a little different, you can hire a company to help you create a video biography. There are many firms that will take you

step by step through the entire process—helping you decide on the purpose of the video, conducting the interviews, shooting and editing the video, and transferring it to DVD/VHS. Most people who go through this process find it to be an incredible experience.

Where to Get Started

The decisions you choose to make and those you ignore or overlook for your estate plan will have long-lasting and permanent ramifications. Don't let the significance of estate planning prevent you from getting started. Would you fail to jump to action if you saw a friend choking because of the long-lasting ramifications of helping him? Of course not! You'd immediately do whatever you could to help. When it comes to your estate plan, just jump in and get started. The details will work themselves out with time and with the help of an experienced estate attorney.

There are many sources—software packages, trust "factories," insurance brokers—that offer "estate planning." This section will discuss the disadvantages to using these sources over an experienced estate attorney.

1. **Computer software.** There are numerous software programs that advertise they can help you create a Will, living trusts, POAs, and other estate planning documents "from the privacy of your own home." They claim that—for $29.95 or less—you can download a program and within a few minutes have an entire estate plan. Unless you have very few assets and no children, I would not recommend using software programs to create your Will and would never recommend its use to create POAs or living trusts.

   Your estate plan is too important to leave to a piece of software. According to the manufacturer of one such program, "This software is not a substitute for the advice of an attorney. Negotiating or drafting legal documents yourself could save you money on attorney fees, but may also expose you to risks. The facts of your personal situation along with your state's specific laws and changes in the law that may have occurred after the production of this software make it advisable to consult an attorney before finalizing any legal documents." I couldn't have said it better myself.

2. **Trust "factories."** Trust factories are pretty easy to spot. You'll often see them advertise free estate-planning seminars on late-night television or in local newspapers. They talk up the benefits of living trusts and explain how you can save thousands of dollars. These seminars are nothing more than sales pitches for their living trusts. For a couple hundred dollars, they claim to create a "customized" estate plan for you. Unfortunately, their estate plans are cookie-cutter documents with nothing but general boilerplate language. It can be very tempting to consider an inexpensive service like this but remember, the goal is not to save as much money as possible in creating the plan. It is to have a solid estate plan that meets your needs when the time comes. If you're incapacitated in the hospital, would you rather have a boilerplate POA that is written in generalities or one that was crafted specifically for your needs and the laws in your state?

3. **Insurance brokers.** Insurance brokers sell an extremely valuable product. There is nothing inherently wrong with them or the products they provide but, just as you wouldn't ask a Chevy salesperson for advice on a Ford, you shouldn't go to an insurance broker for estate planning. To try to avoid the "life insurance salesman" stigma, many insurance brokers are calling themselves "estate planners" or telling people that they provide "estate-planning strategies." Regardless of their new title, insurance brokers view the world through life insurance–tinted glasses. If they sell life insurance, feel free to go to them to buy life insurance but do not use them to plan your estate.

If you are serious about providing for your loved ones, only work with an experienced attorney who specializes in estate planning. Would you go to a general practitioner for heart surgery? Of course not! You'd choose the best heart surgeon you could find and afford. You'd want someone who eats, breathes, and lives heart surgery, not someone who performs heart surgeries, mends broken bones, and removes tonsils. This is obvious when it comes to health care, but it isn't as obvious when it comes to law.

There are a lot of general practitioner attorneys who will draft an estate plan just as quick as they will help you fight a traffic ticket or sue your neighbor. Do yourself and your loved ones a favor by hiring an attorney who specializes in estate planning (sometimes called a "trusts and estates attorney") to help you with your estate documents.

Action Steps

I think we all agree there are more fun and uplifting things to think about than death and estate planning. That's why I want you to get through this chapter as quickly as possible so you can get back to living your life. Before you move on and start Day 6, let's make sure you've done everything you can for your family and loved ones.

Go through the Action Steps below and put a check mark in one of the following boxes for each one.

What's the Purpose of Estate Planning?

1. ☐ COMPLETED   ☐ NEED TO COMPLETE   ☐ DOES NOT APPLY

Identifying your purpose for beginning your estate plan is the antidote to inertia. Get clear on why you want an estate plan and how one can help you and your loved ones. For each of the three most common reasons for estate planning, answer the following questions:

How will an estate plan provide for your loved ones?

How will an estate plan help you achieve your goals?

How will an estate plan help you?

2. ☐ COMPLETED   ☐ NEED TO COMPLETE   ☐ DOES NOT APPLY

Identify the reasons stopping you from starting or completing your estate plan. Did you relate to any of "The Top Ten Excuses People Use to Avoid Creating an Estate Plan"? If you did, reread those sections and address your reason.

The Essentials—Will

Don't Currently Have a Will?

1. ☐ COMPLETED   ☐ NEED TO COMPLETE   ☐ DOES NOT APPLY

If you are single, have few assets, don't care where your assets go when you pass away, and have no children, you don't need a Will.

2. ☐ COMPLETED   ☐ NEED TO COMPLETE   ☐ DOES NOT APPLY

If you are married, have a modest estate, would like to direct where your assets go when you pass away, or have children—you need a Will. Find an experienced estate attorney to help you draft a Will. It won't cost much and the peace of mind that comes from knowing you are protecting your family will be worth it.

Currently Have a Will?

3. ☐ COMPLETED   ☐ NEED TO COMPLETE   ☐ DOES NOT APPLY

Review and update your Will and other estate plan documents with an estate attorney annually or immediately following major events.

Have you moved to another state?

Has the value of your assets changed?

Have you had children or do you have new grandchildren?

Have you or any of your beneficiaries married, divorced, or separated?

Has anyone in your family passed away?

Are there any legal or tax changes?

Do you have any personal changes to make to your Will—such as wanting to name a new executor or guardian?

The Essentials—Power of Attorney (POA)

Don't Currently Have a POA?

1. ☐ COMPLETED   ☐ NEED TO COMPLETE   ☐ DOES NOT APPLY

Hire an estate attorney to create a POA for financial management and health care. Your attorney can help you determine what type of POA is best for your situation.

Currently Have a POA?

1. ☐ COMPLETED   ☐ NEED TO COMPLETE   ☐ DOES NOT APPLY

Unless you created a POA recently with a good estate attorney, I would recommend that you have it reviewed. There are many different types for different purposes. You might think you're protected by your current POA, but it might not be right for your situation. In any case, you must make sure you have a financial POA and a Health Care POA, either as separate documents or as part of one document.

Optional Estate Planning Documents

1. ☐ COMPLETED   ☐ NEED TO COMPLETE   ☐ DOES NOT APPLY

   Consider creating an organ donor document under the Uniform Anatomical Gifts Act if you have strong feelings either way about donating your organs.

2. ☐ COMPLETED   ☐ NEED TO COMPLETE   ☐ DOES NOT APPLY

   Consider writing a "What I want you to know" letter or autobiography. If you are uncomfortable writing but are committed to the concept, hire a company to create a video biography.

Update Your Online Financial Makeover Account

1. ☐ COMPLETED   ☐ NEED TO COMPLETE   ☐ DOES NOT APPLY

   Before you do anything else, update your Six-Day Financial Makeover account at www.SixDayFinancialMakeover.com.

CHAPTER 10

Protect Your Assets

Hardworking people fall victim to costly lawsuits every year, often losing hundreds of thousands of dollars. A large court judgment works as a "reverse" lottery. In an instant, your way of life can change dramatically. Everything you've worked for—your house, your car, and your investment accounts—disappear. Protecting your assets against this type of loss is more important now than ever before.

If you are serious about protecting your financial and physical assets, you must read this chapter. It will provide you with a clear understanding of personal liability insurance, as well as home safes and safe-deposit boxes.

Should I read this chapter?

	TRUE	FALSE
1. I've never considered protecting my assets.	☐	☐
2. Asset protection is just for the ultra-wealthy.	☐	☐
3. I don't currently have an umbrella liability insurance policy or am not sure if I have enough coverage.	☐	☐
4. I'd like to learn when home safes and safe-deposit boxes are appropriate and where I should store my documents.	☐	☐
5. I'd like to learn why asset protection is important.	☐	☐

If you answered any of these questions TRUE, you should read this chapter.

Chapter Toolbar

Cost to Implement Advice	Likelihood of Needing Strategies in Chapter	Need Professional Advice?	Website Tools
$250	1 2 3 4 5 6 7 8 9 10 Not Likely Very Likely	♀ ♀ ♀ ♀ ♀ No Definitely	No

---

You need to protect your assets. You may be thinking that "asset protection" is something only the Beverly Hills crowd needs. It's true that there are a lot of fancy asset protection techniques such as offshore trusts and Swiss bank accounts, but there are also a couple of really simple techniques everyone should do to protect their assets from both men in suits (lawsuits) and men in masks (burglars).

Even if (and maybe even especially if) you don't have many assets to protect, one of your primary objectives should be to protect what you've worked so hard to achieve. You've put a lot of work into your financial makeover, but regardless of how much you save or how you invest, it is worthless if it is taken from you. Every day you go without protecting your house, car, checking account, and investment accounts is one more day you are jeopardizing everything you've worked so hard to achieve.

Protecting Your Assets from Lawsuits

The frequency of lawsuits is shocking, but despite the numbers, no one believes it will happen to them. Too many people use our legal system as their personal lottery. Frivolous lawsuits are not just a problem for big corporations or the rich. They affect people from all walks of life. With a baseless claim and a contingency attorney, anyone can sue you.

The purpose of protecting your assets from frivolous lawsuits is to safe-guard what you've worked your whole life to achieve. It is not meant to defraud creditors or shield your money from illegal activities. Just as it is someone's legal right to sue, it is your legal right to protect what you have from the countless lawsuits disrupting the lives of so many. Protecting your assets using liability insurance is entirely legal, ethical, and even affordable.

Umbrella Liability Insurance

The best way to protect your assets is to avoid a lawsuit, but because we live in a society where you can be sued by anyone for anything, the next best thing is to have someone else pay for your defense and, if needed, the judgment. Where can you find someone who will do this for you? The an-swer is a personal liability insurance policy and it's easier than you might think to get this protection.

A personal liability policy is designed to protect you against judgments from property damage, bodily injury, and personal injury lawsuits. The per-sonal liability policy is sometimes called an "umbrella" liability policy be-cause it sits on top of your automobile and homeowner's insurance policy and covers claims that are either not covered by these policies or that are beyond the limits of these policies.

Here's an example. Amy has a holiday party at her house. One of the guests slips on a patch of ice on Amy's driveway and breaks her hip. The guest sues Amy for $1.2 million and wins.

WITHOUT A PERSONAL LIABILITY POLICY

$1,200,000	Amount of judgment Amy owes
-$ 300,000	Homeowner's insurance liability limit
-$ 0	Amount of umbrella liability coverage
$ 900,000	Amount of judgment Amy still owes
$ 400,000	Amy's house
-$ 275,000	Amy's investment and bank accounts
$ 225,000	Amount Amy *still* owes after selling everything she owns

WITH A $1 MILLION PERSONAL LIABILITY POLICY

$1,200,000   Amount of judgment Amy owes

−$ 300,000   Homeowner's insurance liability limit

−$1,000,000   Amount of umbrella liability coverage

$ 0   Amount of judgment Amy owes

In the first example, where Amy doesn't have an umbrella liability policy, her homeowner's liability policy paid the maximum and Amy was responsible for paying all amounts above the limit—in this case, $900,000. A lifetime of hard work, saving, and responsible investing was gone in the two seconds it took her guest to slip on a patch of ice.

In the second example, Amy was smart enough to have a $1 million umbrella liability policy. In this case, her homeowner's policy paid up to its limit and then the umbrella liability policy came into action and paid up to its limit. As a result, Amy's assets were safe from this judgment.

What to know before you buy a personal liability policy

A personal liability policy is pretty straightforward, but you should be aware of a few issues:

- **Primary insurance underlying limits.** It is important to remember that a personal liability or umbrella policy requires underlying liability limits on your primary automobile and homeowner insurance policies. Make sure you know what limits are needed and if your homeowner and automobile coverage limits are sufficient. For example, if your automobile policy has a $300,000 limit and your umbrella policy begins coverage at $500,000, there is a gap of $200,000 that neither policy covers; you will be responsible for paying this amount if there is a judgment. The easiest solution is to increase the limits on your automobile and homeowner policy to eliminate the gap.

- **Typical coverage.** Most umbrella liability policies provide coverage for one home and two automobiles only. If you have multiple residences, more than two automobiles, watercraft, etc., make sure they are listed under the umbrella policy.

- **Defense costs.** The good news is that defense costs are usually covered by umbrella policies; the bad news is that this coverage may be included in the limit of the policy. For example, if you have a $1 million umbrella policy but your defense costs $350,000, you will only have $650,000 remaining if you lose the lawsuit. If your policy includes defense costs within its limit, consider purchasing a higher liability limit.

How much umbrella liability insurance is necessary?

Umbrella liability insurance starts at $1 million in coverage and goes up from there. This limit meets most people's need and shouldn't cost more than a few hundred dollars a year. If your net worth is greater than $1 million, I would recommend obtaining an umbrella policy that at least matches your net worth. For example, if your net worth is $2.5 million, I would recommend a $3 million umbrella policy.

There are special situations in which you should consider purchasing more coverage:

- **Appreciating assets.** If you have rapidly appreciating assets, get enough coverage to protect the future growth of the assets.

- **Teenagers.** Teenagers can put a family's assets at risk, especially if they drive. Your assets are in jeopardy against lawsuits that result from your children's behavior.

- **High-risk activities.** If you entertain often, serve alcohol, drive carelessly, host events at your home, or conduct other similar activities that increase your chances for a lawsuit, consider purchasing more insurance.

Bodily injury and personal injury lawsuits frequently result in multi-million-dollar settlements. Umbrella liability insurance is an inexpensive way to safeguard what you've worked so hard to achieve.

Protect Your Assets from Burglars and Fire

The threat of a home burglary or fire is real. Home safes and safe-deposit boxes should be a part of your financial makeover. It's not enough to dream big, save, invest, and have insurance. You need to protect your valuables, too. Not all safes provide the same quality of protection. This section demystifies home safes and provides concrete advice on which documents you should keep at home and which documents you should keep in a bank's safe-deposit box.

I have personally experienced loss from both fire and burglary. Both occurred when I was young, but I remember it like it was yesterday. The total financial loss to my family (after insurance proceeds) was minimal, but the emotional loss was great. A check from your insurance company can't replace sentimental items.

The two most common and practical ways to protect your documents are a safe-deposit box and a home safe. Professional document and property storage companies will keep your documents safe, but for the majority of people, a safe-deposit box and a home safe are sufficient.

Home safes

A residential fire occurs every seventy-nine seconds[1] and more than four million homes are burglarized each year in the United States.[2] The threat is real—six billion in assets are lost each year to fire. Your asset protection plan needs to guard against the threat of aggressive lawyers as well as physical threats such as fire and theft. Protecting against physical danger is simple and the losses are avoidable with an appropriate home safe.

This section will address the various types of home safes, which type you need for your situation, what the ratings mean and the minimum rating required, and what should and shouldn't be stored in a home safe.

There are fire safes and there are burglar safes. There are also fire/burglar safes. A fire safe offers little protection against burglary. Conversely, a burglar safe provides little protection from a fire. To fully protect the contents of a safe, you must make sure the safe is rated for superior protection against both fire and burglars.

The safe's rating is very important. It must be "UL" rated. The UL is Underwriters Laboratories, a not-for-profit product safety testing and certification

---

1. Michael J. Karter Jr., "Fire Loss in the United States During 2002," National Fire Protection Association, September 2003. www.nfpa.org/assets/files/pdf/osfireloss02.pdf (accessed May 12, 2005).

2. Patsy Klaus and Cathy Maston, "National Criminal Victimization Survey, 2003," Bureau of Justice Statistics, June 1, 2005. www.ojp.usdoj.gov/bjs/pub/sheets/cvus/2003/cv0384.csv (accessed May 25, 2006).

organization established in 1894. They have the "undisputed reputation as the leader in U.S. product safety and certification." Many products attempt to suggest UL certification without actually earning the UL stamp of approval. Be aware of claims like "built to UL standards" or "materials comply with UL standards." This doesn't mean the safe is UL approved. To ensure your safe offers the maximum protection available buy only UL-rated safes.

Underwriters Laboratories provides ratings for the following two characteristics:

1. **Fire Resistance**—This rating includes two numbers such as UL *350-1*.
   The first number is a measure of the maximum temperature the inside of the safe will reach. For example, a rating of 350 means that the inside of the safe will not reach a temperature over 350 degrees.
   The second number represents the amount of time the safe will not exceed the temperature rating. For example, a rating of 1 means the safe is protected at the stated temperature for at least one hour. A safe rated UL 150-2 means the inside of the safe will not exceed 150 degrees for at least two hours.

2. **Burglary Resistance**—There is only one number for this measurement. Underwriters Laboratories uses the initials "TL" to denote burglary and tamper resistance. The TL will be followed by a number. The number represents the minutes the safe can withstand someone trying to break into it using a variety of tools such as a hammer, chisel, high-speed drill, saw, or diamond grinding wheel.
   For example, a safe rated TL 30 means the safe is protected from a variety of tools for at least 30 minutes.

An adequate home safe that protects against fires and theft will have a UL 350-1 TL-30 rating or better.

WHAT SHOULD BE STORED IN A HOME SAFE

While a top UL-rated safe installed properly in your home is not a guarantee against fire or burglary, it is a very important step forward. Having taken that step, you can feel reasonably confident in storing the following approved items in your home safe:

- Cash
- Wills

- Trust documents

- Powers of attorney

- Real estate deeds

- Jewelry

- Stock and bond certificates

- Video inventory (copy)

- Firearms

- Precious metals

- Asset inventory (copy)

- Important documents (tax returns, insurance policies, birth/marriage certificates)

Safe-deposit boxes

Having a good home safe shouldn't stop you from having a safe-deposit box at your bank. There are many advantages to having both. Some documents should be stored at home and others are better kept within a bank's vault.

Safe-deposit boxes come in a variety of sizes and are an inexpensive way to protect certain documents and property. Each safe-deposit box has two separate locks. You receive a key to open one lock and the bank keeps a key for the other lock. Both keys are required to open the box. You specify who has authorization to access your box, and then it is the bank's responsibility to monitor and control access to only those who are approved.

ADVANTAGES

- **Protection**—Bank safes provide superior fire and theft protection.

- **Monitoring**—Most banks are under twenty-four-hour surveillance.

- **Control**—The bank controls who can access the safe.

- **Some Privacy**—The bank doesn't know the contents of your box.

DISADVANTAGES

- **Inaccessible**—You can only access the contents in your box during regular bank business hours. You will be unable to reach the contents in your box after hours or on bank holidays. Do not keep anything in your safe-deposit box that you may need immediately.

- **Sealed at Death**—Most banks don't seal boxes at death anymore, but they can still make it very difficult for you to get access to a box upon the death of the owner. Inflexible bank rules can make a time of grief even more difficult.

- **Inconvenient**—A home safe can be accessed in seconds. A safe-deposit box requires planning and a special trip. Store documents and jewelry that you use often in your home safe.

- **No Insurance**—Most banks do not hold insurance for the contents of safe-deposit boxes.

- **No Creditor Protection**—A safe-deposit box provides no asset protection in the case of a lawsuit judgment or if you need to pay back taxes. In those cases, other individuals will have access to the contents of your box.

The following documents can be stored in a safe-deposit box:

- Cash

- Wills (copy)

- Trust documents (copy)

- Powers of attorney (copy)

- Real estate deeds (copy)

- Jewelry

- Stock and bond certificates

- Video inventory (copy)

- Precious metals

- Asset inventory (copy)

- Important documents (tax returns, insurance policies, birth/ marriage certificates)

You've come this far in your financial transformation, so don't stop now. Invest in a home safe and a safe-deposit box. Go down the list of Action Steps below—you'll be glad you did.

Action Steps

One of the things I love most about computers is the "undo" function. You can really screw up a document or spreadsheet, but with a click of a button, it's back to the way you started. When it comes to protecting your valuables, you don't get to hit an "undo" button. The threat of getting sued is absolutely real. A burglary or fire can happen tonight. You can't wait until you get sued or burglarized to start protecting yourself—it will be too late.

Go through the Action Steps below and put a check mark in one of the following boxes for each one.

Umbrella Liability Policy

1. ☐ COMPLETED   ☐ NEED TO COMPLETE   ☐ DOES NOT APPLY

Call the insurance company that provides your automobile and home-owner's insurance. It is best to buy an umbrella policy from the same company that provides your automobile and homeowner's coverage—otherwise multiple insurance companies may argue about who should pay a claim. If one company covers everything, there won't be a dispute about who should pay. Ask them what liability limits are currently on your automobile and homeowner's policy.

2. ☐ COMPLETED   ☐ NEED TO COMPLETE   ☐ DOES NOT APPLY

Tell them you are interested in obtaining an umbrella liability policy. Ask them if the defense costs are included in the policy limits. It is okay if they are, you just need to know so you can determine the appropriate amount of insurance you need. Ask them for a quote on an umbrella liability policy with a limit of at least your net worth ($1 million liability limit is the minimum). Consider a higher limit if you are in a high-risk category.

3. ☐ COMPLETED   ☐ NEED TO COMPLETE   ☐ DOES NOT APPLY

Ask them how much it will cost to increase your automobile and home-owner's insurance liability limits so there is no gap in liability coverage. The total cost of the umbrella policy is the cost to raise your limits on your automobile and homeowner's policy plus the actual cost of the umbrella policy.

4. ☐ COMPLETED   ☐ NEED TO COMPLETE   ☐ DOES NOT APPLY

Increase your automobile and homeowner's limits (if necessary) and purchase the umbrella policy.

5. ☐ COMPLETED   ☐ NEED TO COMPLETE   ☐ DOES NOT APPLY

Specifically add extra vehicles, homes, watercraft, etc. to the policy if not already covered.

Home Safes

1. ☐ COMPLETED   ☐ NEED TO COMPLETE   ☐ DOES NOT APPLY

Purchase a fire- and burglar-resistant home safe. The safe must have a UL rating. A safe "built to UL standards" is not UL rated.

    If you are only storing paper documents, jewelry, or other physical assets, a safe rated UL 350-1 or 350-2 should be sufficient. If you are safe-guarding media such as floppy disks or tape backup, you will need a UL rating of 150-1 or 150-2.

    The safe must be burglar resistant. Get a TL rating of at least 15 and possibly 30. If the contents of the safe will exceed $100,000, consider a torch-resistant safe.

2. ☐ COMPLETED   ☐ NEED TO COMPLETE   ☐ DOES NOT APPLY

Keep these documents in your home safe:
    Cash
    Wills
    Trust documents
    Powers of attorney
    Real estate deeds

Jewelry
Stock and bond certificates
Video inventory (copy)
Firearms
Precious metals
Asset inventory (copy)
Important documents (tax returns, insurance policies,
   birth/marriage certificates)

Safe-Deposit Boxes

1. ☐ COMPLETED   ☐ NEED TO COMPLETE   ☐ DOES NOT APPLY

   Rent a safe-deposit box from a bank.

2. ☐ COMPLETED   ☐ NEED TO COMPLETE   ☐ DOES NOT APPLY

   Store these items in your safe-deposit box:
   Cash
   Wills (copy)
   Trust documents (copy)
   Powers of attorney (copy)
   Real estate deeds (copy)
   Jewelry
   Stock and bond certificates
   Video inventory (copy)
   Precious metals
   Asset inventory (copy)
   Important documents (tax returns, insurance policies,
      birth/marriage certificates)
   Reminder: Do not store items you may need to access immediately in a
safe-deposit box.

Update Your Online Financial Makeover Account

1. ☐ COMPLETED   ☐ NEED TO COMPLETE   ☐ DOES NOT APPLY

   Before you do anything else, update your Six-Day Financial Makeover
   account at www.SixDayFinancialMakeover.com.

PROTECT WHAT YOU'VE EARNED

CHAPTER 11

Protect Your Identity

The FBI lists identity theft as one of the fastest growing crimes in the United States. Over 10 million Americans will be victims this year alone and criminals are getting more sophisticated in their attempts to strip you of vital personal information. Their success can mean hundreds of lost hours, thousands of wasted dollars, and a scarred credit report for you.

Protecting your identity is just as important in your financial make-over as setting goals, saving, and investing. So far you've protected against accidents, sickness, disability, death, lawsuits, fire, and burglary. Finish your financial transformation by protecting your identity. In this chapter you will learn how identity thieves get your information and how you can protect yourself.

Should I read this chapter?

	TRUE	FALSE
1. I value having good credit.	☐	☐
2. I don't have a secure mailbox.	☐	☐
3. I usually throw away credit card offers and other junk mail.	☐	☐
4. I've never thought much about identity theft.	☐	☐

TRUE   FALSE

5. I'd like to learn how thieves steal identities and
    how I can protect myself.   ☐   ☐

If you answered any of these questions TRUE, you should read this chapter.

Chapter Toolbar			
Cost to Implement Advice	**Likelihood of Needing Strategies in Chapter**	**Need Professional Advice?**	**Website Tools**
$50–$200	1 2 3 4 5 6 7 8 9 10 Not Likely Very Likely	↑ ↑ ↑ ↑ ↑ ↑ No Definitely	Yes

Are you worried about identity theft? Most Americans are. Identity theft is the number one concern among consumers who contact the Federal Trade Commission.[1] Forty-two percent of all complaints to the FTC are regarding identity theft.[2] The fear is justifiably real.

The FBI says identity theft is one of the fastest growing crimes in the United States. Over 27,000 individuals become victims every single day. That is almost ten million victims per year![3]

Identify theft might seem like an unorthodox topic for a financial make-over book, but Day 6 is dedicated to protecting your assets. We've examined a number of strategies you can implement to safeguard property, both from lawsuits and from physical threats, but one more asset needs to be pro-tected . . . your identity.

Identity theft is a federal crime where one person's identification is used unlawfully by another person for criminal activities. Most often this occurs

---

1. Robert Moritz, "When Someone Steals Your Identity," *PARADE* magazine, July 6, 2003.

2. Federal Trade Commission, "2004 National and State Trends in Fraud and Identity Theft," January 22, 2004, p. 3.

3. Federal Trade Commission, "Identity Theft Survey Report," September 2003, p. 4.

when a thief steals a credit card, a bank statement, or a Social Security number. Once the criminal has this information, your existing accounts are vulnerable and new accounts can be opened and exploited. Thieves can use your personal information themselves, or they can sell it to other criminals.

Criminals will often take advantage of existing accounts by making large purchases on your credit cards, withdrawing money from your bank accounts, writing checks, obtaining loans, and even applying for unemployment benefits or tax refunds. They also frequently open new credit card accounts in your name and make thousands of dollars in charges on those new accounts.

Once they've stolen your information, thieves typically change the mailing address on one of your existing credit cards or one they've illegally established in your name. They can then spend thousands of dollars over several months—paying just the minimum balance, until they've charged up to the card's limit. Since the account statements and past due notices are going to a different address, you don't suspect anything is wrong until it is too late.

In a wired world where our paychecks are automatically deposited, where we pay for goods with a debit or credit card, and where our names are secondary to an account number, "identity" is a concept that has nothing to do with our values or personal lives and everything to do with the strings of numbers tied to our lives. Unfortunately, the efficiency and ubiquity of a digital identity have made it easy, and profitable, for criminals to quickly steal the account numbers that tie us to our assets.

> According to the FTC, the top ten states with the highest per capita rates of identity theft reported are (1) Arizona, (2) Nevada, (3) California, (4) Texas, (5) Florida, (6) New York, (7) Oregon, (8) Colorado, (9) Illinois, and (10) Washington.
> The state with the lowest per capita identity thefts reported? South Dakota. North Dakota, Vermont, Maine, and West Virginia also report low per capita identity theft.

What's the Big Deal About Identity Theft?

If you are asking the question, you have never been a victim. Identity theft is more than an inconvenience; it can be emotionally and financially devastating.

According to a 2003 survey by the Identity Theft Resource Center:

- **Lost Time**—The average victim spends six hundred hours recovering from this crime. For many, time is their most precious resource. When finding an extra hour to spend with the family can be difficult and an afternoon of free time nearly impossible, where are you going to find an extra six hundred hours?

- **Lost Income**—Based on a typical fifty-hour work week, six hundred lost hours represents three months of lost productivity. Thousands of dollars can be lost in time spent reclaiming your identity and repairing the damage. How much income would you lose if you took the next three months off?

- **Lingering Effects**—Even after the crime is discovered, victims struggle with the impact of identity theft. The ongoing effects can include increased insurance or credit card fees, difficulty securing a job, higher interest rates, and battling collection agencies and issuers who refuse to clear records despite substantiating evidence of the crime. This particular theft can follow you for more than ten years after the crime was first discovered.

- **Emotional Impact**—The emotional impact on victims is likened to that felt by victims of more violent crimes. Some victims feel dirty, ashamed, and embarrassed. Others report a split with a significant other or spouse and of being unsupported by family members after experiencing identity theft.

- **Initial Shock**—Approximately 85 percent of victims found out about the crime due to an adverse situation such as denied credit or employment, notification by police or collection agencies, or huge credit card bills for goods never ordered. Only 15 percent found out through a positive action taken by a business that verified a submitted application or a reported change of address.

The time to repair your credit can be staggering. Closing accounts, opening new accounts, and pleading your case to doubting creditors can be frustrating and emotionally grueling. In addition to the potential lost income, clearing your name can cost thousands of dollars. You may be denied jobs and loans, even after you provide an explanation. You may even be arrested for crimes committed in your name.

Incredibly, half of all identity theft crimes go unnoticed for a month, and one in ten go undetected for two or more years! You could be one of those unaware victims right now. You should do everything you can to protect yourself from this costly, yet rapidly growing, crime.

Are You at Risk of ID Theft?

Certain practices make you more vulnerable to identity theft. If you answer "Yes" to two or more of the following questions, you are in a high risk category and you should take immediate action to protect yourself.

(1) Do you often receive "preapproved" credit card offers in the mail?

(2) Do you receive "convenience checks" from your credit card companies in the mail?

(3) Do you throw away statements, convenience checks, or preapproved offers without first cross-shredding them?

(4) Do you carry your Social Security card in your wallet or purse?

(5) Is your mailbox unsecured or unlocked?

How They Do It

Twenty percent of victims have a pretty good idea how their information was obtained—usually the result of a stolen purse or wallet. This statistic should scare you: a full 80 percent of identity theft victims have no idea when or how their private personal information was accessed.

Identity thieves are more sophisticated than the average burglar. They employ several techniques to make you their next victim. New words and phrases have been created to describe their unscrupulous tactics, including "Dumpster diving," "skimming," and "pretexting." However, thieves have no qualms about using old-fashioned tactics like stealing your purse or wallet, too. With a little understanding of their methods, you will be well on your way to successfully protecting yourself from these crooks.

- **Dumpster Diving**—Thieves rummage through your garbage in search of account statements, Social Security numbers, phone numbers, receipts, passwords or PINs, and other documents with your personal information.

- **Skimming**—Thieves slide your credit card through a small electronic device that captures the account number and your personal information. This is used at restaurants and other locations where you voluntarily give your credit card to someone (e.g., waiter) and do not have constant visual access to its whereabouts. Perpetrators use a small handheld device, about the size of a credit card, and in less than two seconds can swipe the information from your card.

- **Pretexting**—Thieves contact their victim and pose as a representative of a bank, investment company, credit card company, employer, government agency, etc. and attempt to "verify" account numbers, passwords, PINs, Social Security numbers, and credit card numbers. It is easy for a thief to obtain your credit card statement from your trash and convince you he is a customer service agent from your credit card company. Thieves may even pose as a representative from the fraud protection division (under this guise you will be more inclined to cooperate with their questions). When they tell you your charge for $329.65 on March 3 at Best Buy didn't process correctly, why wouldn't you believe them?

- **Old-Fashioned Theft**—Thieves are still adept at stealing purses and wallets. They use the credit cards to make large purchases and use whatever other personal information they find. I had one credit card stolen from a health club gym locker secured by a fairly heavy-duty lock. They didn't steal my entire wallet, just one credit card. I was lucky that I discovered it within a couple of hours, but at that point they had already been on a shopping spree with my card.

- **Mail**—Thieves will steal mail from mailboxes in the middle of the day—sometimes even posing as mail carriers. Your mail contains a treasure trove of information for the identity thief—bank statements, credit card bills, investment reports and balances, preapproved credit card convenience checks, and new checks just to name a few.

- **Employment**—Thieves will use the information that their employers rightfully have about you for their own gain. This can occur at organizations that have your personal information in databases or files, such as banks, brokerage firms, and credit card companies.

- **Credit Reports**—Thieves know a credit report contains more personal information in one document than almost any other, and can use this information fairly easily to pose as someone who has a legal right to your credit report such as a prospective landlord or employer.

- **Enemy Within**—Thieves often know their victims, according to the FTC. Roommates, hired help, and landlords all have access to your home and personal information. The FTC states identity theft within families is fairly common and that people are vulnerable to this crime often when ending relationships with roommates and spouses.

How to Protect Yourself from Identity Theft

- **Review Account Statements**—Unauthorized activity can often be detected by looking at your bank, brokerage, credit card, and other account statements. It will require more than a quick glance—take a few minutes to review each charge. Highlight any charge, withdrawal, or suspicious activity, and immediately contact the company that issued the statement. Because of the proliferation of identity theft, almost all credit card companies have entire divisions set up to support the investigation of fraudulent account charges.

- **Use a Shredder**—Any receipt, account statement, "preapproved" credit offer, or document with your Social Security number, account number, or any personal information other than your name and address should be shredded. In order to receive the maximum protection, you should use a cross-cut shredder. You can buy an adequate cross-cut shredder for under one hundred dollars.

- **Protect Your Social Security Number**—Don't keep your Social Security card in your purse or wallet and don't provide your Social Security number on applications; although many forms ask for it, rarely do you need to provide it. When applying for a loan, a credit card, or job, it is usually safe to provide your Social Security number. If your number is listed on your checks, have new checks printed without your number—it is not necessary and certainly makes it easier for thieves to steal your identity.

- **Secure Your Mail**—Get a mailbox with a lock that allows the postal carrier to deposit mail but requires a key to retrieve the mail. Your mailbox contains a wealth of personal, valuable information that identity thieves can easily exploit. Deposit outgoing mail at a post office or in a postal collection box. If you will be away from home for more than five days, call the U.S. Postal Service at 800-275-8777 and ask for a "vacation hold."

- **Password Protocol**—Don't use obvious passwords such as your address, date of birth, anniversary date, Social Security number, or phone number and do not keep a list of passwords in an accessible location. Passwords containing a combination of letters and numbers are best. For example, "tennis1992" is a better password than just "tennis." Do not use your mother's maiden name as a password. A lot of companies still ask for the customer's mother's maiden name as protection, but it provides absolutely no protection from an identity thief since thieves can discover this name fairly easily. Instead, ask the company if you can use a password you've created.

- **Freeze Your Credit**—Depending on which state you live in, you can place a "security freeze" on your credit to prevent new credit from being issued without your prior authorization. Go to the three major credit reporting agencies (see below) to learn more.

- **Keep Personal Information Personal**—Protect yourself from "pretexting" by avoiding giving personal information over the phone or by email or mail unless you know the source is legitimate. If you get a call from someone who claims she is with your credit card company, get her extension and call her back by using the phone number provided on your account statement.

- **Cancel Unnecessary Credit Cards**—Do you really need eight credit cards? Flip the card over, call the toll-free number on the back, and cancel the card. It will take less than two minutes and serves as one more way to safeguard your identity. Ironically, canceling your credit cards may hurt your credit score. To learn how your credit score is calculated and to improve your score, read the book *7 Steps to a 720.*

- **Monitor Your Credit Report**—This is a must. The easiest and most effective method is to hire a company to do this for you. For example, IdentityGuard (www.identityguard.com) is one company that will provide quarterly credit reports and daily monitoring with alerts if new accounts are opened, inquiries are made, or addresses are changed. Make sure you use a credit monitoring service that reviews activity from all three credit bureaus: Equifax, Experian, and TransUnion.

Warning Signs

Be on the lookout for these potential signs of identity theft. If any one of these occurs, take immediate steps to make sure you are not a victim.

- If you fail to receive a monthly credit card or account statement, an identity thief may have changed your mailing address so you won't receive the bills containing the fraudulent charges. Make sure you receive all of your bills and account statements every month. Simply check off the statements as you receive them. If you don't receive a statement, you will be able to act quickly in response.

- If you receive new account correspondence or a new, unsolicited credit card, there is a good chance that a thief applied for the account using your identity.
- If you have good credit but are inexplicably denied for a loan or credit card, there may be unauthorized activity in your name affecting your credit report.
- If you get a call from a debt collector or credit card company regarding unwarranted unpaid bills or late payments, you may already be a victim. Get as much information as possible and place a freeze on any new purchases.

Four Steps If You Become a Victim

1. **Report the fraud to all three credit reporting agencies.** Call each of the agencies below and ask that a "fraud alert" be placed on your report. When you place a call to one bureau concerning fraud, that bureau is supposed to notify the other two bureaus, but I suggest notifying them yourself to be safe. Instruct them that no new lines of credit should be issued in your name without first asking you. All conversations should be followed with a letter sent certified mail, returned receipt requested.

    Equifax
    Fraud Hotline: 800-525-6285
    www.equifax.com
    P.O. Box 740256, Atlanta, GA 30374

    Experian
    Fraud Hotline: 888-397-3742
    www.experian.com
    P.O. Box 1017, Allen, TX 75013

    TransUnion
    Fraud Hotline: 800-680-7289
    www.transunion.com
    Fraud Victim Assistance Division,
    P.O. Box 6790, Fullerton, CA 92634

2. **Close fraudulent accounts.** After you call the credit bureaus, you will receive an updated credit report free of charge. Review these reports very carefully. Immediately close all accounts that have been

fraudulently opened or accessed. Ask if the company accepts the FTC-sponsored ID Theft Affidavit. It is an easy form to document identity theft and can be found at www.SixDayFinancialMake over.com.

If your checkbook has been stolen or you suspect someone is forging your checks, notify your bank immediately. Most banks will have a fraud dispute form. If not, follow up with them in writing. In addition, you should contact the check verification companies below and alert them of the fraud:

TeleCheck
800-710-9898

Certegy, Inc.
800-437-5120

If you are working with an identity theft monitoring company such as IdentityGuard, contact them for assistance and guidance. Again, following any conversation, send a letter or have the FTC Affidavit sent via certified mail with return receipt requested.

3. **File a report with the police.** The FTC recommends you file a report with your local police department and the police department where the identity theft occurred. Make sure you get a copy of the report— your bank or credit card company may need it. If you can't get a copy of the report, at least get the report number for your records.

4. **File a complaint with the FTC.** Although this probably won't benefit you immediately and directly, it will help the FTC and other government agencies track down and prevent identity theft. You can file a complaint at www.consumer.gov/idtheft or you can call their special complaint hotline at 877-IDTHEFT (877-438-4338).

Action Steps

If you've got a lot of time and money to waste, you can skip this chapter's Action Steps. Otherwise, it might be a good idea to protect yourself from one of the fastest growing crimes in the United States.

Go through the Action Steps below and put a check mark in one of the following boxes for each one.

Protect Yourself from Identity Theft

1. ☐ COMPLETED   ☐ NEED TO COMPLETE   ☐ DOES NOT APPLY

Develop a system for reviewing all account statements in a timely manner.

2. ☐ COMPLETED   ☐ NEED TO COMPLETE   ☐ DOES NOT APPLY

Purchase a cross-cut shredder and begin shredding receipts, account statements, "preapproved" credit offers, credit card convenience checks, and other sensitive documents.

3. ☐ COMPLETED   ☐ NEED TO COMPLETE   ☐ DOES NOT APPLY

Become stingier with your Social Security number. Unless you are applying for a loan, job, or lease, don't be so quick to give it away.

4. ☐ COMPLETED   ☐ NEED TO COMPLETE   ☐ DOES NOT APPLY

Buy a secure mailbox that prevents unauthorized people from removing your mail.

5. ☐ COMPLETED   ☐ NEED TO COMPLETE   ☐ DOES NOT APPLY

Cancel unused and unwanted credit cards.

6. ☐ COMPLETED   ☐ NEED TO COMPLETE   ☐ DOES NOT APPLY

Sign up for a credit monitoring service that checks all three credit bureaus, such as IdentityGuard's CreditProtectX3 service.

If You Have Become a Victim

(Detailed steps can be found on page 274.)

1. ☐ COMPLETED   ☐ NEED TO COMPLETE   ☐ DOES NOT APPLY

Report the fraud to all three credit reporting agencies.

2. ☐ COMPLETED   ☐ NEED TO COMPLETE   ☐ DOES NOT APPLY

Close fraudulent accounts.

3. ☐ COMPLETED ☐ NEED TO COMPLETE ☐ DOES NOT APPLY

File a report with the police.

4. ☐ COMPLETED ☐ NEED TO COMPLETE ☐ DOES NOT APPLY

File a complaint with the FTC.

Update Your Online Financial Makeover Account

1. ☐ COMPLETED ☐ NEED TO COMPLETE ☐ DOES NOT APPLY

Before you do anything else, update your Six-Day Financial Makeover account at www.SixDayFinancialMakeover.com.

Conclusion

Congratulations!!! You completed your Six-Day Financial Makeover! You clarified your goals, overcame limiting beliefs, set your finances on autopilot, invested for success, protected your family from disaster, provided for your loved ones, and protected your assets. If you're like most readers, you probably still have a number of unfinished Action Steps, and that's okay. Take a break and take a deep breath. After all, this is Day 7 and everyone knows what happens on the seventh day . . . you rest. (If God rested, you can, too!)

While you're resting, it might be a good time to think about how far you've come and about how much you've improved your financial health. It might also be a good time to think about how you can improve the lives of others. Your financial transformation won't be nearly as rewarding unless you give back.

Giving back can mean different things to different people, and there isn't just one way to do it. Do what feels right for you. There are people across town and around the world who need your help. There are churches and charities that need your money to continue their mission and to support their cause. Gifting helps others, teaches your children the value of giving, feels good, and if that's not enough, you might even get a big fat tax deduction from doing it!

Giving is also easy. When you bought this book you gave back. How's that? I'm going to give 10 percent of every dollar I make from this book to my church.

Hopefully your financial makeover wasn't painful, but I'm sure you don't want to go through this process again and again and again. To ensure this will be your one and only financial makeover, you've got to review your financial situation and occasionally make minor adjust-ments. If you experience major life changes such as a marriage, divorce, children, and/or new goals, expect that your finances will also have to go through some changes to stay optimized.

The book's patent-pending website (www.SixDayFinancialMakeover.com) will help you stay on the right path and was designed to help you translate the words on these pages into a real and positive improvement in your life. If you've been tracking your progress and Action Steps through the website, keep up the good work. If you haven't used the website yet, it's not too late. It takes just a moment to create an account, and it's free. There are many valuable tools, quizzes, and videos that are available only on the website.

Also, you can sign up for the monthly personal finance newsletter I author called "Six Steps or Less . . . to Financial Success" at www.SixStepsOr Less.com.

It's been my pleasure to guide you on this financial journey. If you'd like to share the success of your financial transformation or have any comments, I'd love to hear from you. Send me an email at robert@pacificawealth.com.

About the Author

Robert Pagliarini, MSFS, CFP, is the president of Pacifica Wealth Advisors, a boutique investment and financial-planning firm in Southern California serving some of America's most affluent individuals and families. Called a "financial bodyguard" and "financial motivator" by his clients, Robert has spent the past decade demystifying saving, investing, and insurance, as well as retirement, estate, and tax planning to protect his clients and help them achieve their most important goals.

Robert has worked with clients from nearly all backgrounds and levels of wealth—from stay-at-home moms to top executives, and from clients just starting to accumulate assets to those with more than $100 million. Robert shares his unique and most effective strategies in *The Six-Day Financial Makeover.*

Raised in a poor family by a single mother of five, Robert was inspired to pursue a career in financial planning to help women and ordinary families experience a greater sense of security and financial independence.

Aiming to teach people from any background how to focus their financial planning around tangible goals, Robert has been able to give readers a greater sense of achievement and purpose every day they go to work.

Robert is a graduate of UCLA's personal financial planner program, holds a degree in psychology, is a Certified Financial Planner practitioner, and is one of just a few thousand worldwide to have earned a master's degree in financial services.

Robert has developed a reputation with the media for breaking down complex financial topics into easy-to-understand and action-based advice. Robert has been interviewed by *Money* magazine, *Newsweek*, American Public Media's *Marketplace*, CNN, *The Wall Street Journal*, the Associated Press, Dow Jones Newswires, the *Los Angeles Times*, the *Chicago Tribune*, *Woman's Day*, and many others.

He has served on the board of the Financial Planning Association of Los Angeles and as a deacon at Bel Air Presbyterian Church. Robert lives with his beautiful wife, Elizabeth, and their daughter, Alexandra "Bean," in Orange County, California. Robert can be contacted at robert@pacificawealth.com.